THE SHADOW OF THE OBJECT

A member of the Independent Group of the British Psycho-Analytical Society, Christopher Bollas is a truly independent thinker. He finds his own way through the tribes of contemporary psychoanalysis, not as a follower, but as a single wanderer through the United States, England and France, mainly. Not that he denies his debts towards some of his elders such as Winnicott, Marion Milner and others. He has learned from them that, above all, psychoanalysis is an experience which cannot be accounted for in the style that belongs to mechanical experiencing. The title of his book, borrowed from Freud, marks his preference toward the language of metaphor. His thought is nourished not only by what his patients taught him, but as much with what the giants of universal literature wrote about. If his style bears the marks of his training outside psychoanalysis, he never forgets that the patient is not, as Winnicott said once, a poem, or a novel, but a person who enjoys and suffers and with whom it is essential to relate.
André Green

The essential paradox of man rests in two realities. Man is his own subject and object. And man is the maker of his loss. The 'shadow' of loss has haunted the imagination of humanity, in writers from Aeschylus to Samuel Beckett. Freud gave loss a different aetiology and outlook. Melanie Klein and Donald Winnicott have clinically extended Freud's tentative vision into a coherent humane epistemology of loss. Reared in this last tradition, Christopher Bollas reveals to us new figures of loss, and narrates them with an enviable style. Yet for me the virtue of Bollas's book resides in his acceptance that loss is a loss is a loss.
Prince Masud Khan

The Shadow
of the Object

Psychoanalysis of the
Unthought Known

CHRISTOPHER BOLLAS

 *'an association in which the free
development of each is the condition
for the free development of all'*

Free Association Books / London / 1987

First published in Great Britain in 1987 by
Free Association Books
26 Freegrove Road
London N7 9RQ

British Library Cataloguing in Publication Data

Bollas, Christopher
   The shadow of the object : psychoanalysis
   of the unthought known.
   1. Object relations (Psychoanalysis)
   I. Title
   616.89'17   RC506

   ISBN 0-946960-59-3
   ISBN 0-946960-60-7 Pbk

Typeset by Rapidset and Design Ltd, London WC1

Printed and bound in Great Britain by
A. Wheaton & Co. Ltd, Exeter

CONTENTS

I dedicate this book
to my father, Sacha,
and to my mother, Celeste

ACKNOWLEDGEMENTS

EARLIER versions of some of the following chapters are reproduced here in revised form by kind permission of *The International Journal of Psychoanalysis*, *The Annual of Psychoanalysis*, *The Nouvelle Revue de Psychanalyse*, and *Contemporary Psychoanalysis*: 'The transformational object', *Int. J. Psycho-Anal.* 60:97–107; 'On the relation to the self as an object', *Int. J. Psycho-Anal.* 63:347–359; 'Moods and the conservative process', *Int. J. Psycho-Anal.* 65:203–212; 'Expressive uses of the countertransference', *Contemp. Psychoanal.* 19:1–34; 'Loving hate', *The Annual of Psychoanal.* 12–13:221–237.

Chapter 2 is a synthesis of parts of two articles: 'The aesthetic moment and the search for transformation', *The Annual of Psychoanal.* 6:385–394; and 'L'esprit de l'object et l'epiphanie du sacre', *Nouvelle Revue de Psychan.* 18:253–262. Chapter 11 is partly based on 'Comment l'hysterique prend possession de l'analyste', *Nouvelle Revue de Psychan.* 24:279–286.

I also thank the International Universities Press for permission to include my chapter on 'Normotic illness' which appears in *Clinical Applications of Winnicott's Theory*, eds M. Gerard Fromm and Bruce L. Smith, to be published in 1987.

These essays were all presented in earlier form to the students and faculty of the Istituto di Neuropsichiatria Infantile of the University of Rome, and I am grateful for the creative response I have received. I would also like to thank J-B. Pontalis, editor of the *Nouvelle Revue de Psychanalyse* for inviting me to contribute to his journal. He encourages a freedom of thought and expression that is rare in the world of psychoanalytical publications.

I am pleased to thank Dr Daniel P. Schwartz, Medical Director of the Austen Riggs Center, and Murray M. Schwartz, Dean of the School of Humanities and Fine Arts of the University of Massachusetts, for giving me the space and time to complete this work. I owe a very special debt to my secretary, Betty Homich, for her intelligent and good-humoured handling of the author and his manuscript.

I thank Gregorio Kohon for urging me to write this book in the first place, and my wife Suzanne for her support and critical comments. Many people were kind enough to read the manuscript and I am grateful for their efforts, in particular to Laurie Ryavec, Lawrence Hedges, and Sara Beardsworth, and to my publisher Robert Young.

I owe a very great deal indeed to the psychoanalysts who educated, supervised, and analysed me, and the sensibilities of Paula Heimann, Marion Milner, Masud Khan, and Adam Limentani have had a profound effect on the way I practise and imagine psychoanalysis.

Thus the shadow of the object fell upon the ego, and the latter could henceforth be judged by a special agency, as though it were an object, the forsaken object. In this way an object-loss was transformed into an ego loss and the conflict between the ego and the loved person into a cleavage between the critical activity of the ego and the ego as altered by identification.

Sigmund Freud

INTRODUCTION

I N the early 1950s Paula Heimann, a member of the British Psycho-Analytical Society, posed a simple question that became crucial to the practice of psychoanalysis in what has come to be called the 'British School' of psychoanalysis (see Kohon, 1986). When listening to the patient's free associations (or broken speech), and tracing the private logic of sequential association as all psychoanalysts had done up until then, she asked: 'Who is speaking?' We can say that up until this moment it had always been assumed that the speaker was the patient who had formed a therapeutic alliance with the analyst, and therefore that he was a neutral or working speaker who was reporting inner states of mind. This assumption comprised the classical view of analytic narrative. But Heimann knew that at any one moment in a session a patient could be speaking with the voice of the mother, or the mood of the father, or some fragmented voice of a child self either lived or withheld from life.

'To whom is this person speaking?' Heimann then asked. The unconscious admits no special recognition of the neutrality of the psychoanalyst and, given the unending subtleties of the transference, Heimann realized that at one moment the analysand was speaking to the mother, anticipating the father, or reproaching, exciting or consoling a child – the child self of infancy, in the midst of separation at age two, in the oedipal phase, or in adolescence. 'What is the patient talking about and why now?', she added.

Heimann and other analysts in the British School, all of whom had been deeply influenced by the work of Melanie Klein, analysed the object relations implied in the patient's discourse. The patient's narrative was not simply listened to in order to hear the dissonant sounds of unconscious punctuation or the affective registrations that suggested the ego's position and availability for interpretation. The British analyst would also analyse the shifting subjects and others that were implied in the life of the transference.

In the middle 1950s Margaret Little added other questions that complemented Heimann's earlier position. She said that each analyst at any moment should be asking how she is feeling, why she is feeling this, and why now. The transference enactment was now linked to the countertransference and a 'discourse of object relating' had been discovered. By the end of the 1950s analysts in the British School were attending very carefully to the 'continuous interplay' between the patient's transference and the analyst's countertransference, and the theory of projective identification was increasingly utilized to study the way in which the analysand uses the analyst as an object in the transference in order to put the analyst into the patient's mind, compelling the analyst to relive with the analysand the nature of the patient's early life and to exist with some feeling inside his internal object world. This development of a discourse of object relating in turn deepened the analysand's transference usage of the analyst, as he had discovered a receiver for infant and child communications; in turn, this permitted the analysand to regress into early child experiences within the illusion that is psychoanalysis. The contributions of Michael Balint, D.W. Winnicott, Marion Milner and Masud Khan were important to the analytic community's understanding of the handling of the regressed patient.

To those questions that Heimann and Little developed we must add Bion's musings. Bion wondered **what** is speaking or transpiring, **in what form**, and **linked to what**. This position, heavily cast in the Kleinian interest in the first year of life, helped analysts in the British School to listen to the more interpersonal object relations (of mother speaking to child, or child to father) and to the elements of the psyche addressing each other, sometimes in an intersubjective field, but often in a purely intrapsychic domain. The element of fear could be passed from the analysand to the analyst so that if the patient then registered guilt, he established some link between these two elements. It would take time and continuous reflection on this and many other discourses before the analyst could fully understand what the patient was saying.

Ever since I began clinical work with autistic and schizophrenic children, I have been interested in understanding the representation of one's being through object relations as well as narrative content. The autistic child cannot tell you how he feels or what his psyche is made of; he can only show you, and this he does quite well if the clinician is willing to be used as an object and to be guided via his own internal world through the subject's memory of his object relations. I do not wish to cast aside the necessity of sustaining the classical view of material, a view that places great emphasis on the logic of narrative sequence to guide the analyst in forming an interpretation of the patient's inner preoccupations. Nor do I underestimate the important contributions of the school of Lacan and the emphasis on the word in psychoanalysis. But neither the classical nor the Lacanian view addresses the play of the subject and other in the transference and the character of that part of the psyche that lives in the wordless world. An autistic child may utter not a word, but his cries, dense preoccupied silence and his mimetic use of people is his language. He lodges himself inside the other, compelling the other to experience the breakdown of language (and hope and desire).

The autistic child taught me how to attend to this wordless element in the adult. The chapters that follow all focus in one way or another on the human subject's recording of his early experiences of the object. This is the shadow of the object as it falls on the ego, leaving some trace of its existence in the adult.

The object can cast its shadow without a child being able to process this relation through mental representations or language, as, for example, when a parent uses his child to contain projective identifications. While we do know something of the character of the object which affects us, we may not have **thought** it yet. The work of a clinical psychoanalysis, particularly of object relations in the transference and the countertransference, will partly be preoccupied with the emergence into thought of early memories of being and relating. An exploration of this feature of psychoanalysis, of the reliving through language of that which is known but not yet thought (what I term the unthought known), is the subject of this book.

In part one of this work I examine the infant's experience of his first object. This is, of course, the mother, who is nevertheless known less as a discrete object with particular qualities than as a process linked to the infant's being and the alteration of his being. For this reason I have termed the early mother a 'transformational object' and the adult's search for transformation constitutes in some respects a memory of this early relationship. There are other memories of this period of our life, such as aesthetic experience when a person feels uncannily embraced by an object.

Another way of remembering the early years of life is through our own idiom of thinking about and talking to ourselves. I explore our relation to the self as an object and focus especially on the transfer of the maternal care system into the self care system. The relation to the self as an object is clearly an important feature of our lived life, but is no more explicit than in the dream, when the dreaming subject (the experiential subject inside the dream) is **the object** of the dream script. I consider the fact that in the dream we are subject and object, and I examine how the dreaming subject is handled or managed by the unconscious ego, an object relation that expresses significant features of the mother's logic of caretaking.

I also formulate the notion of the trisexual: a unique individual who makes it his life work to remember for others. This person sided with the nature of the early object world which he embodies in his own particular manner of courting and loving someone.

In the second part of the book I continue to examine our memories of early life, this time concentrating on childhood rather than infancy. It is my view, for example, that children who are 'inside' a family experience which is beyond comprehension cannot successfully organize such experience into phantasies that hold the subject, so they store the 'self state' determined

by the unknown situation. This conservation of self states is often the stuff of moods, some of which are untransformed 'being states' stored by the individual, perhaps awaiting that day when they can be understood and then either transformed into symbolic derivatives or forgotten. I continue to examine the person's conservation of experience in the chapter on 'Loving hate', where I argue that only in hating the other can certain people discover a true relation to the object, a fact that requires them to conserve rather than destroy the other. This particular method of finding some meaning through hate can be contrasted with the children of normotic parents, people who have an abnormal need to be normal. In the chapter on 'Normotic illness' I discuss a new emphasis in illness in which the subject seeks desubjectification in order to become a commodity object in the object world. In part, the child becomes normotic because the parent deflects the child's subjectivity into material objects, a form of parental pathology that might be compared with 'extractive introjection', when one person steals part of another person's mind.

The third part of the book forms an examination of how people remember these early experiences through the transference and the countertransference. I provide as many clinical illustrations as possible in order to illuminate how an analyst works within the framework of the Independent Group of the British Psycho-Analytical Society. It is my view, and one shared by many British psychoanalysts, that the analysand compels the analyst to experience the patient's inner object world. He often does this by means of projective identification: by inspiring in the analyst a feeling, thought or self state that hitherto has only remained within himself. In doing this the analysand might also re-present an internal object which is fundamentally based on a part of the mother's or father's personality, in such a way that in addition to being compelled to experience one of the analysand's inner objects, the analyst might also be an object of one feature of the mother's mothering, and in such a moment the analyst would briefly occupy a position previously held by the analysand.

This brings me to a caveat. I focus on the analysand's memory of early childhood. Although I do not discuss how to differentiate between the actual mother and the mother constituted out of unconscious phantasy, I do think psychoanalysts must try to distinguish between representations of the actual and fantastical. The mother spoken of or implied through object relations in the transference will, of course, always be a composite of the actual and the fantastical, but this should not deter the analyst from endeavouring to collect the details and analyse the trace of the actual mother. I do not think it is a matter of answering the question: 'Yes, but how do we ever know what the mother was **really** like?', for there is an inevitable but essential conflict between two systems of representation and two objects (or two mothers). One system of internalization and representation will register the actual mother and father, while another system of internalization and representation will reflect the dynamically unconscious mother who embodies the analysand's projections. The historical and the fantastical, the actual and the imaginary, are engaged in an endless and inevitable dialectic. To give up the effort to speak about actual history (as opposed to the history of phantasy) is to absent oneself from this dialectic and inevitably, in my view, to diminish the richness and complexity of human life. Some of a patient's internal mental representations of a mother, for example, will more or less accurately register the true nature of this mother's personality reflected in her mothering of this child, while other mental representations will carry projective identifications of the infant's internal world. Sometimes there will be both an accurate representation and a container for projective identifications. At other times, an analysand will use mental representations of the actual mother for dynamically unconscious reasons, as, for example, when a person masochistically submits to the mother's sadism, in order to extract from the analyst (and world) a compensatory psychic litigation: a settlement.

Since my interest is to identify the adult's memory of his early environment, I tend to emphasize the actual mother. In this respect, I do not believe it is simply a matter of identifying a

particular characteristic of a mother's personality, but more a question of analysing the maternal process. A woman who would ordinarily
be a 'good-enough mother', as Winnicott puts it,
may have suffered a severe blow in life, perhaps
the death of a mother or sister following the birth of her child – an
unfortunate but all too frequent deal of fate in one's life – and this
may be sufficient to disturb her mothering of a particular infant.
Although her mothering may be very disturbed for a period of
time she might recover to become a good-enough mother. The effect of her disturbed mothering, however, will be retained in the
structure of the child's ego and may be 'remembered' in the transference relation to an analyst many years later.

I do not discuss how one might analyse the presence of the
actual mother's mothering. I look forward to doing so in another
work. It is, however, not simply a matter of indicating to the
patient that he had a disturbed mother and stating how her disturbance has affected him. Such an explanation would not help a
patient because, as we know, each analysand **organizes** his actual
experience into material for omnipotent mental activity, such as
projection. A patient who was the object of disturbed mothering
will in himself be a disturbed and disturbing person, a feature
which must inevitably be taken up in the transference as a reflection of himself. The analyst should not modify the intensity of the
transference by referring the patient back to his mother and to
his early life until the analyst has confronted and analysed the
nature of the analysand's mental life within the transference.

In the following chapters I employ the terms **ego, subject and self**
in ways that vary slightly from their use by other psychoanalytic
theoreticians. I shall therefore define my use here, although I
prefer to keep in mind the fact that such terms and their definitions are not cast in clay.

When I refer to the **ego** I draw attention to that unconscious
organizing process that reflects the presence of our mental structure. When Freud abandoned the effort to integrate his topographical and structural models of the mind, he did so partly
because he realized that the id could not simply be associated with

the unconscious and the ego with the preconscious, since the mental forces engaged in the act of repressing an unwanted mental content are as unconscious as the repressed content. How could one account for these two unconsciouses? It would be interesting to trace the history of the problem from that point in Freud's writing, but my intention here is to argue that the unconscious ego differs from the repressed unconscious in that the former refers to an unconscious form and the latter to unconscious contents. The unconscious form, or idiom of the ego, evolves from the inherited disposition which is there before birth, a design that distinguishes and differentiates the 'personalities' of neonates. There is a dialectic between this inner core and the environment. I think that Winnicott was partly wrong to link his concept of the true self to the id and the idea of the false self to the ego, although it is clear what he was trying to work out in this manner, a theory that bears striking resemblance at times to Lacan's work. But by stating that the true self or the inherited disposition is on the side of the id, he failed to account for the organizing idiom of each infant and the factor of personality, which I think is more of an ego process than an id procedure. I regard the ego, for example, as part of the true self, which in its entirety must also include the id. The infant's ego develops and establishes a highly complex system of organization all of which precedes the 'birth' of the subject or the presence of the self.

Since the ego is a mental structure that evolves from the dialectic of the internal and the external, ego structure constitutes a history of the development of the person. All ego attitudes, feelings and operations indicate, even if we cannot grasp it, the trace of an object relation.

The **subject** arrives on the scene rather late in the day. By the time we are capable of a meaningful interpretation of our existence, and the meaningful presence of others, we have already been constituted via the ego's negotiation with the environment. Although I agree with the Kleinian theoreticians that phantasy exists from birth (and probably **in utero**), and although it is likely that something like the psyche (a term Winnicott uses to describe the presence of an internal world that is determined by the soma

and eventually external objects) is present at the
beginning of life, I do not think that internal

phantasy or psyche determines the structure of
the ego. I think it is almost the opposite: phantasy reflects the ego.

The ego is the constitutive factor in the unthought known. We
are in possession of complex rules for being and relating, processes that reflect the dialectic of the inherited and the acquired.
In the primary repressed unconscious we know these rules, but as
yet only some of them have been thought. A very significant portion of our existence is predetermined by this unthought known,
and a psychoanalysis will bring the unthought known into
thought, through the experience and the interpretation of the
transference and countertransference.

A patient does not simply represent his internal world to the
analyst in narrative. He uses the analyst as a transference object
and this usage is further articulated through the analyst's
countertransference. The patient processes us, organizes us and
establishes his idiolect of usage over time. These procedures are
the work of the unconscious ego, and only by confronting (occasionally facilitating) and analysing the patient's ego procedures
can we bring into consciousness, and make psychically available,
what has been buried as a deep structure. The psychoanalytic act
is, in a way, a mental derivative of the ego, since through psychoanalysis the ego is encountered and known.

The person's self is the history of many internal relations.
Each infant, child, adolescent and adult (through the life cycle)
experiences the – theoretically infinite – parts of the self articulated through the interplay of internal and external reality. Once
any one part is objectified (in thought or in feeling) it thereupon
comes into existence. There is no one unified mental phenomenon
that we can term self, although I shall use this term as if it were a
unity; it is true to say that all of us live within the realm of illusion
and within this realm the concept of the self has a particularly
relevant meaning. Over a lifetime we objectify, know and 'relate
to' the many different states in our being. Emotional and psychological realities bring with them self states which become part of
our history. The concept of self should refer to the positions or

points of view from which and through which we sense, feel, observe and reflect on distinct and separate experiences in our being. One crucial point of view comes through the other who experiences us.

From the multifarious vantage points which in turn allow many objectifications of our being into self states, we establish over a long time a sense of this relation. It has continuity over time and is in possession of its own history. We are also aware of its limitation, all the more significant because in theory we should have a limitless self, but in reality we discover the bounds of our significance.

Each of the following chapters evolves in some specific way from a problem or a matter of interest that occurs in the clinical situation. I keep a notebook where I enter ideas that focus my thinking. The concept of the transformational object, for example, emerged from my interest in the intrinsic therapeutic factor of the analytic space and process, and I developed this idea in my notebooks from 1973 through 1977.

When I practise psychoanalysis, seeing ten people a day five days a week, my daily frame of mind is akin to a meditative state. I find it difficult to think reflectively about a session immediately upon its completion, although I can record brief notes that mark some moment of significance I wish to remember. In the evening after work, while driving in my car, listening to music or simply engaging in the pleasant humdrum of ordinary life, an idea derived from work with a patient will cross my mind. I enter the idea in my notebook without straining to push myself beyond what I know exactly at that moment. I prefer it this way because it allows me to imagine an idea without, as it were, knowing exactly what I mean. I often find that although I am working on an idea without knowing exactly what it is that I think, I am engaged in thinking an idea struggling to have me think it. I hope this book is true to and reflects that private and isolated struggle.

I   The Shadow
       of the Object

1 The transformational object

WE know that because of the considerable prematurity of human birth the infant depends on the mother for survival. By serving as a supplementary ego (Heimann, 1956) or a facilitating environment (Winnicott, 1963) she both sustains the baby's life and transmits to the infant, through her own particular idiom of mothering, an aesthetic of being that becomes a feature of the infant's self. The mother's way of holding the infant, of responding to his gestures, of selecting objects, and of perceiving the infant's internal needs, constitutes her contribution to the infant-mother culture. In a private discourse that can only be developed by mother and child, the language of this relation is the idiom of gesture, gaze and intersubjective utterance.

In his work on the mother-child relation, Winnicott stresses what we might call its stillness: the mother provides a continuity of being, she 'holds' the infant in an environment of her making that facilitates his growth. And yet, against this reciprocally enhancing stillness, mother and child continuously negotiate intersubjective experience that coheres around the rituals of psychosomatic need: feeding, diapering, soothing, playing and sleeping. It is undeniable, I think, that as the infant's 'other' self, the mother transforms the baby's internal and external environment. Edith Jacobson suggests that

> when a mother turns the infant on his belly, takes him out of his crib, diapers him, sits him up in her arms and on her lap, rocks him, strokes him, kisses him, feeds him, smiles at him, talks and sings to him, she offers him not only all kinds of libidinal gratifications but simultaneously stimulates and prepares the child's sitting, standing, crawling, walking, talking, and on and on, i.e., the development of functional ego activity. (1965, p. 37)

Winnicott (1963b) terms this comprehensive mother the 'environment' mother because, for the infant, she is the total environment. To this I would add that **the mother is less significant and identifiable as an object than as a process** that is identified with cumulative internal and external transformations.

I wish to identify the infant's first subjective experience of the object as a transformational object, and this chapter will address the trace in adult life of this early relationship. A transformational object is experientially identified by the infant with processes that alter self experience. It is an identification that emerges from symbiotic relating, where the first object is 'known' not so much by putting it into an object representation, but as a recurrent experience of being – a more existential as opposed to representational knowing. As the mother helps to integrate the infant's being (instinctual, cognitive, affective, environmental), the rhythms of this process – from unintegration(s) to integration(s) – inform the nature of this 'object' relation rather than the qualities of the object as object.

Not yet fully identified as an other, the mother is experienced as a process of transformation, and this feature of early existence lives on in certain forms of object-seeking in adult life, when the object is sought for its function as a signifier of transformation. Thus, in adult life, the quest is not to possess the object; rather the object is pursued in order to surrender to it as a medium that alters the self, where the subject-as-supplicant now feels himself to be the recipient of enviro-somatic caring, identified with metamorphoses of the self. Since it is an identification that begins before the mother is mentally represented as an other, it is an object relation that emerges not from desire, but from a perceptual identification of the object with its function: the object as envirosomatic transformer of the subject. The memory of this early object relation manifests itself in the person's search for an object (a person, place, event, ideology) that promises to transform the self.

This conception of the mother being experienced as transformation is supported in several respects. In the first place, she assumes the function of the transformational object, for she constantly alters the infant's environment to meet

his needs. There is no delusion operating in the
infant's identification of the mother with transformation of being through his symbiotic knowing; it is a fact, for she actually transforms his
world. In the second place, the infant's own emergent ego capacities – of motility, perception, and integration – also transform his
world. The acquisition of language is perhaps the most significant
transformation, but learning to handle and to differentiate between objects, and to remember objects that are not present, are
transformative achievements as they result in ego change which
alters the nature of the infant's internal world. It is not surprising
that the infant identifies these ego achievements with the presence
of an object, as the failure of the mother to maintain provision of
the facilitating environment, through prolonged absence or bad
handling, can evoke ego collapse and precipitate psychic pain.

With the infant's creation of the transitional object, the transformational process is displaced from the mother-environment
(where it originated) into countless subjective-objects, so that the
transitional phase is heir to the transformational period, as the
infant evolves from experience of the process to articulation of
the experience. With the transitional object, the infant can play
with the illusion of his own omnipotence (lessening the loss of the
environment-mother with generative and phasic delusions of self-
and-other creation); he can entertain the idea of the object being
got rid of, yet surviving his ruthlessness; and he can find in this
transitional experience the freedom of metaphor. What was an
actual process can be displaced into symbolic equations which, if
supported by the mother, mitigate the loss of the original environment-mother. In a sense, the use of a transitional object is the
infant's first creative act, an event that does not merely display
an ego capacity – such as grasping – but which indicates the infant's subjective experience of such capacities.

THE SEARCH FOR THE TRANSFORMATIONAL
OBJECT IN ADULT LIFE

I think we have failed to take notice of the phenomenon in adult
life of the wide-ranging collective search for an object that is

identified with the metamorphosis of the self. In many religious faiths, for example, when the subject believes in the deity's actual potential to transform the total environment, he sustains the terms of the earliest object tie within a mythic structure. Such knowledge remains symbiotic (that is, it reflects the wisdom of faith) and coexists alongside other forms of knowing. In secular worlds, we see how hope invested in various objects (a new job, a move to another country, a vacation, a change of relationship) may both represent a request for a transformational experience and, at the same time, continue the 'relationship' to an object that signifies the experience of transformation. We know that the advertising world makes its living on the trace of this object: the advertised product usually promises to alter the subject's external environment and hence change internal mood.

The search for such an experience may generate hope, even a sense of confidence and vision, but although it seems to be grounded in the future tense, in finding something in the future to transform the present, it is an object-seeking that recurrently enacts a pre-verbal ego memory. It is usually on the occasion of the aesthetic moment, which I describe in the next chapter, that an individual feels a deep subjective rapport with an object (a painting, a poem, an aria or symphony, or a natural landscape) and experiences an uncanny fusion with the object, an event that re-evokes an ego state that prevailed during early psychic life. However, such occasions, meaningful as they might be, are less noteworthy as transformational accomplishments than they are for their uncanny quality, the sense of being reminded of something never cognitively apprehended but existentially known, the memory of the ontogenetic process rather than thought or phantasies that occur once the self is established. Such aesthetic moments do not sponsor memories of a specific event or relationship, but evoke a psychosomatic sense of fusion that is the subject's recollection of the transformational object. This anticipation of being transformed by an object – itself an ego memory of the ontogenetic process – inspires the subject with a reverential attitude towards it, so that even though the transformation of the self will not take place on the scale it reached during early life, the adult subject tends to nominate such objects as sacred.

Although my emphasis here is on the positive aesthetic experience, it is well to remember that a person may seek a negative aesthetic experience, for such an occasion 'prints' his early ego experiences and registers the structure of the unthought known. Some borderline patients, for example, repeat traumatic situations because through the latter they remember their origins existentially.

In adult life, therefore, to seek the transformational object is to recollect an early object experience, to remember not cognitively but existentially – through intense affective experience – a relationship which was identified with cumulative transformational experiences of the self. Its intensity as an object relation is not due to the fact that this is an object of desire, but to the object being identified with such powerful metamorphoses of being. In the aesthetic moment the subject briefly re-experiences, through ego fusion with the aesthetic object, a sense of the subjective attitude towards the transformational object, although such experiences are re-enacted memories, not recreations.

The search for symbolic equivalents to the transformational object, and the experience with which it is identified, continues in adult life. We develop faith in a deity whose absence, ironically, is held to be as important a test of man's being as his presence. We go to the theatre, to the museum, to the landscapes of our choice, to search for aesthetic experiences. We may imagine the self as the transformational facilitator, and we may invest ourselves with capacities to alter the environment that are not only impossible but embarrassing on reflection. In such daydreams the self as transformational object lies somewhere in the future tense, and even ruminative planning about the future (what to do, where to go, etc.) is often a kind of psychic prayer for the arrival of the transformational object: a secular second coming of an object relation experienced in the earliest period of life.

It should not be surprising that varied psychopathologies emerge from the failure, as Winnicott put it, to be disillusioned from this relationship. The gambler's game is that transformational object which is to metamorphose his entire internal and external world. A criminal seeks the perfect crime to transform the self internally (repairing ego defects and fulfilling id needs) and externally (bringing wealth and happiness). Some forms of erotomania may be efforts to establish the other as the transformational object.

The search for the perfect crime or the perfect woman is not only a quest for an idealized object. It also constitutes some recognition in the subject of a deficiency in ego experience. The search, even though it serves to split the bad self experience from the subject's cognitive knowledge, is nonetheless a semiological act that signifies the person's search for a particular object relation that is associated with ego transformation and repair of the 'basic fault' (Balint, 1968).

It may also be true that people who become gamblers reflect a conviction that the mother (that **they** had as **their** mother) will not arrive with supplies. The experience of gambling can be seen as an aesthetic moment in which the nature of this person's relation to the mother is represented.

CLINICAL EXAMPLE

One of the most common psychopathologies of the transformational object relation occurs in the schizoid self, the patient who may have a wealth of ego strengths (intelligence, talent, accomplishment, success) but who is personally bereft and sad without being clinically depressed.

Peter is a twenty-eight-year-old single male whose sad expressions, dishevelled appearance, and colourless apparel are only mildly relieved by a sardonic sense of humour which brings him no relief, and by an intelligence and education which he uses for the sake of others but never for himself. He was referred by his general practitioner for depression, but his problem was more of an inexorable sadness and personal loneliness. Since his break-up with a girlfriend, he had lived alone in a flat, dispersing himself during the day into multiple odd jobs. Although his days were a flurry of arranged activity, he went through them in a style of agitated passivity, as if he were being aggressively handled by his own work arrangement. Once home, he would collapse into the slovenly comfort of his flat, where he would prop himself before the TV, eat a scanty meal of packaged food, masturbate and, above all, ruminate obsessively about the future

and bemoan his current 'bad luck'. Every week, without failure, he would go home to see his mother. He felt she lived in order to talk about him and thus he must be seen by her in order to keep her content.

Reconstruction of the earliest years of his life yielded the following. Peter was born in a working-class home during the war. While his father was defending the country, the home was occupied by numerous in-laws. Peter was the first child born in the family and he was lavishly idolized, particularly by his mother who spoke constantly to her relatives about how Peter would undo their misery through great deeds. An inveterate dreamer about golden days to come, mother's true depression showed up in the lifeless manner in which she cared for Peter, since she invested all her liveliness in him as mythical object rather than actual infant. Soon after Peter's analysis began it became clear to me that he knew himself to be primarily inside a myth he shared with mother; indeed, he knew that she did not actually attend to the real him, but to him as the object of her dreams. As her mythical object, he felt his life to be suspended and, indeed, this was the way he lived. He seemed to be preserving himself, attending to somatic needs, waiting for the day when he would fulfil her dream. But because it was mother's myth he could do nothing, only wait for something to happen. He seemed to empty himself compulsively of his true self needs in order to create an empty internal space to receive mother's dream thoughts. Each visit to the home was curiously like a mother giving her son a narrative feeding. Hence he would empty himself of personal desire and need in order to fulfil mother's desire and he would preserve himself in a state of suspension from life, waiting for the myth to call him into a transformed reality.

Because his mother has transmitted to him his crucial function as her mythic object, Peter does not experience his internal psychic space as his own. Inner space exists for the other, so that in reporting inner states of being Peter does so through a depersonalized narrative as this region is not the 'from me' but the 'for her'. There is a notable absence in Peter of any sense of self, no quality of an 'I', nor even of a 'me'. Instead his self representation bears more the nature of an 'it' on an existential plane. Being an 'it' means for him being dormant, suspended, inert. Peter's free associations are accounts of 'it' states: ruminative reports on the happenings of his body as a depersonalized object. His mother's primary concern was for him to remain in good health in order to fulfil her dreams for him. He was consequently obsessed with any somatic problem, which he reported with almost clinical detachment.

Gradually I recognized that the mythic structure (existing in a narrative rather than existential reality) disguised the secret discourse of the lost culture of Peter's earliest relation to his mother. His ego-states were an utterance to mother who used them as the vocabulary of myth. If he was feeling like a casualty because of ego defects and the failure of id needs, it was because he was her knight errant who had fought battles for her and must rest for future missions. If he felt depleted by his personal relations it was because he was a cherished god who could not expect to mix successfully with the masses. If he spoke to his mother with a sigh she responded, not by discovering the source of the sigh, but by telling him not to worry, that soon he would make money, become famous, go on TV, and bring to the family all the wealth that they deserved.

His existential despair was continually flung into mythic narrative, a symbolic order where the real is used to populate the fantastic. On the few occasions when he tried to elicit from his mother some actual attendance to his internal life, she flew into a rage and told him that his misery threatened their lives, as only he could deliver them. He was to remain the golden larva, the unborn hero, who, if he did not shatter mythic function with personal needs, would soon be delivered into a world of riches and fame beyond his imagination.

In the transference Peter spoke of himself as an object in need of care: 'my stomach hurts', 'I have a pain in my neck', 'I have a

cold', 'I don't feel well'. He spoke to me in the
language of sighs, groans, and a haunting laughter which served his need to be emptied of agitated desire and to elicit my acute attention. He
rubbed his hands, looked at his fingers, flopped

his body around as if it were a sack. As I came to realize that this
was not obsessive rumination which served as a resistance, but a
secret discourse recalled from the culture of his earliest relations
to his mother, he found my attention to his private language an
immense relief. I felt that he was trying to share a secret with me
within the transference, but it was a secret utterance that was
prior to language and masked by its enigmatic quality. I could
only 'enter' this sequestered culture by speaking to him in its
language: to be attentive to all groans, sighs, remarks about his
body, etc. Above all, I was to learn that what he wanted was to
hear my voice, which I gradually understood to be his need for a
good sound. My interpretations were appreciated less for their
content, and more for their function as structuring experiences.
He rarely recalled the content of an interpretation. What he appreciated was the sense of relief brought to him through my voice.

Peter's language, which I shared in the beginning of the analysis, reflected the terms of a minimally transformative mother.
Later, when Peter would invite me to become a simple accomplice
in the mother's transformational idiom, I would refuse such
transformations (such as the golden larva myth) in favour of
achievable transformations. As I analysed this transformational
idiom, it gave way to a new culture of relatedness. The constella-
tion had to be broken down through analysis before a new idiom
of relatedness could be established.

Peter's sense of fate, his remaining a potential transformational object to the other, suggests that not only does the
infant require separation and disillusion from the transformational mother, but the mother must also suffer a 'let-down'
brought on by the real needs of the infant, which mitigates the
mother's unconscious wish for an infant to be her transformational object. Peter's mother continually refused to recognize and attend to him as a real person, though admittedly
there was a quality of what we might call covetous mothering. She

possessed him like an alchemist guarding dross
that was her potential treasure. His real needs
went unmet, as mother insisted that Peter fulfil
her sense that destiny would bring her a de-
liverer-child.

DISCUSSION

The search for the transformational object, in both narcissistic
and schizoid characters, is in fact an internal recognition of the
need for ego repair and, as such, is a somewhat manic search for
health. At the same time their idiom reflects a minimally transformative mother, a factor that becomes clear in the often meagre
way they use the analyst in the transference. I will discuss the
analyst's confrontation vis à vis the transfer of the patient's
transformational idiom in the chapters on countertransference.

To be sure, one of the features of such patients is their comparative unavailability for relating to the actual other – their
obtuseness or excessive withdrawnness – but I think such characteristics, reflective of psychodevelopmental arrests, also point
towards the patient's need to assert the region of illness as a plea
for the arrival of the regressive object relation that is identified
with basic ego repair. In analysis this can result in the patient's
almost total inability to relate to the analyst as a real person,
while at the same time maintaining an intense relation to the analyst as a transformational object. What is the patient trying to
establish?

As other authors have pointed out (for example, Smith,
1977), such patients seek a special ambience with the analyst,
where the analyst's interpretations are initially less important for
their content and more significant for what is experienced as a
maternal presence, an empathic response. Indeed, so-called analytic neutrality of expression – ostensibly to mitigate the hysterical or obsessional patient's dread of feeling criticized and to
facilitate the analysand's freedom of association – actually works
in a different way for narcissistic or schizoid patients: they can
become enchanted by it, and may appear oblivious to the actual
content of the interpretation so long as the song of the analytic
voice remains constant. Now, we may look upon this as a compli-

cation in the path of analysability, or we may
recognize that the analytic space (the provision
of the holding environment) facilitates a process
in such patients that leads to the evocation of a
deeply regressed state which may be a part of this

patient's necessary path to cure. Indeed my experience with such
patients is that a regression to this form of object relating often
takes place in the first session of analysis, as the ecology of the
analytic room (analyst, analyst's interpretations, couch, etc.) becomes a kind of asylum.

As I view it, the patient is regressed to the level of the basic
fault, but as each regression points to the region of illness within
the person, it also suggests the requirement of a cure. What is
needed is an initial experience of successive ego transformations
that are identified with the analyst and the analytic process. In
such moments, the patient experiences interpretations primarily
for their capacity to match his internal mood, feeling or thought,
and such moments of rapport lead the patient to 're-experience'
the transformational object relation. He appreciates the analyst's fundamental unintrusiveness (particularly the analyst not
demanding compliance) not because it leads to freedom of association, but because it feels like the kind of relating that is needed to
become well. The paradox is that as the patient regresses into
need, searching for a miraculous transformation, the analyst's
ordinary work of listening, clarifying and interpreting intro-
duces a different idiom of transforming psychic life.

Some clinicians might regard this use of the analyst as a resistance, but if so, I think we overlook the undeniably unique atmosphere we create for relating. The very offer of treatment invites
regressive longings in many patients, as I explore below in chapters 12, 13 and 14. Placing the patient on the couch further
induces a sense of anxious expectation and dependency. Our
reliability, our unintrusiveness, our use of empathic thought to
meet the requirements of the analysand, are often more maternal
than was the actual mother's care. And in such moments, the
patient's identification of the analyst as the transformational object is not dissimilar to the infant's identification of the mother
with such processes. Indeed, just as the infant's identification of

ego transformations with the mother is a perceptual identification – and not a desire – so, too, the
patient's identification does not seem to reflect
the patient's desire for us to be transformational,
but his adamant perceptual identification of the
analyst as transformational object. In the treatment of the narcissistic, borderline and schizoid characters, this phase of the
analysis is both necessary and inevitable.

This stage of treatment is very difficult for the clinician since,
in a sense, there is no analysis of the patient taking place, and
interpretive remarks may be met by a gamut of refusals: from
indifference to polite contempt to rage. One such patient would
often nod politely, say that yes he did see what I meant, indeed
was impressed with how accurate my remark was, but invariably
he would end by saying: 'But of course, you know what you have
said is only technically correct. It doesn't help me with life experiences, so, as such, as correct as it is I don't see what you think
I can do with such a remark.' He was convinced I knew how to
take care of him, and even if it was only for an hour a day, he
wanted me to soothe him. Analysis proper was regarded as an intellectual intrusion into his tranquil experience of me, and I was
for him a kind of advanced computer storing his information,
processing his needs into my memory banks. He was waiting for
an eventual session when I would suddenly emerge with the
proper solution for him, and in an instant remedy his life. I have
come to regard this part of his analysis as that kind of regression
which is a re-enactment of the earliest object experience, and I
think it is folly for an analyst to deny that the culture of the analytic space does indeed facilitate such recollections. If such regressions are a resistance to the analysis of the self, they are
resistances only in the sense that the patient must resist analytic
investigation as premature, and therefore not to the point. In the
transference – which is as much to the analytic space and process
as it is to the person of the analyst – the patient is relating to
the transformational object, that is, experiencing the analyst as
the environment-mother, a pre-verbal memory that cannot be
cognized into speech that recalls the experience, but only into
speech that demands its terms be met: unintrusiveness, 'holding',

'provision', insistence on a kind of symbiotic or
telepathic knowing, and facilitation from thought
to thought or from affect to thought. In these
sessions, then, the primary form of discourse is a
clarification which the patient experiences as a
transformative event. Interpretations which require reflective
thought or which analyse the self are often felt to be precocious
demands on the patient's psychic capacity, and such people may
react with acute rage or express a sudden sense of futility and
despair.

Perhaps because psychoanalytic theory evolved from work
with the hysterical patient (who interpreted the analytic space as
a seduction) or the obsessional patient (who adopted it willingly
as another personal ritual) we have tended to regard regressive
reactions to the analytic space as resistances to the working alliance or the analytic process. Yet the hysteric's sexualization of
the transference and the obsessional's ritualization of the analytic process (free dissociation?) may be seen as defences against
the very 'invitation' of the analytic space and process towards
regression. Thus, in the analysis of such patients, psychic material was readily forthcoming and one could be relatively pleased
that there was considerable grist for the analytic mill, but treatment often continued endlessly with no apparent character
change, or was suddenly intruded upon by archaic or primitive
material. In such cases I believe the analyst was unaware that the
failure of the patient to experience the analytic situation as a regressive invitation was a resistance. Indeed, the analytic process,
in emphasizing the mechanics of free association and interpretation of the patient's defences, could often result in a denial of the
very object relation that was 'offered' to the patient. If the analyst cannot acknowledge that in fact he is offering a regressive
space to the patient (that is, a space that encourages the patient to
relive his infantile life in the transference), if he insists that in the
face of the invitation 'work' must be carried out, it is not surprising that in such analyses patient and analyst may either carry on
in a kind of mutual dissociation that leads nowhere (obsessional
collusion), or in a sudden blow-up on the part of the patient, often
termed 'acting out'.

As I view it, then, the analyst functions as an evocative mnemic trace of the transformational object, because the situation will either induce a patient's regressive recollection of this early object relation or the variations of resistance to it: either denial by sexualization or obsessional ritualization, for example. Indeed, the transference from this point of view is first and foremost a transference reaction to this primary object relation and will help us to see how the patient remembers his own experience of it. There may be a deep regression to an adamant demand that the analyst fulfil the promise of the invitation and function in a magically transformative manner. Or the patient may have enough health and insight into regressive recollections to carry on with subsequent work in the analysis while remaining in touch with more archaic aspects of the self. Indeed I believe that much of the time a patient's passivity, wordlessness or expectation that the analyst knows what to do is not a resistance to any particular conscious or preconscious thought, but a recollection of the early pre-verbal world of the infant being with mother. Unless we recognize that psychoanalysts share in the construction of this pre-verbal world through the analyst's silence, empathic thought and the total absence of didactic instruction, we are being unfair to the patient and he may have reason to be perplexed and irritated.

The transference rests on the paradigm of the first transformational object relation. Freud tacitly recognized this when he set up the analytic space and process and, although there is comparatively little about the mother-child relation within Freud's theory, we might say that he represented his recognition of it in the creation of the analytic set up. The psychoanalytic process constitutes a memory of this primary relation, and the psychoanalyst's practice is a form of countertransference, since he recollects by enactment the transformational object situation. What Freud could not analyse in himself – his relation to his own mother – he represented through his creation of the psychoanalytic space and process. Unless we can grasp that as psychoanalysts we are enacting this early paradigm, we continue to act out Freud's blindness in the countertransference.

The search for transformation and for the transformational object is perhaps the most pervasive
archaic object relation, and I want to emphasize
that this search arises not out of desire for the
object **per se**, or primarily out of craving or

longing. It arises from the person's certainty that the object will
deliver transformation; this certainty is based on the object's
nominated capacity to resuscitate the memory of early ego transformation. In arguing this, I am maintaining that though no
cognitive memory of the infant's experience of the mother is available, the search for the transformational object, and nomination
of the deliverer of environmental transformation, is an ego
memory.

In a curious way, it is solely the ego's object and may, indeed,
be to the utter shock or indifference of the person's subjective
experience of his own desire. A gambler is compelled to gamble.
Subjectively, he may wish he did not gamble, even hate his compulsion to do so. In Melville's *Moby Dick*, Ahab feels compelled to
seek the whale, even though he feels alienated from the source of
his own internal compulsion. He says:

> What is it, what nameless, inscrutable, unearthly thing is it;
> what cozening, hidden lord and master, and cruel, remorse-
> less emperor commands me; then against all natural lovings
> and longings, I so keep pushing, and crowding, and jamming
> myself on all the time; recklessly making me ready to do what
> in my own proper, natural heart, I durst not so much as dare?
> Is Ahab, Ahab? Is it I, God, or who, that lifts this arm? (1851,
> pp. 444–5)

There is something impersonal and ruthless about the search for
the whale, and indeed for all objects nominated as transformational. Once early ego memories are identified with an object that is contemporary, the subject's relation to the object can
become fanatical, and I think many extremist political movements indicate a collective certainty that their revolutionary
ideology will effect a total environmental transformation that will
deliver everyone from the gamut of basic faults: personal,
familial, economic, social and moral. Again, it is not the

revolutionary's desire for change, or the extremist's longing for change, but his certainty that the object (in this case the revolutionary ideology) will bring about change that is striking to the observer.

CONCLUSIONS

In work with certain kinds of patients (schizoid and narcissistic) who exaggerate a particular object-seeking, and in our analysis of certain features of culture, I think we can isolate the trace in the adult of the earliest experience of the object: the experience of an object that transforms the subject's internal and external world. I have called this first object the transformational object, since I want to identify it with the object as process, thus linking the first object with the infant's experience of it. Before the mother is personalized for the infant as a whole object, she has functioned as a region or source of transformation, and since the infant's own nascent subjectivity is almost completely the experience of the ego's integrations (cognitive, libidinal, affective), the first object is identified with the alterations of the ego's state. With the infant's growth and increasing self-reliance, the relation to the mother changes from the mother as the other who alters the self to a person who has her own life and her own needs. As Winnicott says, the mother disillusions the infant from the experience of mother as the sole preserver of his world, a process that occurs as the infant is increasingly able to meet his own needs and requirements. The ego experience of being transformed by the other remains as a memory that may be re-enacted in aesthetic experiences, in a wide range of culturally-dreamed-of transformational objects (such as new cars, homes, jobs and vacations) that promise total change of internal and external environment, or in the varied psychopathological manifestations of this memory, for example in the gambler's relation to his object or in the extremist's relation to his ideological object.

In the aesthetic moment, when a person engages in deep subjective rapport with an object, the culture embodies in the arts varied symbolic equivalents to the search for transformation. In the quest for a deep subjective experience of an object, the artist

both remembers for us and provides us with
occasions for the experience of ego memories of
transformation. In a way, the experience of the
aesthetic moment is neither social nor moral; it is
curiously impersonal and even ruthless, as the
object is sought out only as deliverer of an experience.

As I shall maintain in the next chapter, the aesthetic space
allows for a creative enactment of the search for this transformational object relation, and we might say that certain cultural objects afford memories of ego experiences that are now
profoundly radical moments. Society cannot possibly meet the
requirements of the subject, as the mother met the needs of the
infant, but in the arts we have a location for such occasional
recollections: intense memories of the process of self-trans-
formation.

Although all analysands will experience the analytic space as
an invitation to regress in the care of a transformational object,
and although it may be essential for the analyst to allow the
patient a prolonged experience of regression to dependence (see
below, chapter 14), many patients, as I will take up in the final
part of this book, will invite the analyst into a pathological transformational relation. For example, some analysands create confusion in order to compel the analyst to **misunderstand** them.
This is a negative transformation and may represent the transfer
of a pathological mother-child relation. Of course this must
eventually be analysed, but even here, in the analyst's vigorous
interpretive 'work' I think the patient unconsciously experiences
the analyst as a generative transformational object.

Transformation does not mean gratification. Growth is only
partially promoted by gratification, and one of the mother's
transformative functions must be to frustrate the infant. Like-
wise, aesthetic moments are not always beautiful or wonderful
occasions – many are ugly and terrifying but nonetheless profoundly moving because of the existential memory tapped.

2   *The spirit of the object as the hand of fate*

HOW do we believe? Is not ordinary perception predicated on a conviction that the sensed or the perceived is there for us to apprehend it? If some philosophies challenge the assumption of the verifiable 'thereness' of an external object, or if psychology cautions us that all perception is apperception, it is nonetheless the case that our individual and collective sanities rest on a certain poetic licence, a necessary illusion that the world we discuss is there to be experienced. This necessary illusion underwrites our existence; without this belief in a verifiable perception we would share not only the anxiety but the certitude of one another's madness. We would also be unable to 'correct' one another's perceptions, whether in disagreement in ordinary conversation about the accuracy of the spoken word or to engage in the sheltered industry of literary criticism where we continually shift the meaning of the texts we read. Our collective agreement that the world is shared by us all is matched by another poetic licence, that the terms we use to describe the world are adequate to represent it. The mathematician who writes 'let $X=1$' acknowledges the arbitrary nature of the symbolic. Language functions through illusion.

I do not intend to write about shared beliefs in this chapter, but rather about that occasion when a person is shaken by an experience into absolute certainty that he has been cradled by, and dwelled with, the spirit of the object, a rendezvous of mute recognition that defies representation.

Perhaps the most obvious example of this form of experience occurs during the moment of an unbeliever's conversion to a sacred object; in conversions to Christ, the person usually feels the sudden enclosure of the self by a sacred presence. This may be followed by a sense of being held by the object, and a recognition of some significant change in the environment's light (from ordinary to sacred) or by the accompaniment of polyphonic gongs that on recollection remind the subject of church bells.

The aesthetic moment is a caesura in time when the subject feels held in symmetry and solitude by the spirit of the object. 'What would characterize experience as aesthetic rather than either cognitive or moral,' writes Murray Krieger, 'would be its self sufficiency, its capacity to trap us within itself, to keep us from moving beyond it to further knowledge or to practical effort.' Whether this moment occurs in a christian's conversion experience, a poet's reverie with his landscape, a listener's rapture in a symphony, or a reader's spell with his poem, such experiences crystallize time into a space where subject and object appear to achieve an intimate rendezvous.

While such moments can subsequently be flung into hermeneutical explication, they are fundamentally wordless occasions, notable for the density of the subject's feeling and the fundamentally non-representational knowledge of being embraced by the aesthetic object. Once experienced, these occasions can sponsor a profound sense of gratitude in the subject that may lead him into a lifelong quest for some other reacquaintance with the aesthetic object. The christian may go to church and there hope to find traces of his experience, the naturalist may look for another sighting of that rarest of birds that creates for him a moment of sudden awe, and the romantic poet walk his landscape hoping for a spot in time, a suspended moment when self and object feel reciprocally enhancing and mutually informative.

THE HAND OF FATE

Why does the aesthetic moment evoke in us a deep conviction that we have been in rapport with a sacred object? What is the foundation for this belief? It occurs, in part, because we experience this uncanny moment as an event that is partially sponsored by the object. Further, we cannot calculate when we will have an aesthetic experience. It is almost inevitably a surprise. This surprise, complemented by an experience of fusion with the object (icon, poem, musical sound, landscape, etc.), of feeling held by the object's spirit, sponsors a deep conviction that such an occasion must surely be selected for us. The object is 'the hand of fate'. And in our induction by the object we are suddenly captured in an embrace that is an experience of being rather than mind, rooted in the total involvement of the self rather than objectified via representational or abstract thought.

The aesthetic moment is an experience of 'rapt, intransitive attention' (quoted in Krieger, 1976, p.11), a spell which holds self and other in symmetry and solitude. Time seems suspended. As the aesthetic moment constitutes a deep rapport between subject and object, it provides the person with a generative illusion of fitting with an object.

A form of déjà vu, it is an existential memory: a nonrepresentational recollection conveyed through a sense of the uncanny. Such moments feel familiar, sacred, reverential, but are fundamentally outside cognitive coherence. They are registered through an experience in being, rather than mind, because they express that part of us where the experience of rapport with the other was the essence of life before words existed. As I shall explain later, the aesthetic moment constitutes part of the unthought known. The aesthetic experience is an existential recollection of the time when communicating took place primarily through this illusion of deep rapport of subject and object. Being-with, as a form of dialogue, enabled the baby's adequate processing of his existence prior to his ability to process it through thought.

THE FIRST HUMAN AESTHETIC

The mother's idiom of care and the infant's experience of this handling is one of the first if not the earliest human aesthetic. It is the most profound occasion when the nature of the self is formed and transformed by the environment. The uncanny pleasure of being held by a poem, a composition, a painting, or, for that matter, any object, rests on those moments when the infant's internal world is partly given form by the mother since he cannot shape them or link them together without her coverage.

The infant has his own intrinsic 'form', given the design of his

inherited disposition, and his own cognitive
abilities (ego capacities) bias his subjective experience of reality. But as I have said earlier,
these internal transformational abilities are
identified with the mother. This first human aes-

thetic informs the development of personal character (which is
the utterance of self through the manner of being rather than the
representations of the mind) and will predispose all future aesthetic experiences that place the person in subjective rapport
with an object. As I have indicated in chapter 1, each aesthetic
experience is transformational, so the search for what Krieger
terms the 'aesthetic object' is a quest for the transformational object. The transformational object seems to promise the beseech-
ing subject an experience where self fragmentations will be
integrated through a processing form.

Depending on whose representation of the person's subjective
experience of infancy we read, we either focus on the person's
capacities (development of cognition, motility, adaptive defences, ego capacities), his incapacities (arising from inherent
deprivation and subsequent psychic conflicts) or both. No doubt
the infant has an internal structural tendency at this point of
being, as Piaget argues, but without a facilitative mother, as
Winnicott stresses, the infant's nascent ego capacities will suffer,
perhaps irreparably. This is objective fact.

The infant, however, is neither objectively aware of his own
ego capacities, nor of the mother's logic of care. If he is distressed, the resolution of discomfort is achieved by the appari-
tional-like presence of mother. The pain of hunger, a moment of
emptiness, is transformed by mother's milk into an experience of
fullness. This is a primary transformation: emptiness, agony,
and rage become fullness and content. The aesthetic of this experience is the particular way the mother meets the infant's need
and transforms his internal and external realities. Alongside the
infant's subjective experience of being transformed is the reality
that he is being transformed according to the mother's aesthetic. I
believe that he incorporates the milk, the new experience (fullness) and the aesthetic of handling. The baby takes in not only the
contents of the mother's communications but also their form. In

the beginning of life, handling of the infant is the primary mode of communicating, so the internalization of the mother's form (her aesthetic) is prior to the internalization of her verbal messages. Indeed, I believe that Bateson's notion of the double bind, where message is contradicted by mode of delivery or vice versa, formulates the conflict between the form as utterance and the content as message. The infant is caught between two contradictory experiences.

The mother conveys her aesthetic by her style of being with the infant – feeding, diaper changing, soothing, crooning, holding and playing – and it is the entirety of her way of being present with the baby that constitutes the phenomenology of her transformation of the infant's being. With a 'good-enough mother' a tradition of generative transformations of internal and external realities is established. Continuity of being is maintained.

Winnicott writes that this experience takes place in what he terms a 'facilitating environment' which includes the mother's system of care that protects the infant from either internal or external impingement. The baby is primarily protected against impingements which might lead him to replace being taken care of with precocious mental processes that interrupt and dissolve being by means of premature thought and vigilance. Murray Krieger (1976), a literary critic, describes a similar process when he writes about the aesthetic experience. 'I have tried to establish, then, that to the degree that an experience is functioning in the aesthetic mode, we find ourselves locked within it, freely and yet in a controlled way playing among its surfaces and its depths' (p. 23). Like Winnicott's facilitating environment, Krieger's 'aesthetic mode' holds the self within an experience of reverie or rapport that does not stimulate the self into thought. Writes Krieger: 'Would not such an object have, as a major objective, the need to keep us locked within it – to keep us, that is, from escaping into the world of cognitive or practical concerns?' (p. 12).

I agree with Krieger, but we may also ask an obvious question. What are the origins of this experience? The aesthetic experience is not something learned by the adult, it is an existential recollection of an experience where being handled by the maternal

aesthetic made thinking seemingly irrelevant to
survival.

Eventually, under ordinary circumstances,
the maternal aesthetic yields to the structure of
language, and at this point being can be spoken.
The mother's facilitation of the word-forming experience,
together with the infant's grasp of grammatical structure, is the
most significant transformation of the infant's encoded utterance. Until the grasp of the word, the infant's meaning resides
primarily within the mother's psyche-soma. With the word, the
infant has found a new transformational object, which facilitates
the transition from deep enigmatic privacy towards the culture of
the human village.

When the transformational object passes from the mother to
the mother's tongue, the first human aesthetic, self to mother,
passes towards the second human aesthetic, the finding of the
word to speak the self, or as a Lacanian might argue, the word's
discovery of the self. As it was mother's style of transforming the
infant's being that constituted the first human aesthetic, so too, I
believe, wording will handle and transform the moods of the self
and constitute further terms of that individual's personal aesthetic.

Thus the first human aesthetic passes into the idiom of formal
aesthetics, as the mother's aesthetic of care passes through her
tongue, from cooing, mirror-uttering, singing, story telling and
wording into language.

As part of this extraordinary transition we bear the structure
of the maternal aesthetic with us in several ways. Embedded in
Heinz Lichtenstein's notion of the 'identity theme' (1961) is not
only a thematics but an aesthetics. Our internal world is transformed by the mother's unconscious desire into a primary theme
of being with her that will affect all future ways of being with the
other. In an earlier paper (Bollas, 1974) I argued that a person's
character is a subjective recollection of the person's past, registered through the person's way of being with himself and others. I
would add that character is an aesthetic of being, as we have
internalized the structure of our existence, the phenomenological
reality of the maternal aesthetic. We have internalized a process,

a forming and transforming idiom, as well as the thematics of mother's discourse. Whenever we desired, despaired, reached towards, played, or were in rage, love, pain or need, we were met by mother and handled according to her idiom of care. Whatever our existential critique of her aesthetic, be it generative integration into our own being, compliance followed by dissociated splitting of our true self, or defensive handling of the aesthetic (denial, splitting, repression) we encountered her idiom. Indeed, the way she handled us (either as accepting and facilitating or refusing and rigid or a mixture of both) will influence our way of handling our self, as I explore in chapter 3. In a sense, we learn the grammar of our being before we grasp the rules of our language.

In a 'good-enough' situation the mother as transformational object manipulates the environment to make it correspond to human need, but this does not preclude the internalization of a frustrating aesthetic. As this experience is internalized into the structure of the ego, the self seeks transformational objects to reach relative symmetry with the environment or to re-create traumatic gaps in the symmetry. A person wants to express to a quizzical friend why he appears to be depressed. 'Are you angry about something?' asks the friend. 'No,' he replies, 'I'm not angry. I'm bewildered by a letter I've received.' The word 'anger' is not an adequate transformation of the mood to the word; it will not make the external expression generatively symmetrical with the internal impression. The word 'bewildered' does, and the subject feels relieved and may be understood. This no doubt reflects a need based on experience of a good-enough transformational process, while we know that in another situation another person might need to be misunderstood in order to experience relief.

If failure occurs, let us say at the point of acquiring language, words may become meaningless expressions of the child's internal world. They may feel useless, or, if the rules of the family prohibit words which speak the mood of the self, they may feel dangerous. Failure to transform the infant's internal moods into language may facilitate the schizoid character position, where language is dissociated from feeling, and where the moods of the internal world are almost exclusively registered in the subject's way of being. True self states then are manifested through the 'language' of character, held within the self, whereas compliant or abstract thought representations are placed into the word. As such, the subject's internal or private self is continually dissociated from his executant self. An aesthetic moment for such an individual may occur when he faces a formidable and confusing external object that establishes an internal confusion in the subject, providing him with an uncanny feeling of the awful and the familiar, an experience where this aesthetic object seems to demand resolution into clarity but threatens the self with annihilation if the subject seeks to speak it.

LITERARY EXAMPLES

An example of the aesthetic experience described occurs in Herman Melville's novel *Moby Dick*, when Ishmael is captured by the confused portrait of a whale in the Spouter Inn. It is Ishmael's captivation by the awesome representation of a large hovering mass about to impale itself on a ship that constitutes his aesthetic moment. He cannot define what he sees, despite his efforts to throw the experience into thought, for the experience of his captivity is outside cognitive apprehension. When he does transform this experience into a word, 'whale', he can leave the painting and is released. Because Ishmael can experience aesthetic moments – he is captured by paintings, sermons, books on whales, the whale itself, and idiomatic presences of others (Queequeg for example) – he dwells in the aesthetic moment with a transformational other: the object that captures and places him under the deep spell of the uncanny. Ishmael therefore reflects the creative alternative to Ahab, who scans the seas for a concrete transformational object (Moby Dick), because he occupies Melville's position – that of the artist who is in the unique position to create his own aesthetic moments and find symbolic equivalents to psychohistorical experiences that henceforth (as text or painting) become a new reality.

Perhaps it is fitting to illustrate the reverie of the aesthetic moment by quoting at some length from one of the most popular stories read to English school-children: *The Wind in the Willows*. A children's story is a kind of transitional fiction, a text that emerges from a world of the child's fantastical certitudes and captures this magic through its fairy-tale plotting and serene narrative voice. Children's fiction is replete with moments of horror, awe, fascination and suspense. Self and environment are mutually transformative as if something of the child's sense of ontogenetic metamorphosis is registered in the fiction he reads. Often, as in *The Wind in the Willows*, the tale is about a journey, a picaresque adventure that is faithful to the child's appreciation of his own psycho-somatic transformations.

The Wind in the Willows is a tale of discovery. A homely and frightened little mole is befriended by an adventuresome if rather reckless water rat who insists that they travel down the river to discover the world. One morning just before dawn they are rowing quietly downstream. Suddenly the rat is startled by what he feels is some ethereal sound. 'So beautiful and strange and new,' he says. 'Since it was to end so soon, I almost wish I had never heard it. For it has roused a longing in me that is pain, and nothing seems worthwhile but just to hear that sound once more and go on listening to it forever.' The mole has heard nothing but he is respectfully alert to new possibilities. He asks his friend, the rat, what has happened, but the rat is transported into a dream state. 'The rat never answered, if indeed he heard. Rapt, transported, trembling, he was possessed in all his senses by this new divine thing that caught up his helpless soul and swung and dandled it, a powerless but happy infant in a strong sustaining grasp.' This experience – an aesthetic moment – feels new and strange, yet it arouses a 'longing'; its immediate impact is not cognitively linked to any previous mental experience, yet affectively it evokes the past. Then the author, in the position of the omniscient identifier of the psychic locations of his characters, says that the rat is 'transported', possessed, like a 'powerless but happy infant in a strong sustaining grasp'. The writer knows how to identify this type of experience for the child reader; he invokes the imagery of the infant being held by the mother and places the

aesthetic moment in the space between the infant
and the caretaker.

39

THE SPIRIT
OF THE
OBJECT

THE SPIRIT OF PLACE

In my view the aesthetic moment is an evocative
resurrection of an early ego condition often brought on by a sudden and uncanny rapport with an object, a moment when the subject is captured in an intense illusion of being selected by the
environment for some deeply reverential experience. This holding experience sponsors a psycho-somatic memory of the holding
environment. It is a pre-verbal, essentially pre-representational
registration of the mother's presence. As with the rat and mole,
the experience cannot be properly linked to any discrete object,
but is placed instead with a notion of what the object thought to be
sponsoring the event should be like: awesome and sacred. The
reader of *Wind in the Willows* discovers that in fact Rat and Mole
are experiencing the sun rise, but they cannot see the sun, they
only experience its effect on their environment. The object casts
its shadow on the subject. In much the same way the infant experiences the mother as a process that transforms his internal
and external environment, but he does not know that such transformation is partly sponsored by the mother. The experience of
the object precedes the knowing of the object. The infant has a
prolonged sense of the uncanny, as he dwells with a spirit of place
the creation of which is not identifiable.

It is possible to see how the reduction of spiritual experiences
to the discrete administration of **the mother** always strikes us as
somehow an insult to the integrity of uncanny experience, as the
sacred precedes the maternal. Our earliest experience is prior to
our knowing of the mother as an object in her own right.

CLINICAL ILLUSTRATION

A young man in psychotherapy, Jonathan (see chapter 4 for
further discussion of this patient), was born into a wealthy family
dominated by an ambitious mother who refused to give up her
active social life for the care of her new infant. She hired a nanny,
and the infant was passed from one figure to another, from
mother to nanny, from nanny to mother, during the first five

years of his life. He is very fond of his mother, who is associated with warmth, smell, soft clothing and tranquillity. He has no memory of his nanny. As he says: 'Just a blank. I remember nothing.' Now, he has what I believe to be an aesthetic experience that utters the terms of the first human aesthetic. As he wanders through the city, every so often he will see a young man, always in a bus or car, who is going in the opposite direction (a momentary presence) who evokes a sudden feeling that he is the person who can 'transform' him. He considers such moments to be the most glorious moments of his life, because they fill him with a 'transcendental' sense of 'exquisite harmony', even though they are followed by a sense of blankness and despair. This transformational object appears and disappears; it promises deliverance but yields absence and blankness. As Jonathan has discovered in the psychoanalysis, the search for this transformational object and the nature of his aesthetic experience belong to an existential memory of his experience of the maternal aesthetic (the past called into the subject's being). When he was with mother he was filled with a sense of joy; when she left him to the nanny, he felt blank and deserted.

Transformational-object-seeking is an endless memorial search for something in the future that resides in the past. I believe that if we investigate many types of object relating we will discover that the subject is seeking the transformational object and aspiring to be matched in symbiotic harmony within an aesthetic frame that promises to metamorphose the self.

3   *The self as object*

O NE of the features of Winnicott's psychoanalytic sensibility is to look within the patient for the infant who lives within a maternal holding environment and to ask how patients communicate their knowledge of this experience through the transference. In living with borderline, schizoid and narcissistic character disorders, Winnicott knew that he was immersed in the patient's unconscious reconstruction of a child's environment, and I understand that it was a feature of his technique to adapt himself to the patient's ego defects and characterological biases in order to allow for the transference to evolve without the impingement of a premature use of analytic interpretation. From this experiencing of the early infant environment, the analyst could then interpret the past as it was re-created through the transference.

People bear memories of being the mother's and father's object in ego structure, and in the course of a person's object relations he re-presents various positions in the historical theatre of lived experiences between elements of mother, father and his infant-child self. One idiom of representation is the person's relation to the self as an object, an object relation where the individual may objectify, imagine, analyse and manage the self through identification with primary others who have been involved in that very task.

I find the concept of the relation to the self as an object to be of considerable use to me in my clinical work with patients, and although this idea is present in psychoanalytic theory (particularly in Milner, 1969; Modell, 1969; Schafer, 1968; Kohut, 1977; Khan, 1979; and Winnicott, 1965), I do not think it has been adequately conceptualized and it does not appear to be as prominent a feature in our interpretive formulations to our patients as it might be.

Winnicott (1965) said that there is no such thing as a baby without a mother. He also thought that there was no adult without a baby and mother portion or, as I mean to emphasize, there is no adult who, in relation to himself as an object, is not existentially through self management, or representationally through self objectification, managing certain aspects of himself as a mother or father does a child.

INTRASUBJECTIVE SPACE AND THE
RELATION TO THE SELF AS OBJECT

It is an ordinary feature of our mental life to engage in subvocal conversations with oneself. As I have been planning this chapter, for example, I have thought from the second person pronoun objectifying myself to say: 'You must include Winnicott and Khan because much of your thinking comes from their work.' Even if a second pronomial identification is absent it may be implicit, as for example, when I think 'don't forget to provide ordinary examples of this phenomenon before going into more complex clinical examples': the 'you' is implied. This constant objectification of the self for purposes of thinking is commonplace. It is also a form of object relation, as Freud so sagely understood when he evolved his theory of the superego to identify that part of the mind that speaks to us as its object. Naturally this intrasubjective relationship will change according to the person's state of mind. If I write on a topic in my notebook I am more relaxed and permissive of the fanciful idea than when I write for a lecture. Much of psychoanalysis is about the nature of intrasubjective relations to the self as an object – those relations that are biased by instinctual forces and superego activities, and those relations reflective of integrative ego activities.

The intrasubjective relation to the self as an object is not just a cognitive division enabling us to widen the parameters of thought and action, nor is it simply an intrapsychic objectification of the play of instincts, desires, reproaches, inhibitions, and mediative activities. It is a complex object relation and we can analyse how a person holds and relates to himself as his own internal and external object.

On a recent trip to Rome to deliver a paper I had

several occasions for working through different

issues in the management of myself. While leaving

the plane and heading for a taxi I was anxious

about not making my hotel on time. I had been

thinking in the first person for much of the flight: 'I will do this, prepare that, see this, visit so-and-so,' but as the taxi went slowly, my anxiety increased and I required some brief holding activity. I said to myself: 'Damn it, the taxi is too slow and I will be late [anxiety increases]. Look: there is nothing you can possibly do about it, so stop worrying [slightly modified]. But people will be kept waiting [re-emergence of anxiety]. Don't be silly [unfortunate use of a bit of psychopathy]. Anyway, there is nothing you can do and what will upset your friends here is if you arrive in a state, so leave it be.' This mental work is an example of holding, which is a feature of the total aspect of self management that we are engaged in during our lifetime. As a result of this brief spell of self objectification, expression of anxiety and reassurance, I was able to enjoy the taxi ride to the hotel and to arrive for the lecture in a good-enough state of mind.

A day after my arrival in Rome, when I was sitting in an outdoor café, a beautiful woman walked by, to which I responded subvocally: 'look at that, will you!', a remark to the self as object that can certainly be read in many ways.

It would be interesting to give further thought to the phenomenology of this intrasubjective relation. How do our patients, for example, handle themselves as an internal object within intrasubjective space? What is the nature of their ability to give expression to their affects, to bear internal conflict, to mediate between instinctual demands and superego prohibition, and to facilitate a good-enough solution to the conflicts between the areas of the mind? What is their conscious and unconscious experience as the object of their self management?

A patient, Michael, came for treatment because of the termination of a love relationship. One of the more remarkable features of this young man was his virtual incapacity to realize his wishes. If, for example, he thought to himself on a Friday afternoon that he would go to a film that night, the wish was never followed up by those ordinary activities (buying a film guide, selecting a film, planning how to get to the cinema) typical of most of us. Inevitably he felt some frustration but never linked his recurrent sense of despair to this failure in self management. On a Saturday morning he might feel lonesome and think of going for a walk, and he might even go so far as to get his coat on and walk out of the front door, but he would only get to the newsagent where he would buy a paper and return to his house to peruse the newspaper in a desultory state. One of the aspects of this man's despair was his failure to have an internalized space for the reception of his own wishes, another space for the mediation of any conflict between wishes, practicalities or inhibitions, and another mental space for the facilitation and management of the partial gratification of the wish.

Another patient, Adrienne, is a hard-working professional woman who, upon leaving work, enters a world of fantastical daydreams. She has a never-ending 'novel' of stable and interesting imaginary characters who live on an alien planet. She spends hours each night imagining a life for the main character who is involved in intrigues and close escapes from danger, and as Adrienne develops complex relations with the other characters many of them become the object of separate fantastical scripts that go on for months. During her work day, which she manages quite competently, Adrienne does engage in intrasubjective relating, but frequently, when she is upset with herself, she addresses herself as 'she'. 'She' has done something wrong, or 'she' would be condemned. It emerged that her feelings, when addressing herself as 'she', were in identification with the sound of her mother's voice, whom she can recall punishing her quite frequently for the smallest of mistakes.

I am particularly concerned to emphasize the necessity of asking how each person relates to himself as an object within intrasubjective space. Who is speaking? What part of the self is speaking and what part of the self is being addressed? What is the nature of this object relation? Is it a good-enough object relation? Is instinct permitted representation? In what way? As a demand? Or are instinctual needs elaborated into the wish so that they become part of the subject's range of desire? Is

desire represented in coherent ways so as to be
syntonic with the other parts of the self, or is
sexuality communicated in a persecutory manner, perhaps through the structure of the per-
verse, which could constitute a breakdown in the intrasubjective
object relation? The content of the desire is less my concern here
than the fate of the handling of the content within an internal
object-relational setting. Each person who possesses a capacity
for intrasubjective relating is an object of his own self management, and the nature of how the self is handled as an object of
one's own management is worthy of scrutiny.

THE MANAGEMENT OF THE SELF
AS AN OBJECT

In a perfectly ordinary way we are constantly engaged in acts of
self management, from our choice of vocation to our choice of
clothing; from the perception and facilitation of our needs to the
management of our own personal realities for the partial gratification of those needs; from our recognition of, and planning for,
holidays to our differing abilities to recognize and confront economic and familial realities.

The way in which we position ourselves in space and in time
may partly reflect how we were originally situated spatially and
temporally in relation to our parents. A patient may, for
example, indicate through awkward body gait and social ill ease a
primary discomfort at having to occupy space in the first place. I
can think of one patient whose manner of walking and talking was
so arhythmic and hesitant that it became a crucial feature of the
analysis, and it is helpful to understand the evolution of this
characterological development to see how the patient's way of
handling the self as an object may reflect the lack of ordinary
spatial-temporal co-ordinates in the parent's handling of the
patient when an infant. It is my view that when I was with this
patient I was witnessing the patient's transference of a maternal
care system to the self as an object.

The relation to the self as object is a complex object relation,
and also expresses one's unconscious phantasies, but my emphasis

in this chapter is solely on that aspect of this relation that constitutes a partial transfer of the maternal care system. Each person's spatial-temporal idiom reflects the integrative work of unconscious phantasy, which in turn reflects the ego's record of the infant's early experience of his place in the object setting. This body memory conveys memories of our earliest existence. It is a form of knowledge which has yet to be thought, and constitutes part of the unthought known.

Another patient, Mark, who is quite grandiose, inevitably cannot say no to an invitation to display his intellectual wares to any interested party. The result is that he is enormously over-committed. Such a burden however is unconsciously motivated because it serves to defend him against any form of personal celebration of his own intelligence and creativity. Instead he offers up a very worn-out person, overly critical of his performance on any occasion, and if he celebrates anything, it is the idiom of the performer who is perpetually dragged on to the stage for yet another exhausting performance. How can this be if in fact it is Mark who has arranged these events? As I have understood it, he creates a facilitating environment (the schedule of overcommitted duties) that appears to handle him in a demanding manner: 'Tomorrow you must do this, the day after that you must do that, next week you will have to go north, etc.' The dynamics of such a relation to the self as an object are of course complex and they could be due to any number of internal relations. In his case, he dreads that should he be found to enjoy his abilities, someone will wrongly assume that he wishes to live an independent life, when in fact he unconsciously prefers to be symbiotically bound to an object that demands he fulfil its needs. As it is, this relation to himself as an object re-creates his mother's own narcissistic uses of him, which he found quite pleasurable in many ways, and it biases his own way of handling himself as an object in his life.

THE DREAM AS SETTING FOR THE
RELATION TO THE SELF AS OBJECT

As I shall explore in the next chapter, dream space differs from intrasubjective subvocal space, since the former is an hallucinatory event while the latter is a mode of conscious objectification of psychic states within a relationship. In the dream one portion of the self is represented through an illusion that the experiencing subject in the dream is the entire self,

while the other portions of the self may be represented through the dream events and other aspects of the dream script. My question is 'How is the experiencing subject handled as an object by the dream script?' In other words, as we become accustomed to the nature of our patient's dream life, how is the dreamer managed as an experiencing subject within his hallucinated scripts? In asking this question, I am departing from the classical notion of the dream content as only a manifest content which hides the latent true meaning. The dream experience constitutes an object relation in its own right and can be examined as such in terms of the dreamer-subject's experience of the dream event.

Some dreamers rarely script desire into their dreams, and the dreaming subject may only have tasks to perform in his dream experience. Other dreamers may overestimate themselves, and the self in the dream is beset with a multitude of sexual objects which sustain excitation but mitigate orgasmic-type experiences. Other dreamers may script dreams which are so sequentially bizarre and disconnected in manifest logic that the self has a perpetual sense of anxiety over the utter bewilderment of his dream script. Some may be scripted to have an initial experience of partially satisfied desire only to have it interrupted by some upsetting event, such as the emergence of a rival or rejection by the love object. Yet others may script nightmares so frequently that they fear sleeping and dreaming itself, as their experience of the dream script is that it always contains a potential terror against the self. Whatever the dreamer's experience of the dream script, it is relevant to our psychoanalysis of the person's relation to himself as an object **to consider the dream space as a particular kind of unconscious holding environment** in which the dreamer may be the object of a presentation of desire, guilt, and historical notation, from an unconsciously organized and interpretive portion of the self. Therefore, when thinking with the patient about his dreaming self's experience of the dream, it is useful to consider his emotional reality within the dream and the thoughts he had while 'inside' the dream event.

Day dreams lie somewhere between dreaming proper and intrasubjective relating, and are occasions for the subject's location of an objectified portion of himself in a script. In these conscious fantasies we may once again ask how the person handles himself as his own object. What range of experiences are provided? What is the nature of the self as object relation?

INTERSUBJECTIVITY AND THE RELATION TO THE SELF AS OBJECT

While it might not be accurate to maintain that each of us chooses a friend or a mate or a peer environment as an expression of our relation to the self as object, it can certainly be said that our external world evokes unconscious elements of the self as object relation,[1] and that our experience of reality is therefore influenced by those unconscious associations elicited by environmental conditions. To be overly simplistic for a moment, if Tom is a rather passive and dependent chap he may choose Harry as a friend, for Harry is an active and aggressive fellow who objectifies a split-off fragment of Tom's self with which Tom is only now brought into relation by virtue of his relation to Harry. How Tom relates to Harry has its own indigenous and circumstantial truths, but it also yields how Tom relates to those elements of himself that he has split off and finds in Harry. If Mary marries Jim and projects her need for self idolization into Jim, whom she insists is ideal, and who in turn idolizes her, he is projectively identified with a role which he must either fulfil or incur Mary's extreme displeasure. In this relationship, it is questionable whether Mary is really relating to Jim or to Jim as a split-off fragment of her own self; in this way the relationship simply lives out her unconscious relation to herself as object.

The way people interact reveals implied or tacit assumptions about their relation to the self as object. Each person forms his own 'culture' through the selection of friends, partners and colleagues. The totality of this object-relational field constitutes a

type of holding environment and reveals important assumptions about the person's relation to
the self as an object at the more existential level
of self management.

Martin came for treatment because he felt he
was too envious and too isolated. I discovered that he felt slightly
depersonalized each day when he left his home and rode on public
transport to work. He would become anxious if anyone looked at
him on his way from his house to the bus stop, and if the bus was
late he would become angry. When walking from the bus to the
underground, he was particularly conscious of anyone walking
towards him, and he felt a mixture of anxiety and anger. He was
always unusually angry whenever the train was behind schedule
and when it did come he always sat in the same carriage, with a
newspaper open to protect him from potential engagement with
other people. His watch, which informed him of the bus, underground and train schedules, and his knowledge of sequential time
– that everything happened in a pattern – and his use of place (the
bus stop, train platform, carriage, etc.) were used to hold him
and facilitate his passage from an extremely protective home environment to work. In effect, he converted certain objects into
cathected reassurances. His watch, a bus with a particular number, the train carriage and a route to his office were spoken of
with great affection, while the people he encountered en route
were inevitably irritating and intrusive. Martin had managed to
create a type of schizoid holding space that managed his anxieties. He was only partly conscious of the fact that the relation
to his holding environment also bore a relation to himself as an
object, but eventually he articulated with greater clarity his conscious sense of the self who was being managed by this arrangement of the external object world. As he conceived of himself as
awkward and unacceptable to his fellow travellers, he related instead to the schedule, buses, underground, trains and the different locations along the way, and in this relation he conceived of
himself as an agreeable co-ordinator of the transport system. If
all worked well he was a happy traveller tuned into the system of
travel. If there was a hitch, he was the irritated and knowledgeable critic from within the system. He had in fact established

something of a symbiotic relation to the non-human environment which could within reason be predictable and, so long as it was, he was able to fit in and feel comforted by it. The entire phenomenon was that sort of relationship where the self is comforted as an object in spite of, and because of, distresses occasioned by the human environment.

THE EVOLUTION OF THE RELATION TO
THE SELF AS OBJECT

In the early months of each baby's life the mother communicates complex rules for being and relating to her infant. In the first years of life the mother and father 'instruct' the child in being and in relating through the handling of him as an object. Since there is little psychological sense of differentiation between the baby and his external objects, there is also little differentiation between the infant's internal instinctual processes and the parents' environmental handling of the baby's internal needs. The situation allows for instinctual and parental processes to evolve together, since any significant instinctual paradigm will be linked experientially with a syllogism of parental care: the internal and the external feature in a dialectic that eventually biases the structure of the ego. If each baby has an internal structuring tendency (an early ego function) then the baby assimilates through experience rules communicated to him from the mother and father about the handling of the instinctual drives and needs (another ego function).

In a sense, ego structure is a form of deep memory, as this structure is derived from experiences between the baby and the mother. One crucial feature of the structuring process – in addition to the indigenous elements of the baby's inherited traits – is the infant's internalization of the mother's handling of him as her object. For each schema from the baby's inherited disposition there is a schema of maternal coverage. The baby and then the child internalizes as structure a process that is a dialectically negotiated composition of his own instincts and ego interests and the mother's handling of them.

Ego structure is the trace of a relationship.

The complex relation that each of us has to the self as an object begins in the first hours of life when we are

the objects of parental perception, reception, facilitation, initiation and object presentation. Indeed it may begin in utero. Every stage in ego and libidinal development involves the infant in a relationship in which he is the object of parental empathy, handling and law. Every infant, therefore, internalizes into the ego those processes in which he is the other's object, and he continues to do so for a long time. Our handling of our self as an object partly inherits and expresses the history of our experience as the parental object, so that in each adult it is appropriate to say that certain forms of self perception, self facilitation, self handling and self refusal express the internalized parental process still engaged in the activity of handling the self as an object.

Through the experience of being the other's object, which we internalize, we establish a sense of two-ness in our being, and this subject-object paradigm further allows us to address our inherited disposition, or true self, as other. We use the structure of the mother's imagining and handling of our self to objectify and manage our true self.

When Winnicott writes about a relation between a false self and a true self, he addresses elements of the phenomenology of the relations to the self as an object. The false self is derived from the mother's communication of her assumptions about existence while the true self, the object of this care, is the historical kernel of the infant's instinctual and ego dispositions.

To some extent, each subject (the experiential and reflectively aware area of the person) is the object of his own unconscious ego processes. As the mother was the transformational object 'known' as a complex process of care, so as the infant develops, the ego assumes the transformational function, as it inherits the processes of the mother's supplementary ego care. The historical subject arrives on the scene after the rules have been established, and one feature of human conflict is the perpetual struggle and interplay between the historical subject and his ego procedures. In no other place than the dream does this fact seem so clear. In the dream experience the experiential subject is 'confronted' by the ego's processing of the day's experiences and by the instinctual and historical associations evoked by the day's events. As such the dream is a remarkable rendezvous between the two domains of existence, our conscious co-ordination of lived experience involving perception and integration of the observed, and our unconscious reading of life. When the dreaming subject lives amidst the dream event, the person encounters that oddity of human existence: the subject is face to face with the process of being and relating that constitutes his psychic structure and may, for example, dismay, anger, perplex or please his subjective sensibility. The knowledge derived from the dialectic of the infant's true self and the subtle syllogisms of maternal and paternal presence and care constitutes part of what will later be known but not thought. This unthought known is not determined by abstract representations. It is established through countless meetings between the infant subject and his object world, sometimes in tranquillity, often in intense conflict. Through these meetings the infant's needs or wishes negotiate with the parental system and a compromise emerges. Ego structure records the basic laws which emerge from these meetings and its knowledge is part of the unthought known.

CLINICAL EXAMPLES

Marianne is a twenty-five-year-old art historian who came for analysis after a spell of psychotherapy with me. She is the only child of two well-to-do parents who had several children by former marriages. Raised by seven nannies during her first five years, she describes her mother as a very arrogant woman who masked personality confusion by using the social configurations granted to her class falsely to suggest competence and assuredness. She recalls that her mother was highly critical of her behaviour and remembers that she tried to comply with her mother's wish to see her daughter as a young, brilliant socialite when she was but a child. Her father was a somewhat remote man who came to life when delivering some pompous address to the family. Unfortunately his eloquence was misplaced, for no one listened to him, and he betrayed little concern that this discourse was not received. In spite of his pomposity, Marianne rather liked her father and she can recall trying to emulate him.

Marianne found it exceedingly difficult to nar- rate her life to me in the analysis. For years she had deposited fragments of feeling and thought into a multitude of friends, all of whom were part of some loose community, although most of them were located in different parts of the world. Typically she would visit a friend in one country and tell that person a bit about another friend, usually something nasty. When she sensed that she might be wearing out her welcome, she would travel to visit another friend and disclose something 'unfortunate' about herself or another friend. One result of Marianne's depositing of herself into different people was to preserve through this splitting an unintegration in herself. The splitting was, however, externalized and lived out by her, for she cognized the different feelings and thoughts she had about herself and others in terms of who it was that knew about a particular thought or feeling. Therefore although she was preserving a split in the self, she was also maintaining a split in her objects, each of which acted as a limited container for diverse thoughts or feelings. Inevitably her moods shifted, from those hypomanic flights to a friend who lived in another land, to a depressive feeling that occurred when she felt that she had to move on before the friend rejected her. The only exception to this pattern was the relation to her husband, who tolerated her vindictiveness and spitefulness and who converted it into a form of play. In gratitude for his survival she became deeply attached to him.

From the historical material presented to me I knew certain facts which established a broad frame of reference. When the mother dismissed the nannies, she did so for no apparent good reason – one day she would find herself simply in the mood to get rid of nanny. She showed a passing interest in her daughter, not reflective of any mothering impulse or nurturance as it was more like an inspection of her daughter's social and intellectual potential. She had absolutely no tolerance for her daughter's naughtiness and simply walked from the room imperiously whenever Marianne played up.

In the course of her analysis it became clear that she

recreated aspects of her infantile environment when she deposited feelings and thoughts into different holding persons. Parts of herself were contained in different holding environments, much as, when a child, she was held by a dispersed colony of nannies. The lack of a stable mothering process simply facilitated the widening of ordinary splitting, the frustrations of this instability increased her destructive instincts and gave a certain urgency to the splitting process. She seemed to be saying to herself in her contemporary life: 'It is too risky to inform anyone of my presence, as it will lead to a desolating rejection. I will move from person to person and make from a collection of persons a collated object which is more within my control.' In a sense, then, she defended herself against a fear of rejection and a desultory depressive state by reversing the passive dread of a state of disorienting confusion occasioned by unintegration, and actively preserving splits and in a sense nurturing them by visiting the containers.

There was another feature to her externalizations. She had a capacity to tantalize her friends with either destructive bits of gossip or by actively seducing different men. This tantalizing was frequently accompanied by a pseudo-admiration of her friends, particularly the men, whom she appeared to hold in high regard. This often led the man to become sexually aroused and she would have a brief affair which in one way or another she made known to different persons. In this case she defended herself against a pervasive sense of emptiness by occupying herself with false encounters; she expressed a grandiose contempt for what she unconsciously experienced as a man's narcissistic self infatuation by causing him an erection and then by dropping him, an act which intruded upon the man's self love, as she imagined it. She also used excitement to medicate herself against an underlying depression.

I understood her use of excitement to be her conversion of the occasional visit from the mother in early infancy into some form of current relation in which she could once more experience the excitement which fused with the mixtures of anxiety and rage occasioned by the mother's sporadic visits. Thus the fragmentation of herself may have expressed elements of her early infantile environment, and her erotization of the splitting into external objects indicated some sexualization of the marginal presence of the mother who may have been known by what she sponsored in her baby (anxiety, frustration, excitement and rage).

By preserving a multitude of containers all over the world to hold different bits of herself, she created an environment which handled her in much the way that the mother's created world managed her. Her true self was to be without an other who could both bear her and nourish her out of her destructive self cancellation. In essence she said to herself, 'You are to keep all feelings and thoughts about the other outside the relationship'. By feeling false when in the presence of any one container, she related to herself as the mother handled her in infancy: 'You are not to say what you feel, and you are to appear as if you agree with the false presentation of events.' By tantalizing her male friends, and by intriguing her female friends through gossip, she injected into her life doses of excitement which were the trace, at an experiential and unconscious level, of the presence of the mother. Furthermore, these excitements inevitably brought her a sense of despair since whatever triumphs she accomplished were only momentary: the men went back to their women, the women returned to their moral scruples.

The father's relation to her was present in her self as object relation by virtue of a certain fatuous self handling. She unsuccessfully attempted to enshrine herself amidst her own pompous discourse, but usually broke up her spells of self inflation by yelling at herself to shut up and be quiet. I understood this to re-create aspects of her relation to her father whose narcissistic self infatuation, which she partly envied, also led her to want to destroy it in him by standing between him and the mirror of his own discourse, sticking her tongue out at him.

Her self hatred served another purpose. The moments in her being that I refer to were not as persecutory as they might sound; she seemed to be idealizing and then denigrating in an almost pleasurable manner, as if she was trying to bring two splits together by using herself as an object of both affects. In those moments, I think she was not unlike the infant who handles a transitional object in this manner; she loves and hates intensely. In Marianne's case, she became a transitional object to herself, and the pleasurable dimension enabled her to tolerate certain thoughts and feelings that would otherwise be persecutory. Thus, as the object of this form of self management, she was the receiver of her own ego splits which were allowed co-existence through unconscious cathexis of herself as a kind of transitional object. This feature of the analysis enabled me to understand that what appeared to be a negative therapeutic reaction, when she seemed to need to preserve her illness, was in fact her unwillingness to give up her use of herself as her own transitional object, co-ordinating her affects.

Adrienne, mentioned earlier (see above, p.44), has been in analysis for two years. In her mid-twenties, she has managed, in spite of her good looks, intelligence and giftedness, to ensure that she is unapproachable. Initially, her analysis was characterized by mournful sessions in which she claimed she could not possibly continue her work and that she would certainly have to give in her notice. She contracted some kind of illness that ostensibly necessitated absence from work and a lengthy period of recuperation. Although a considerable amount of progress has been achieved in her analysis I have always been aware of a silent and secretive relation that Adrienne possesses to herself as her own object, a relation that is so dense and absorbing that she has little internal space for the reception of new experiences or for the initiation of desire from within herself. In a sense, her self-as-object relation can be seen by the way she enters the analytic space. She always brings with her several large shopping bags and articles of clothing, which she places in different parts of the room, thus creating what I think of as a kind of shell of observable objects around her. She lies on the couch with such comfy familiarity and possessiveness that it is hardly a couch at all, but more an assumption on her part that has corporeal realization when it suits her. When she talks to me about herself, she does so in such an odd way that for a long time I have struggled to try to identify this strange quality. I was intensely annoyed at the way she spoke to me and yet I could not understand why, since she was quite undemanding and even polite. Eventually I understood that I felt she was talking to me as if I were an object that she had always possessed. By this I do not mean that she is like that sort of patient who assumes you know what is going on inside her mind; rather, I had the superficial status of an independent object but the object of a fussing old granny who is feeding her cat. She talked to me as if I were a well-known object, and I was aware of a countertransference response in which I felt annoyed and slightly claustrophobic.

Fortunately I had some assistance in coming to terms with my own countertransference. Adrienne had provided me with details of her parents, and I believe that her relation to herself was partly a continuation of her mother's relation to her as the mother's object. In short, her mother was totally absorbed in the care of Adrienne throughout her childhood, constantly fussing over her, always finding some reason why she need not go out of the house to play with the other children, and forever attentive to her somatic complaints – and a faithful advocate of the Adrienne to be: a remarkable figure who would one day realize herself through some significant intellectual accomplishment. Adrienne saw little of her father, as her mother insisted throughout her childhood (until she was ten) that Adrienne should be tucked into bed by 7:00 each night, some 10 minutes or so before her father got home from work. Since her father left the house each morning by 6:30, she saw him only at the weekends. Even then her mother would not let father take Adrienne out for walks or to church without grilling him about what time he would be back and so on. Much of the time spent with her mother was filled with mother's endless talk conveyed in a secretive manner about 'life'; she chatted about the neighbours, their children, their wives' and husbands' pasts, about the ways of the world. Naturally, much of this was very absorbing for her small child.

It was clear to me that Adrienne somatized conflict in order to regress into a mother-child relation, where she was the object of a mothering part of her that was always presenting herself with medicines and comforting words. I also came to realize that Adrienne's relation to herself was so comprehensive that it formed an intense resistance in the transference. Any insightful moment in the analysis was inevitably processed through 'mother' who spoke to her as a child, and she would quite literally have a conversation with herself in which the mothering part would say, 'Don't listen to him; he's just trying to upset you,' and the little girl part of her would feel tearful and hurt, and quite angry with me.

Whenever she felt the slightest touch of anxiety or depression in reaction to work situations, she withdrew into the relation I have been describing. The mothering part of her would say: 'Look, you don't have to take this kind of treatment from X. Just tell them you don't feel well and go home. And when you are home, just have a cup of hot chocolate and crawl into bed and get good and comfy.' In response to this voice, she would feel understood and would regress, often quickly! She would leave work in tears, to the acute embarrassment and bewilderment of her colleagues, and occasionally she would telephone me in a tiny little voice choked with tears and suicidal exhaustion to tell me she could not go on.

By persistently working with her in the transference and by utilizing my countertransference, I was able to help her, but I have no doubt in my mind that it was the understanding of her transference of the maternal care system to herself as an object of that care that sponsored a breakthrough in her analysis. Indeed, once I aligned myself with the part of her that felt suffocated by this transference to herself as an object, she began to experience what I think it is fair to term a countertransference, that is, she began to feel irritated and thwarted by her own handling of herself, an affective state that eventually became critical in the establishment of her true self feelings and needs.

Harold is a highly gifted man in his mid-thirties who strikes his colleagues and friends as considerably dynamic and creative. In fact, he needs a stimulus in order to react to something, so that truly creative living is not possible. He can only respond to a problem in a dynamically efficient way. Analysis of his character has revealed that he continues to utilize his mother's traumatically intrusive presence by fostering problems to

which he, the baby object of this maternal introject, must respond. The result is an exceedingly efficient false self system. The mother's traumatizing influence is sustained in his transference of this element to himself as the ever-traumatized object of maternal impingement. The nascent countertransference response to this transference, which I see as an indication of true self presence, is revealed in his stammering, in sudden depressions, and in fitfully agitated states of anguish.

Stewart is a depressed man in his mid-forties. One of the striking features of his character is the way that he alternates between insightful self holding and scatty, highly abstracted statements that bear little relation to his internal reality. I believe that these opaque abstractions, formulated in circuitous intellectual designs, constitute his absence from self knowing. Although, of course, we might conceptualize his defences as those of denial, isolation of affect and intellectualization, my discovery in the analysis has been to realize how his alternation between self holding and absence from self relating partly reflects his mother's alternating attentiveness and distraction during his early years of life. He transfers the maternal care system to himself as the object, and his not infrequent frustration and rage at losing contact with himself is in the nature of a countertransference, a specific reaction to the transference of the maternal care system.

DISCUSSION AND CONCLUSION

It is my view that each person transfers elements of the parents' child care to his own handling of himself as an object. In that transference to the self as an object, the person represents the interplay of the inherited (true self) and the environmental that featured in the structuring of the ego. In the relation to the self as an object the person re-creates elements of the mother's facilitation of his existence. The structure of the ego is a form of deep constitutive memory, a recollection of the person's ontogenesis, and, although it may have little to do with the mother as the patient knows her in her whole object sense (as a person), in some respects it informs us of how she mothered this particular baby. It is her active presence, her deep instruction, her activities as a transformational object, that the baby integrates into that psychic structure that constitutes the ego; in this grammar of the ego are stored the rules for the handling of the self and the objects. When that structure coheres, if even marginally, the baby will begin to express his knowing of his being through fantasy, thought and object relating. This unthought known constitutes the core of one's being and will serve as the basis of subsequent infantile and child phantasy life.

A person's character, then, is in its deepest respects the idiolect of the subject's ego grammar. It will be observable in the way the person uses others as his objects (ordinary transferences) and how he relates to and handles himself as an object (self as object transference and countertransference). This use of the other and the self as objects is obviously a process, so we may say that character is a process, one that expresses the subject's historical experience of the primary objects. The baby does not internalize an object, but he does internalize a process derived from an object. The mother's and father's process of care, which demonstrates their complex conscious and unconscious rules for being and relating, constitutes the facilitating environment and is the matrix which serves as a space for the infant's projections and for his introjections.

The psychoanalytic process is a unique therapeutic procedure because it enables the person to represent the transference to the self as object and to crystallize those features of being and relating which are countertransferential expressions. At the core of the psychoanalytic situation is the person's narrative relation to himself as an object for reporting and reflecting upon. Each analysand narrates his life and tells the analyst about himself as an object in dreams and in family relations, as an evolved object with a past and a history, as a participant in small and large social groups, and as an experiential presence within the psychoanalytic relation. The point of view which the patient reveals in his narration establishes crucial aspects of the transferences to the self as object and those countertransferences evoked.

In describing the self involved in a dream, the patient may express a mood of shock or disgust with the self, or in reporting the details of his relation to colleagues he may have to reflect with dismay and despair about aspects of his behaviour. In these moments, he objectifies and relates to himself as an object. Frequently his reproaches or enthusiasms will be followed by another response which is a reaction to his own narration – a reaction, that is, to the transference aspects of the relation to the self as object, and his responses will be in the nature of a countertransference.

In the psychoanalytic situation the patient is also the object of the analysis. We know that the analyst will be initiating the patient in a new relation to the self as object, one that makes use of unconscious features of the self-as-object relation and does so in the context of the ordinary transference to the analyst. When the patient lives through the discourse of the transference experience within the analytical setting, a discourse where the transference addresses of the patient's object world and defensive make up both implies an other and evokes aspects of the self and other within the analyst's countertransference, the person gradually discovers the private language of the self. He knows through the idiolects of his use of the object who his primary object is, what the assumptions of this object are in terms of being related to, and what this implies about the object's assumption about the self and its other. He knows what he is saying to this object and how he has partly organized himself as a person in the terms of this relationship. As the analyst notes for his patient whom he, the analyst, is becoming, in terms of the other implied by the patient's transference and the other collected in the analyst by the countertransference, the patient becomes aware of how he invites or compels the other to be deformed. As the patient becomes aware of this process of deformation of the other and the self as objects, and as the analyst speaks up for that object whom he is made to be, the patient gradually hears news of himself through the experience of

SO-C*

the other. This process includes both the analyst as other and, paradoxically, the patient as object of his own transference, as other to himself. Until this moment the person has been speaking a dead language, its meaning unknown to himself and frequently experienced by, but unknowable to, his friends. The grammar of this discourse lies memorially buried as the structure of the ego awaiting the analyst's use of the analytic space to rediscover the patient's discourse, a language composed of rules derived from interactions between the child and his mother and father. As I hope to make clear in chapters 10-14, the many transferences and countertransferences re-create aspects of the infant's and the mother-father's being. By rediscovering this dead language the patient can now occupy that position that the analyst has been occupying; the analysand can now receive his own discourse. In the revival of this lost discourse, first the analyst listens and then the patient is there to hear news from the self and its others.

The discourse of character is no longer emptied into the external object world where its representation is enigmatic and its reception fosters bewilderment. Its syntactical cohesion is no longer torn by divorces from the object. The discourse is now uttered to an internal other, that other constituted in the patient through identification with the function and psychosomatic trace of the analyst. In a very real way, along with the intelligent interpretive caretaking of the analyst, this allows the patient an opportunity to find a more generative way of holding the self as an object of care. In the space where that holding occurs there is an intra-subjective rendezvous, where an archaic language of character is received and interpreted; there the patient finds a dwelling place where even the severest of illnesses can be held in nurturant care. The creation of a space for the reception of the discourse of character and the functional accomplishment of the holding of the self as an object of one's nurture are perhaps the two most essential contributions a clinical psychoanalysis can make to the human subject. Part of the unthought known has been determined by the infant's meetings with the maternal process and this knowledge can come into thought proper in the transference

which is an occasion when subject and object
meet, and where the analyst is specially trained
to note the logic of expectation in the patient's
use of him as an object.

Each patient's symptomatology has in the
first place foreclosed the possibility of true subjectivity. The borderline lives through violently split self representations that are
housed in external objects that preoccupy him in a paranoid universe. The hysterical patient has cast herself into an externalized
theatric, where desire is dissociated from gratification and where
her true life objects are denigrated as currency or payment for an
unattainable idealized object. The schizoid patient has long since
absented his affective true self and cast himself into false self discourse through vigilant ego precocity; he lives in a world mentally
processed to such a degree that in that place he enjoys remarkable omnipotence and total isolation. The narcissistic patient
lives in the melancholy celebration of idolized self and idealized
object representation, enraged if this universe is not confirmed in
lived experience, but so anaesthetized against object relating that
his life is a chronicle of pain and despair. If we look closely at our
patients we would probably all agree that each has his or her own
sense of existence but that, by virtue of the persistent pathology
of their defences, they live by disowning the self.

In the sequestered space of a psychoanalysis, the analyst
coheres the defences through the transference-countertransference interpretations into a relationship (to the primary object)
that has been lost. In that moment, or in the accumulation of
these moments, the analyst restores to the patient what I believe
we can term genuine or true subjectivity: that understanding of
oneself that permits us sentient knowledge of the originating activity behind our experiences of ourself and our objects.

4   *At the other's play:*
to dream

FOR Freud, the dream is an emblematic arrangement of veils articulated by the unconscious, and the task of psychoanalysis is to read the discourse of the dream by translating its iconographic utterance into the word. As Pontalis (1974) and Khan (1976) have pointed out, the classical notion of the dream as only the road to something else (the unconscious) has unfortunately resulted in some neglect of the dream as a lived experience.

I regard the dream as a fiction constructed by a unique aesthetic: the transformation of the subject[2] into his thought, specifically, the placing of the self into an allegory of desire and dread that is fashioned by the ego.[3] From this point of view, the dream experience becomes an ironic form of object relation, as the part of the self in the dream is the object of the unconscious ego's articulation of memory and desire. The arrangement of this intrasubjective rendezvous is one of the major accomplishments of the dream experience, an object relation partly contingent on the aesthetic function of the ego. Finally, I think the person's experience in the dream is based not only on instinctual representations, but on what I believe are ego memories, a view that suggests the ego fulfils a highly idiomatic and creative function when it re-presents these memories in the dream.

As the subject's experience inside the dream is usually not as the director of the theatric but as an object within a fantastical play, the dream setting provides us with an ironic form of object relation, with the subject as the ego's object. In part, the subject is the object of the ego's representational formation of needs, memories, desires and daily experiences, and, for this reason, we may say that as the subject is the object of the ego's transformation into play of memory and desire, the ego sponsors a character who plays the self in the recurrent theatre of the dream.

One of the aesthetic accomplishments of dream work is the dream setting, the establishment of an environment composed of imagery that leads the dreamer into the dream experience. There are two ways in which we need to view this dream environment. We may translate it from imagery into word, from dramatic experience into thematic nucleus, an endeavour exhaustively outlined by Freud. We may also focus on the implications of the dream setting's management of the subject as a form of object relation. This suggests that we inquire how the dreamer is handled by the ego, a structural and aesthetic consideration that can complement our posing questions about the dream's thematic content, much as we might distinguish between the thematic and the aesthetic properties of a poem. A poem is a unique way of forming a theme, and poetic handling becomes as important as the theme it presents; similarly a dream is a special technique of forming meaning, for the dream not only speaks us – it handles us.

According to Freud, the motivating urge of a dream is an infantile repressed wish. Without the presence of a repressed wish, other dream thoughts – for example memories of past events and thoughts from the day's experience – will not be constructed into a dream. We need the inspirational drive of the wish to fuse a multitude of thoughts into the living theatre of the dream. 'Our theory of dreams,' writes Freud, 'regards wishes originating in infancy as the indispensable motive force for the formation of dreams' (1900, p. 589). The dream event seems to have been arranged by an Other whom Freud nominates as the infantile part of the self. Objectively, of course, we know this Other is part of us, that it is not distinctly separate from our being; subjectively, the experience is that the Other casts us, both throwing light on our thoughts and placing us in a drama each night. Freud did not ignore this subjective truth, this otherness of the dream author:

A second factor, which is much more important and far-reaching, but which is equally overlooked by laymen is the following. No doubt a wish-fulfilment must bring pleasure; but the question then arises 'To whom?'. To the person who has the wish, of course. But, as we know, a dreamer's relation to his wishes is quite a peculiar one. He repudiates them and censors them – he has no liking for them, in short. So that their fulfilment will give him no pleasure, but just the opposite; and experience shows that this opposite appears in the form of anxiety, a fact which has still to be explained. Thus a dreamer in his relation to his dream-wishes can only be compared to an amalgamation of two separate people who are linked by some important common element. (1900, pp. 580–1)

In many of our dreams, although we may temporarily enjoy the illusion of managing the dream event, we recognize that we are inside a drama that has a bewildering logic of its own. Not only do such moments often not feel of our own making, but they may be repellent and disturbing occasions that deny any semblance of our subjectivity and seem to underline precisely the opposite: our rather passive presence as an object cast into some bizarre drama without any recognizable script.

To create this dream fiction requires an aesthetic: a mode of transforming thought into dramatic representation. Although Freud sees dream formation as a kind of industrial enterprise (he likens the dream thoughts to an entrepreneur and the wish it evokes to capital), it is foremost a theory of aesthetics (how the thematic is transformed by the poetic). He himself suggests this in one of his countless definitions of the dream when he writes that a dream is 'the form into which the latent thoughts have been transmuted by the dream-work' (1900, p. 183). He compares the dream to the literary text:

As regards the dimensions of dreams, some are very short and comprise only a single image or a few, a single thought, or even a single word; others are uncommonly rich in their content, present whole novels and seem to last a long time. (1900, p. 91)

In the sense that the dream experience is a highly sophisticated form of theatre that challenges all our critical capacities, the ego which fashions the dream setting reflects an organized and avowing unconscious whose discourse, as Lacan has argued, is structured like a language: the speech of a visual theatric that both represents and veils thought. The syntactical forms of this Other are the dream, the joke, the fantasy, the symptom, the intrusive gap in the subject's discourse, and the meta-discourse of all object relating.[4]

Just as Freud asked his patients to achieve a 'negative capability', to suspend assumption and prejudice and to report the thoughts that came across the mind, free association suspended the narrative structures of secondary process thought and permitted the analyst and analysand to witness the patterns of thought (metathought) and the gaps in the reportage. Through the patient's suspension of criticism and the analyst's recognition of the recurrent resistances to this suspension, traces of the discourse of the Other could be identified through a critical activity similar to literary criticism. Most importantly, lacunae in reporting came to be seen as a synecdoche of resistance to speaking the repressed. The poetics of the unconscious demonstrated a Wordsworthian insistence that the ordinary was invested with mystery, that the immediacy of explicit meaning yield to the hermeneutic of the underlying theme; that imagery, syntax and aesthetic of organization be taken as another (repressed) discourse. Utilizing this literary criticism, the subject discovered a thematics and poetics of self that had been veiled from him. Indeed, the neurotic symptom, which comprises an idea with a new form, is a salient example of the interplay of thematics and poetics, so the analyst functions as someone attending to the dialectic of meaning and form in the person.

Because the manifest dream text is considered to be an encoded representation of the dream thoughts, many psychoanalysts have been misled into thinking that the dream seeks mute privacy, that it intends to defy comprehension. **Veiled in enigma, the dream invites curiosity!** Precisely because of its 'allegorical structure, its discontinuous ideational imagery, bizarre juxtapositions and surrealistic faces', the dream compels the dreamer to fill in the gaps within its text. What Fletcher writes of allegory, we may say of the dream: 'the art of allegory will be the manipulation of a texture of "ornaments" so as to engage the reader in an interpretative activity' (Fletcher, 1964, p. 130).

The veil deceives. It also tantalizes.

The dream text is a primordial fiction. What Freud discovered and then neglected was the notion of the dream space as a night theatre involving the subject in a vivid re-acquaintance with the Other. He did acknowledge that a person is capable of being profoundly affected by the dream – 'We know from our experience that the mood in which one wakes up from a dream may last for the whole day' (1915, p. 85) – but he did not fully recognize that the fundamental contribution of the dream to human sensibility was its offering a place for this interplay of self and Other. I say that he did not fully recognize this because although he discovered it, indeed founded a clinical space which framed this dialogue, he established this as a scientific rather than aesthetic event. However fruitful the theoretical contributions of chapter 7 of the *Interpretation of Dreams* have been to psychoanalytic metapsychology, they have obscured the aesthetic discovery of the dream space as theatre.

There was a kind of sleuth-like sensibility about Freud. Give him a text and, as Ricoeur (1970, p. 32) has pointed out, he would regard it with suspicion. Like Ahab in Melville's novel *Moby Dick*, Freud wanted to break through 'the pasteboard mask of all outward presentiments'. 'The conception of dream-elements tells us,' he writes, 'that they are ungenuine things, substitutes for something else that is unknown to the dreamer (like the purpose of a parapraxis), substituting for something the knowledge of which is present in the dreamer but which is inaccessible to him' (1915, p. 113). This leads him to regard the dream text as a pernicious and deceitful representation that hides the ' "genuine" thing behind' (p. 151). In one of his last statements on the dream he proposes that

what has been called the dream we shall describe as the text of the dream or the **manifest** dream, and what we are looking for, what
we suspect, so to say, of lying behind the
dream, we shall describe as the **latent** dream
thoughts. (1933, p. 10, author's emphasis)

Even though he has paid homage to the dream work, Freud says
of its created text that

it is bound to be a matter of indifference to us whether it is
well put together, or is broken up into a series of disconnected
separate pictures. Even if it has an apparently sensible ex-
terior, we know that this has only come about through dream-
distortion and can have as little organic relation to the
internal content of the dream as the façade of an Italian
church has to its structure and plan. (1915, p. 181)

He warns us that we must not be impressed with the literary function of the dream work since it 'can do no more than condense,
displace, represent in plastic form and subject the whole to a secondary revision' (1915, p. 182). Yet, we may justly say that such
processes are indeed the seed of fiction and may be an aesthetic
necessary to induce the ego's participation in and recollection of
the dream.

Dream thoughts cannot engage us, only the dream experience
can. Indeed, Freud himself suggests this:

Here we have the most general and the most striking psychological characteristic of the process of dreaming: a thought,
and as a rule a thought of something that is wished, is objectified in the dream, is represented as a scene, or, as it
seems to us, is experienced. (1900, p. 534)

Freud did not adequately distinguish the dream experience from
the dream text; at times we are explicitly led to believe that the
subject's experience of the dream is not important. Freud restricted himself to an analysis of the dream text – specifically to identifying the dream thoughts that sponsored the dream – in order to
translate the image back into the word.

Freud's idea was to bring a repressed idea into consciousness – to the word. I think we must search for the presence of the unthought known which refers to the unrepressed unconscious. We must search for an entirely new experience to find representation of the unthought known. I suggest here that the ego's management of the subject in the dream setting represents some aspects of the infant-child's early experience as subject and object. Later I will examine how analysis of the transference and countertransference reveals another system of representation of the unthought known.

The dream text, then, is nothing more than the awakened subject's transcription of the dream experience into language, a narrated tale of a dramatic experience. In a way, it is the subject's narrative of the Other's fiction, or, more accurately, a **reversal of the dream experience**: whereas the subject was inside the Other's fiction – without memory of any alternative existence – in the dream experience, the Other is inside the subject's narrative when he fashions a dream text. This process of **emerging** from a dream through different layers of fiction complements a similar process of **entry** into the dream experience. As Freud conceived it, we begin with thoughts that occur to us during the day. We might term this our conscious day narrative. As we sleep, this narrative evokes earlier experiences, specifically infantile desires – a process that occurs because sleep is regressive to the hallucinatory stage of thought. Our day narrative meets with the regressive transformation of the night discourse. This discourse of the Other transforms our conscious thoughts into emblematic theatre and is guided by the culture of the dream experience: a space where the Other's desire is to be gratified, where the subject's conscious thoughts are not to be violated, and where the Other takes the subject's day narrative and transforms it into a night fiction, so that the subject is compelled to re-experience his life according to the voice of the unconscious.

It is the art of the ego's invention of the dream setting that provides us with the possibility for a dream experience, and this setting is the accomplishment of what we might justly call the aesthetic function of the ego: that facility to synthesize wish and thought, and to transform the synthesis into a dramatic mask, along with the induction of the subject to the experience. The term dream work belongs to the individual features of this synthetic process – to condensation, displacement, symbolization and secondary elaboration. The notion of the dream aesthetic belongs to the use of these functions in the composition of a dream setting that will lead the subject into a dream experience.

Dream thoughts do not constitute a dream experience. The dream experience is a conditional event, it cannot occur without the creation of a dream setting. The setting is the world of thought and wish transformed into imagery of place. The dream experience is the dreamer's subjective experience of being while inside the dream theatre, an experience of being that will be contingent on the nature of the theatre and the possibilities of setting within that theatre.

Of any dream that induces a dream experience we may ask: 'What kind of world does the dream provide for the dreaming subject?' 'How does it handle the dreaming subject within the dream?'. This handling is beyond the synthetic function of the dream work. It points towards the dream aesthetic as the expression of an ironic style of object relating – specifically, the style whereby the subject (as dreamer) relates to himself as object (as the dreamed).

When the subject experiences the dream setting we may say that he is being handled by the dream aesthetic, that the ego (an unconscious organizing process) arranges the place where the Other speaks, a fantastical environment that will be either favourable or unfavourable to the subject's desire. This ego process will manifest itself through the dream imagery of the setting, for the nature of this setting may influence the subject's capacity to experience the dream, specifically to yield to the dream imagery or to resist it, to be gratified or to be horrified. The decision about the nature of the dream setting – that moment when the ego chooses how it will populate the dream space – is what Khan (1976a) means by the dream experience, an experience that he takes to be prior to the subject's experience in the dream setting, when what we might call the ego attitude is settled. In the unremembered climate of this attitude, the ego transforms thought into setting and the dramaturgy of the subject dreamed by his ego is enacted.

It is this settling of an ego attitude that is crucial to the dreamer's dream experience, since it is the moment when the ego 'decides' how to invite the subject to experience the dream, a curious moment that has vast implications. Were we to study a subject's dream world systematically we would certainly discover how each dreamer's ego handles the subject and what this reveals of the person's relation to himself as an object. We may ask how the ego transforms the subject's desire. Is it made reachable in the setting or unreachable? The ego's 'attitude' towards the dream theme and the subject to whom the theme will be presented constitutes an aesthetic choice. We are talking essentially of the **handling** of different themes (instinctual, memorial, etc.), of especially recurrent styles of processing particular themes, and, when we talk of such idioms, I believe we are noting what we might term ego memories derived from basic ego structures. It is an occasion when the thought known (the subject) is encountered by the unthought known (the ego), a recurring moment of being transported back through time into the dense dialectic of our inherited being and the logic of the environment.

As I have said in the previous chapter and in the introduction, ego structures emerge in the earliest months and years of life when the ego develops 'rules' for processing intrapsychic and intersubjective experience. These rules are developed as mother and child negotiate paradigms for processing all of life's experience. This is the 'grammar' of the ego, and this deep structure generates the forms of the self's existence-structure, or what we might call the character of the subject. The structure of the ego is the self's shadow, a silent speech that is unheard by the subject until he enters the echo chamber of psychoanalysis. There the person discovers this densely structured grammar of the ego that speaks in the psychoanalysis through dreams, parapraxes, phantasies, and most especially through the nature of the transference, where the subject attempts to set up what for him is the

trace of the basic paradigmatic situation, where
basic ego structures have been established (the
unthought known). Needless to say, the patient is
often embarrassed by this and may come to regard his unconscious self, or his true self, as
aggravating.

In the dream, ego structures express themselves primarily in
aesthetic rather than thematic ways, that is, through the processing of the instinctual and memorial themes, and this is most
obvious in the choice of the dream setting. How does the ego represent desire or aggression to the subject? Does the dream aesthetic represent dream thoughts in impossible (nightmare)
settings or, obversely, does it condense so many thoughts into
archetypal images that the subject feels he is among symbols of a
culture that transcends his idiom of representation? Does the ego
give the subject time to experience the dream imagery, or is it so
hurried as to make perception or recognition of the imagery impossible, thereby truncating the experience of the dream? Is the
ego so obsessional that the dream imagery is inevitably a kind of
ruminative collation of highly abstracted landscapes of thought:
the so-called problem-solving dream experience which belabours
the subject during the night?

CLINICAL EXAMPLE

I will briefly outline a clinical example to illustrate this way of
considering dreams and dreaming. Jonathan is a bisexual youth
of twenty-three. He is the eldest of four children and the child of
distinguished parents. He was born while both parents were
graduate students and was placed with a nanny who looked after
him while his mother attended classes and worked on her disser-
tation. He appears to have complied with this split parenting and
to have developed a precocious self that left both parents pleased
both with his progress in school and with what they took to be a
beguiling personal character. In fact, Jonathan was able to develop in this manner only by splitting off from his character those
aspects of his phantasy life that expressed desperate need or
acute rage. In the first weeks of his analysis he 'confessed' homosexual phantasies and homosexual events. After this he was at a

complete loss for words. He had no thoughts. Of course I knew that he was thinking and phantasizing, and I thought these were transference thoughts too frightening for this compliant person to report. The analysis would have been acutely uncomfortable for him had he not been able to report his dreams, which were inevitably vivid and complex. Since they were dissociated from his conscious life he would rarely provide any association, and only eventually did I use this dissociation in the analysis. We began to regard the dream as the utterance of an unknown speaker, the split-off self which we acknowledged to be like an other to him. In this way, although he could not associate to his dreams, he became curious about them, and accepted that by engaging in a dialogue with this other he was hearing from himself. Since I could rarely interpret the thematic meaning of the dream without associations, I was compelled to see if I could use the structure, or aesthetic, of the dream to work towards interpretation. Since I could not break down the parts of the dream to find their associative links, I looked at the dream as a totality and studied the dreams over time to see if the placing and replacing of recurrent imagery, settings, personages, etc. could reveal basic paradigms. I am not going to trace that enterprise here, but it was through this practice that I noticed how he lived inside his dream world, and I began to pay attention to the recurrent dream settings and the way he was handled by them.

In one common set of dreams, for example, he was in a desert and next to a lake. Sometimes his wife was there with him, sometimes he was alone, once he was there with his mother and his sister. In one dream the lake was surrounded by a brick wall. He never seemed to take any notice of the lake. He reported its presence, but he never drank from it, for example, and it was the absence of this action which seemed to me more important than what was present in the dream. My observation yielded one potential interpretation which I put to him: that as wife, mother, sister were next to the lake, perhaps his not taking nourishment from the lake reflected the way he split off his needs from potential environmental gratification. This was one way of looking for a theme within the dream. I was equally struck by the fact that his ego continually provided him with potential nourishment, as if the dream setting was offering him something that he could not turn into a dream experience: in this case to drink from the lake. The usefulness of this distinction (how the ego handles the subject) became more important when he reported another dream.

He took a broken antique object, enclosed it in a cellophane bag and placed it gently in a pool of water. This was done in his garden. After this act he felt that the seeds he had planted in the garden would grow and that he would be included in his family. We knew from previous dreams that he often represented himself as broken down. By linking this dream to previous ones, I said that I thought he wanted to place his broken-down self into a womb-like container that would heal it. This was one of the themes of this dream, but what struck me more was the autistic-like act within the dream, an act that was not supported by the dream setting. The bag would not heal the broken pieces of the self. As I noted this, I realized that one feature of his dreams was that he was dissociated from his desire, that the Other offered him a good setting for succour but he could not participate, or that he symbolized his need in an unsupportive setting. This fault in the structure of the self – itself an aesthetic flaw of being rather than a theme of specific phantasy – emerged in the dream setting as an aesthetic problem: his dream experience was out of synchrony with his dream setting. Thus the aesthetic utterance of the dream contradicted the thematic message: 'you wish to actualize your needs, but you can't fit into an environment where this can be done.' Such a contradiction of the thematic by the aesthetic was like the use of ironic delivery (form) contradicting message (theme): 'of course I **just know** you were about to apologize to me,' for example.

If the subject cannot make use of the dream setting, it is equally important to see how the dream setting makes use of the subject, the other side of the issue of how the subject is handled by the ego. Whenever Jonathan dreamed about his family in a domestic setting, the events of the dream became inordinately complicated, and the action speeded up so quickly that the setting made it virtually impossible to have any dream experience other than one of bewilderment and confusion. In what we called the squirrel dream he entered his parents' flat and quickly noticed the new shag carpet on the floor. He was almost yielding to the pleasure of this discovery when his mother pointed to the door in alarm and before he knew it hundreds of squirrels came swarming into the flat through the front door. He tried to chase them away, and there was considerable confusion. Mother screamed and father – apparently in an effort to drive them away – set the curtains on fire, whereupon the entire flat caught fire. To escape, he fell out of a window and seemed to fall for a long time. It was the only moment in the dream thus far when he seemed to have time for thought or being. As he fell past one of his neighbours' windows, he noticed a cake left on the ledge to cool. He grabbed a piece and devoured it hungrily, and the lady thanked him for bringing to her attention that the cake was now ready to eat. Suddenly he noticed he was falling towards the intersection of two cars about to collide. The cars were driven by his sister and brother and one car was followed by a large van that was transporting a house. Eventually we understood the themes of the dream (that the ravenous squirrel represented his desire for his mother countervened by his father's consuming and enraged passion for her), but I will not focus on the themes as utterances but the aesthethic as voice. When the Other presented him inside the setting of the family it created confusion, and it only threw him into peace if the family was away. In dreaming of his family, the complexity and speed of the activities prevented him from completing his experiences, and he wound up merely a reactive mechanism of the madness.

The dream aesthetic is a form conveyed by the structure of the ego, a structure that in Jonathan's case internalized an unintegrated experience of relating to the mother or father, so that when need was aroused in Jonathan towards his mother, what was printed was not gratification but a kind of manic interaction with the environment that was out of everyone's control. The ego handling of the dreaming self – its aesthetic – inherits its now internalized structures from the way the self experienced the

early environment and passes this on in the
dream setting by the way the ego handles the subject. This is not a memory in the proper sense, a
cognitive recollection that becomes available to
the subject's psychic or thematic recovery, but is

an existential memory, a remembering by being, that is internalized into the ego's structure and is manifested in the dream
through the ego's style, or as I choose to denote the phenomenology of its style, into the aesthetic.

I found this aspect of the dream aesthetic very useful in his
analysis – as useful as the varying pregenital or oedipal fantasy
themes revealed by them – because they helped facilitate him
through the negative transference. The unrelatedness to the lake
can be seen as a refusal to make use of the analyst (to drink equals
to internalize) and a reluctance to relate to the dream itself, to
which he has no associations. That is to say, when he produced
some material from his life and I interpreted it to him, he very
often made absolutely no use of it, just as when by the lake in the
dream, he did not use what could help him. On other occasions,
when he produced very confusing, abstract or elliptical remarks,
he demanded a statement from me which was impossible for me to
make, as I had no understanding of his meaning. On those occasions he articulated his need at the one moment when I was fairly
useless. We have come to regard these aesthetic problems as the
voice of the pre-verbal self, that self who internalizes into the
structure of the ego a language of the early relation to mother so
that the structure of the ego is the printing of this dialogue.

DISCUSSION

An ego attitude may derive from ego structure, just as in
Jonathan's dream we may argue that the agitated representation
of events in domestic settings is the ego's attitude towards an
actual family setting with which it cannot cope. That is to say, just
as Jonathan's ego integration was faulty in integrating actual
family experiences, so, too, the ego represented this faultiness in
dreams about the family. Or, to take the lake and desert dream,
the ego represented its dissociation from partaking in what
appears to be available gratification by ignoring the nurturing

function of the lake, or appearing to ignore it. **In the dream the subject is made to re-live the nature of the experience that became internalized and structured the early ego, and this remembering by re-experiencing occurs through the medium of the ego's handling of the subject through the dream setting.** This primary phantasy of the dream lies dormant in the ego's attitude to the dreaming subject and may help us to understand why in some dream experiences the subject is permitted by the Other to feel at one with the dream experience, while at other times the experience is one of radical alienation and captivity. **Experiences in life not only evoke repressed instinctual wishes, they also elicit ego memories: indeed, for each dream that represents an instinctual wish there is also an implicit ego attitude, a memorial record of the ego's handling of the wish.** I think that while the content of the dream reveals the instinctual phantasy, the theme of the dream plot, the composition of the dream setting, and the aesthetic organization of the experience, all reveal the ego's handling of the instinctual wish. Just as the ego's task vis-à-vis the instincts, the superego and reality is one of synthesis – a proto-aesthetic function – so too the ego betrays this aesthetic in the dream representation of the play of instincts, superego replies and day experiences. Each time the dreaming subject is made the object of the ego's attitude, the self re-experiences existential attitudes towards instinct and object that were constituted in the earliest years of life, attitudes no longer available to cognitive recollection, but remembered in the structure of the ego's handling of memories or desires.

Psychoanalysis has long been disposed to regard the voice of the dream as the utterance of a true self, the Other interpreter of our being, and to regard our conscious subjectivity with suspicion. In the inevitable conflict between our conscious interpretation of our meaning and the discourse of the dream, the parapraxis, the symptom or the logic of free association, the analyst is biased towards the verity of the Other's interpretation. The analyst allies himself with that part of the patient that can achieve a negative capability towards the discourse of the Other, in order to be available for the analyst's alliance with the hermeneutic

truth of the Other's interpretation. If our dream
professes one thing about our desires, let us say,
and we disagree with the dream's representation,
it is inevitably the case that the analyst will treat
the patient's disagreement as a denial of the

truth. It is this struggle between our conscious interpretation of
our existence and the Other's discourse which establishes the essential feeling of our being in relation to an other self, a conflict
that can lead us to feel vexed by the analyst who agrees with the
Other's disagreeable comment on our motivation, as if we have
been slighted in favour of the Other.

As I view it, the dream is a unique moment when the person as
conscious subjectivity encounters a fundamentally impersonal
mental process (the language of the unconscious and the ego's
transformation of such language into discourse) which assumes a
personal function when the dream experience is created. I realize
this is patently obvious, that when we dream we face the representatives of our mental processes in the dream formation, but
when we confront night after night the theatre of the unconscious,
and when we are the represented object in the drama, we are witness to the ego's processing of our being. I am less concerned with
instinctual representation in the dream than with the unconscious ego's re-living of the instinct – a re-living that is re-enacted
in the way the ego deals with the wish, a handling of instinct that is
typical of the subject's ego style, and that I have called the aesthetic function of the ego. I think this ego memory is as important
as the instinctual representation, both because it is more available to the dreamer, for it bears the stamp of the characteristic,
the familiar, and because an analysis of the ego's style of transforming memory and desire brings the patient and the analyst
closer to the core, the true self, of the patient.

Of course this point of view suggests a different style of dream
interpretation, as the ego's transformation of the latent dream
thoughts into a manifest text – its aesthetic activity – not only reveals its style of handling memory and desire, but also nec-
essitates that we regard the creative function of the dream. When
we analyse a dream for instinctual content, we begin from the
manifest text and work towards the latent content, using the

content of the manifest text only for the clues to the latent meaning. The style of the dream is immaterial to us. Now in analysing the ego's experience of the instinct, we must work first in the classical manner (locating the latent dream thoughts) and **then we must see how the ego has transformed these thoughts into a dream experience.** We must attend to the creativity of the dream experience, since it is there where we will witness the discourse of the ego experience, a discourse that is the ego's utterance of what I have called the grammar of the ego. To fail to do the latter is to suggest that the person is only constituted from the instinct when we know that each person **interprets** the instinct and that this interpretation manifests itself through the ego's representation of the instinct to the self within the dramaturgy of the dream theatre.

To summarize my point of view, I am impressed that examination of any patient's dreaming life reveals not only typical contents within dreams, but recurrent styles of dreaming. Such modes of handling the varied instinctual and memorial themes of the dream seem to me to be aesthetic accomplishments of the ego, which functions to transform the theme into a dramatic representation where the dreamer will experience the theme. This aesthetic accomplishment reflects the idiom of that dreamer's particular ego attitude towards the theme, an attitude that reveals itself through the way the theme is represented and how the dreaming subject is made to re-experience the dream theme within the dream experience. I am not only struck by the fact that this nightly dramaturgy is an ironic object relation – where the subject is presented with the Other's view of the self. I am also impressed with the fact that such representation is the ego's way of compelling the self to re-experience historical (psychodevelopmental) ego attitudes towards the dream themes. Only attention to what is patterned and aesthetically recurrent (the typical forms of the dream themes) will suggest to the analyst what is fundamentally an historical (memorial) ego experience of the dream and what is not. When we attend to the ego's transformation of dream theme into dramatic fiction, we are indeed acknowledging a creative function in the dream process, and we are wiser, I believe, if we note that the dream does not simply bring us into communication with instinctual or memorial experiences; it brings us into contact with our own internal and highly idiomatic aesthetic: that aesthetic reflected by the ego style typical of each of us.

5   *The trisexual*

I N a footnote to the *Three Essays on the Theory of Sexuality*
(1905) Freud defined three stages in the homosexual's libidinal development. There is first a short but intense fixation to the
mother, then a period when 'they identify themselves with a
woman and take themselves as their sexual object', which constitutes a 'narcissistic basis' from which they proceed to the
homosexual position, when they 'look for a young man who re-
sembles themselves and whom they may love as their mother
loved them' (p. 145). Later Freud was to describe an 'innate bisexual disposition in man' which he claimed was reflected in the
masturbator's identification with both sexes (1908, p. 166).

I believe there is a third position. I refer to that person who
'seduces' members of each sex in order to gain the other's desire
of his self. The object of desire is the person's own self, but a self
hypercathected as part of an erotic family triangle. I propose to
call this individual a trisexual, and I define trisexuality as a state
of desire characterized by identification with and seduction of
both sexes in order to appropriate genital sexuality by redirecting
it into a threesome's love of one.

How is this position imaginable? If the bisexual stance allows
identification with both sexes, the trisexual adds to this a libidinally desexualized body, its gender suspended from the categories
of sexual difference in order to be converted into a vessel for a
transcendent corporeality. In the final stage of trisexual seduction there are three lovers: a man who admires this person, a
woman who seeks him and the trisexual himself, who is sufficiently dissociated to cathect aspects of himself as the object of desire. The trisexual's body image is without gender, it is a body
stance beyond sexuality or, more accurately, the body before the
knowledge of sexuality: a virgin presence, the mother's infant as
sexual object.

The seduced other, in the case of a woman, for

example, finds herself in a curious struggle. Having engaged in a rather intense mutual seduction with the trisexual, she finds herself in a strange competition to earn some right to perpetuate their erotics. As the trisexual gradually desexualizes the relationship and converts the erotic into the familial, she is suffused with some sense of the uncanny. This has happened before. But where? And with whom? And why is it such a sweet loss and an acceptable conversion of the erotic?

Typically, the trisexual makes himself available to a woman or a man as an object of intense fascination. This person is unusually gifted and sensual. He is insightful and knowledgeable. He is often very interested in a wide range of subjects. At the moment of seduction he shows an unusual degree of interest in his lover to be. If he meets someone at a party, his entire attention is devoted to one person, who feels this attention to be sensually enveloping. He takes the woman to his flat and for the next few days or over a week he is a devoted and expert lover. Indeed his knowledge of erotics is so considerable that he draws increasing attention to himself as a fascinating phenomenon. He slowly desexualizes the relation and gradually what had been a relation between two becomes a collaboration in which two people are absorbed in the wonder of one, the trisexual. This abandonment of sexuality is not abrupt, it is gradually superseded by other things. Instead of making love, for example, he might cook a superb meal and follow it with a discourse on the philosophy of life that leaves the lover rather spellbound. On another evening, he might take his lover to meet friends and there enrich her social life, by introducing her to people of some fame and considerable creativity. In short, his partners feel a sense of increased privilege just to be with him, and the transformation of sexuality into shared interests passes, incredibly enough, almost unnoticed.

Gradually the lover becomes aware of the fact that she is only one of many admirers. But this recognition is not traumatizing. For as he removes himself from her as a boyfriend, he has placed her in a colony of interesting people, all of whom seem in awe of him. Any new lover soon finds that her seduction, though of course singular in some sense, is typical in another. His friends appear to have been 'seduced' by him, and are happy to have had such an experience. As the trisexual ends a sexual relation with a lover, any narcissistic blow is muted by her realization that in being loved by him at all she has been placed in very privileged company. Furthermore, she is not just one of many women. For she can see that he has captivated men and women – indeed it looks as if all persons of culture and significance are taken in – so her envy of the others is muted.

Trisexuality differs from ordinary narcissistic self love, as the trisexual seduces both sexes first and then **transforms** their erotic desire into a reverentially admiring gaze. **His power resides in the act of conversion.** A compulsively seductive individual, he seduces and appropriates his lovers to become that psychic income that generates his narcissistic wealth, all of it coming from the exchange of the other's desire into the currency of devotion.

To some extent, of course, trisexuality does constitute the competitive presence of the narcissistic element in sexual life. If we consider the male trisexual, he appears to represent the ordinary trace of the positive oedipus complex when he seduces a woman. On the occasion when he seduces a male admirer, he dramatizes a negative oedipus complex. If he seduces both sexes and identifies with each, he appears to be bisexual. Trisexuality might be considered a third form of oedipal engagement in which the formerly repressed narcissistic position emerges to compete with both the positive and negative oedipal motifs. The trisexual's narcissistic self cathexis is so intense that he allows himself to be loved by a woman, or a man, and then dispels the illusion of love and recedes from the fields of eros. But he does not disappear. Instead, he stands at a distance as if he is the embodied memory of what has taken place. This body of desire no longer signifies sexuality but the memory of gratification. It is not accurate to say that he proceeds to take himself as the object of his own love. It is more to the point to say that he loves his function as the curator of memories.

During the course of his analysis, Sandor would describe many intense involvements with people of both sexes. Although he had no overt homosexual relations with men friends, it was clear that he had romances of a latent homosexual kind. As Sandor is a person with a commanding sensibility and striking good looks, many men were drawn to him. His expressiveness, wit, and 'in' knowledge of aesthetics, philosophy, politics and history guaranteed that he was in exceptional demand. In fact he would often show up for his analytic sessions between exciting engagements so that he would rush to see me and flee afterwards to meet up with friends. Although he allowed himself a regular and substantial amount of time to paint, he spent the rest of his time frequenting clubs, exhibitions and friends' houses. Virtually everyone loved him. Every so often he would have an affair with a woman. Perhaps it is more accurate to say that he would have a fling. For usually he would meet a woman at a party or exhibition and take her home where he would make love to her. He prided himself on being a good lover, and it was clear that the women felt they had themselves a good catch. Within a week or two he would, however, decline any further sexual involvement, but would offer in its stead intense friendships. As with his men friends, so with his women ex-lovers: he was virtually always available, extremely helpful, insightful and wonderful company. During years of analysis, according to Sandor, not one woman whom he transformed from lover to friend ever became angry with him or felt cheated by his subsequent sexual refusal and his colony of lovers. Indeed they seemed to count themselves lucky to have met him and to have had such an intense erotic experience, and they were deeply grateful to him that they could continue a compelling friendship.

A schedule of social engagements like Sandor's would exhaust virtually anyone except him. He maintained a silent but rigorous physical regime to keep fit. Every day he would jog for a few miles. Several times a week he would go to a sauna. He ate very carefully and prided himself on his diet. If he ever smoked, he would berate himself in the session.

Over a period of time, his friends became aware of his personal rituals. In fact, they rather added to his uniqueness, and many imitated his regime. Perhaps when they telephoned him and were spoken to by his hearty tape-recorded message, they imagined him either at the sauna, jogging in the park, at a club or preoccupied with a new lover.

Few knew of his occasional and private anguish, characterized by intense longing for a particular woman whom he found it impossible to seduce. Over the course of the analysis, he reported at least three such thwarted loves. They were exceedingly tantalizing and, like Sandor himself, had 'lovers' of both sexes, but in the end they remained genial isolates who withdrew their body selves from the circuit of copulation. Once, with one such woman, he managed to sleep the night with her, but the possibility of actual intercourse never arose, although in her embraces, kisses and erotic verbalizations, Sandor found himself pushed into a kind of mute erotic frenzy. In the wake of this moment he found himself greatly relieved that the woman still offered him her presence, for he was aware that beneath the veil of their passion resided an intense longing and sadness. Eventually he reckoned that such lusts for a partner constituted a curious act of love of one's double, and the failure to seduce the other acquainted him with that sadness that generated much of his trisexual activity.

Sandor's life history gives us a clue to one of the reasons for the formation of trisexual love. Both of his parents had suffered grievous losses in their childhood and each was deeply nostalgic. Each parent would tell Sandor of their past in great detail, giving their memory a certain intrusive presence in contemporary life. And each parent nursed the other with meticulous care. In subsequent years, Sandor was aware of an intense mutual need and affection between his parents, one so absorbing that neither parent created room for relating to a third person. In a way, an oedipus complex depends to some extent on parental creation of an oedipal space and, if such a space does not exist, then the child's oedipal complex will be deformed. In fact, Sandor's parents were very loving people and I am convinced that he had a close relation to his mother, but they conducted their family life along bilateral lines of affection. If mother

was loving father, then she appeared oblivious
of Sandor. By our reconstructive reckoning,
Sandor turned first to the mother and then to the
father, to form a romance in the oedipal manner,
but neither parent knew how to provide for this kind of love.
Sandor was never given the status of rival, as the threesome of the
family was never conceived. He dealt with this disappointment in
object love by turning to his own body as the object of desire. To
do so required an extraordinary intensification of imaginary life,
and Sandor did this in his oedipal and latency period, always imagining himself to be the heroic object of the other's desire.

Some of Sandor's friends joked that he could have anyone he
wanted in a love life since his many conquests amazed them, but
on several occasions a friend would comment on his apparent indifference to partnering with someone. He seemed to have no
need for the other, at least no personal need, although his active
social life obscured this phenomenon to all but a few of his very
closest of friends.

In analysis it became clear how essential he believed the trisexual position was for him. Passion, heterosexual and homosexual, was only an instrument to entice the desire of the other. His
essential aim was what followed: a reversal of the oedipal situation so that both parents were now in competition with one
another for the sexual love of the child. The trisexual's sexuality
is the immaculate conception of pregenital sexuality. It is the family picture before the knowledge of sexuality erases innocence and
consigns the early family to the vaults of memory. On these
preoedipal grounds there are three objects of desire: the mother
(heterosexual), the father (homosexual) and the child self (narcissistic). The evolution through bisexuality to apparent choice of the
self as the preferred object represents the trisexual's journey in
early life: from oedipal frustration back to preoedipal gratification. The aim of such a preoedipal situation is to compel the
parents to love the child on his own terms: to be endlessly admiring and in awe of his presence. Thus, to some extent, one aim
of trisexuality is to defeat sexuality and to transform it into
admiration.

From the genitals to the eyes.

From intercourse to mutual gaze.

Trisexuality thus expresses a certain kind of infant triumph over the terms of adult sexuality.

By defeating the oedipal space, by transcending a space that never imagined him, never admitted him or allowed him to win (achieve certain identifications) and **lose** (lessen certain libidinal attachments), the trisexual experiences a compensatory power. As we shall see, he embodies in his being a psychic function, and in becoming a function, he personalizes that which is profoundly unconscious and makes it available to the other.

Although he always supplied his thwarted sexual lovers with enough personal gratification to mute serious disappointment, it was nonetheless true that Sandor's friends felt themselves engaged in a curious competition with his body self. In the instant of his apparent love of their body selves, the lover must have felt hopeful and gratified. In the subtlest of ways, Sandor withdrew his sexual cathexis of their body and replaced it with interest. I am sure this did not escape the lover's attention, but possibly his shift of sexual desire from the other's body to his own body may have mitigated their sense that sexuality was leaving the scene, so to speak. Sandor's very considerable expertise in making love was actually an object of interest in its own right. After the tide of orgasmic passion the lover would be in retrospective awe of Sandor's range of sexual caresses and erotic knowledge. His own body self would then become the object of intense interest and gradually the twosome would act out a fantasy: that Sandor's exquisite and passionate expertise could never be given over to the other's desire. Sandor would keep it in a safe place, within himself, not for his own pleasure, but for storage against the inclement weathering of life's disillusions. This augmented the view of Sandor as a remarkable personage since he appeared to take nothing for himself, although he took everything into himself. From his accounts it appeared as if many people counted it a privilege to have been loved by him in the first place. From this place he would cast the shadow of the object on the other.

What is the psychic function of the trisexual's particular form of narcissism? What does he bring to the other?

As each of us has been the object of an intense illusion we might say that we have all been the object of a universal seduction. We have all been the object of maternal love and care, just as each of us has been weaned from this attachment. Is it not possible that the oedipus complex constitutes a double deception? We are invited by our own intrinsic identifications into the illusion of equality of power with a father or mother, only to discover our impotence. And yet isn't the process a procedure which substitutes oedipal desire for preoedipal desire? In desiring to compete and to win, even if one does not win the oedipal struggle, one idiom of desire – the aim to achieve oedipal victory – slips in place of another form of desire, that wish to be in the solicitous and comprehensive care of the mother.

I believe it is inaccurate to say that it is sublimation that resolves the oedipal conflict. Rather, it is participation in the conflict that suggests eventual resolution. Those who cannot resolve the oedipal conflict are probably those who were never admitted into that space in the first place. Not only are they fixed, as is Sandor, in the domain of preoedipal sexuality, but they are also denied that experience of losing, of a generative triumph of the parent's world over the child's life, which, in my view, is an experience essential to repression of earlier forms of desire.

Sandor was denied access to oedipal space and conflict by the symbiotic earnestness of his parents who loved him and cared for him as the future that embodies the past. Both parents were so deeply involved in the reciprocal recollection of their relation to their parents that their memories suffused their relation to Sandor. Although they gave him undivided attention, they often absorbed him in nostalgic, though painful, recollections from the past. Sandor's true oedipal opponents were the ghosts of his ancestors who displaced him in his relation to his parents. But like his parents he erotized the function of memory.

Sandor needs to put a present lover into the past. He prefers to reflect on the lover than to live with her in the present. She must become a memory. From there he can love her without anxiety, the anxiety that an intense involvement in the present will divorce him from affiliation with his parents' erotics. He repeats, then, what his parents seem to have accomplished. He enlivens the present, through a love relation, in order to give it sufficient vividness for it to survive like a beacon in the past. Like his parents, who were preoccupied with their pasts, Sandor vigorously uses the present to create his past.

So Sandor is left to bear the erotic function of memory. He reacquaints his lovers with some prior knowledge, as each of them is revisited by traces of their own infant desire and by the apparitional appearance of that extraordinary object that conferred privilege and gratification in a self-contained moment of time. By using erotic capability the trisexual invites the other into genital sexuality in order to dispel it and compel it to disappear from two-person relating. The trisexual **converts** erotic passion into a living mnemic presence. By soliciting the other's desire, he becomes the master of the other's sexual destiny and signifies the mortality of ecstasy. His body bears the memory of the other's gratifications, and is not the object of desire but its mnemic province. In this respect he has understood the parents' parenting to embody the trace of their parents and their grandparents, as his mother and father unconsciously testify to their need for early maternal and paternal care. This is an erotics of absence.

'I am the memory of what you desire.'

'I am the memory of your desire.'

'I am the desire of your memory.'

In the sweet secrecy of the early loves that are lost to us the trisexual finds his voice. He speaks to us in that place where each of us knows of the love of mother and mother love.

THE NARCISSIST AND THE TRISEXUAL

If trisexuality is a form of narcissism, how does it differ from narcissism proper? The question requires that we consider how it is that a narcissist conducts his erotic life.

Although it is a conventional explanation – in that it is not

particularly psychoanalytic – I think it is useful
to begin by establishing that the narcissist
appears to love only himself. If we imagine that
the narcissist's relation to himself has been a loving one and one of some considerable duration,
then we are closer to the contemporary psychoanalytic understanding of the narcissistic personality if we say that after a while
the narcissist no longer looks into the mirror, but assumes the
other to be the mirror. Kohut (1971) has written about this form
of mirror transference. The narcissist's fragile assumption of the
intrinsic beauty of the self differentiates this particular individual from the trisexual. Where the narcissist assumes love the
trisexual works actively to seduce the other. Modell (1969) has
written an account of the narcissist's effect on the other; in particular, he acquaints us with how boring such a person can be. As
the narcissist assumes he has all that is needed, he expends no
effort. He seeks no object. Objects are assumed to be part of the
self system, a point Kohut makes in his formation of the concept
of the 'self-object'. This assumption is not true of a trisexual. Nor
is the trisexual either overtly self preoccupied or boring. Indeed,
he is usually very interesting, highly seductive and interested in
the other. If anything, he plays Echo to Narcissus.

Further, narcissistic characters tend to seduce the other in
passive ways, by presenting the other with the image of the narcissist's self. One patient who fits this category of person tends to
place himself next to a woman, such that she is meant to fall in
love with his simple presence. She is invited to be curious about
him and to ask him about his life. He obliges by spilling out his life
history, which is fairly interesting, and gradually she falls in love
with the picture he gives her of himself. It is my view that such
narcissistic characters do not yield themselves to the other in a
relationship; instead they give the other a picture of the self that
is equivalent to the object that the narcissist holds of himself. It is
a subtle distinction, but an important one, to note that the narcissist puts an image to the woman, one of his own making, so that
as she contemplates him, she falls in love – if she does at all – with
the image of the self. At all times, the narcissist is in control and
does not surrender to true intimacy. He insists they go hand in

hand in life with him leading. If a woman attempts to seduce the narcissist, and if her seduction is object-differentiated so that she is not simply admiring the narcissist's self, then the narcissistic character can become panicked. With one patient, this became clear when a woman who was very attracted to him also had very different views of him than he had of himself. A struggle ensued. Either she accepted his image of himself as the only possible one, or the relation was to be over. Fight as she might for her image of him, this was effectively refused. Each day when this patient came to a session he would say: 'Can you believe that she said this about me?' Or, 'she thinks I am like . . .'. He was so overcome with narcissistic rage over her different view of him that he was never able to consider the merits of her perception.

For the narcissistic character, either the other falls in love with the narcissist's image of himself – as is he – or there will be no partnership. The image of the self and the self are, of course, not the same; indeed, the narcissist's image of self is ultimately a defence against facing the reality of the self. To be sure, it is true that the trisexual is equally in dread of intimate partnership, but where the narcissist gives the other a picture of himself to be adored, the trisexual gives the other an encapsulated experience to be remembered.

The narcissist: 'In it you have found me wonderful.'

The trisexual: 'In me you have found it wonderful.'

The narcissistic character visits the other with **need** and invites the partner to share in his fulfilment. The trisexual visits the other with memory, with an ache, a jolt, that awakens the loss of something known to the other. The trisexual suggests to the other the intensity of mother love, when the nature of being feels inspired by eros itself. To be the memory of the other's desire, to convert eros from generative procreativity (division into further multiples) into the desire of memory (a unity) is the trisexual's aim.

What family has Sandor created for himself? To him it is not the post-oedipal family, a differentiated group of people with independent desires and interests who are capable of mutuality.

oedipal family. As he converts his lovers into
friends, as he transports them back from differentiated erotics to the spiritualism of uncanny
fusion states, he penetrates frozen memories and
de-represses through acting out the affective state of self in early
object life.

As Gear, Hill and Liendo (1983) have suggested, however, one
of the neglected features in our literature on narcissism is the degree of power and authority that the narcissist aims to exert in his
object relations. By inviting the other to fall in love with his image
of himself, the narcissist aims to control the other's eventual effect upon him. Behind the question, 'Who has the power to establish the version of the self?' lies another: 'Who has the right to
determine the fate of the child self?' It is my view that because of
early conflicts in relation to the mother, the narcissistic character
is determined to **appropriate** the mother's position. He takes
over her function and mothers himself in an intense and rigid
manner. We all assume some aspects of the mother's idiom of
caretaking, in that continuing process of relating to ourself as an
object of our own consideration and care (as I have explored
above, in chapter 3), but in the narcissistic character's case,
there is considerable frustration and rage with this mother, so in
assuming his own care of himself, the narcissist feels a sense of
triumph at gaining control and power over the sources of self es-
teem.

But where the narcissist gains power by assuming control over
his version of himself (and all that comes with it), the trisexual
finds power by refusing authority or direct influence. It is not in
what he acquires or possesses but in what he gives up that the
trisexual gains position. He finds power in appearing to be Echo.
He gives to the other, but in so doing, limits both his function and
the other's influence. He becomes the testimony of memory, the
witness of history, the representation of a repressed area of the
other's self. Former lovers look upon him as storing valued parts
of themselves, and when they meet up, there is always this secret
pleasure of shared memory.

I often puzzled when listening to Sandor's account of his many different lovers, why there was so little protest from anyone. Didn't someone feel exploited? Certainly I think he used people. Then I realized that each of his lovers knew of his specialness in advance. They knew this before they became the object of his seductions. Further, they understood that he was admired and 'loved' by persons of both sexes and no one was in any doubt that Sandor enjoyed being himself. I believe that his lovers were predisposed both to being loved by a **unique person**, by a person of glamour and sensuality, who signified a particular kind of erotics, and to the narcissistic achievement of having 'had' such a fabulous love – to the satisfaction of having used him to their own narcissistic benefit.

Sandor acts out in the course of a few days the whole of preoedipal life. Lovers are born into the relation. They are carried off to a special place (his flat) where they are the object of a kind of bizarre maternal preoccupation. As this love life takes place between two adults, it would appear that mutual love is gratified through genital sexuality, but this is an unconscious representation of an intense feeding situation. As the lover is 'weaned' from this erotics, she is placed in a society where she regards this Sandor-mother from some remove. There appears to be no loss, no regret, no anger. Only a sense of wonder and gratitude. Clearly one can see here how a person like Sandor tries to utilize the illusions of unconditional love to effect a delusion: that such love is indeed there, so much so that the child feels no pain, no loss, no rage. Only by distorting preoedipal life, by exploiting narcissistic self states, can Sandor perpetuate his effect upon his lovers and friends. I think it is likely that Sandor's lovers are aware of the fate that awaits them, and perhaps they too seek an intensification of the past as they know that their love affair with Sandor will only be momentary. Amongst fragile people, or persons who seek to find evidence of the presence of unconditional love, a Sandor can ply his trade. For some he is a second coming.

A trisexual is a rare but unmistakable person. I have distinguished him from an ordinary narcissistic character. It is im-

portant to emphasize that such an individual is
quite glamorous, extremely popular, and known
to be enamoured of himself without being obviously grandiose. A clinician working with such
an individual might seek respite from the com-

plexity of the person's character by assuring himself that a trisexual is actually very shallow. But such a countertransference
judgement would, in my view, reflect a wish on the analyst's part
to simplify the complex and reduce the difficulties of working
with a trisexual. For such a person is genuinely intelligent, gifted,
well educated, insightful, and socially cohesive. He does not
'come across' as a Don Juan. It is quite understandable that he is
often the object of considerable speculation. Try as people might
to understand him, to place him in some collectively known position, they fail. His ability to survive knowing is part of his mystery. So, speculations that he is 'gay' or 'bisexual' do not stick. No
one really knows.

Can we say, then, that people who fall in love with a Sandor
are in any sense of the term in love? The answer must be no. No, if
we mean in the mature sense of love. But love does seem to be
around. It is there as memory, as each of us bears some trace of
early object love. Those who 'fall' in love with a Sandor commit
themselves to something of a mistaken act of identity. Perhaps
these people have an experience rather like all of us do, one time
or another, when, whilst walking along the street in a crowd, we
see a face in the distance. Surely it cannot be! It is X, a childhood
friend, whom we haven't seen in thirty years. The heart races. We
pick up speed. We fumble for words to speak our introduction
after such a long time has elapsed. And in the penultimate moment, as we cry out their name, we find . . . our mistake. Yet we
have also seen our dear friend, and as we walk away from this
scene, no doubt disappointed (even if slightly relieved), we may
find ourselves remembering the many moments spent with our
childhood chum. The same experience, although lived out in an
obviously different way, can occur when we see someone who re-
minds us of a loved one who has died. It can be a shocking but
profound mistake.

Those who fall for Sandor commit themselves to the error of

mistaken identity. The feelings in the lover, however, are often profound and intense, just as in the case of the mistaken identity above. Sandor knows this. It is his function. He knows that he is a figment of memory's desire, and in this he finds a sense of power, significance and compensation.

On a rare and unannounced occasion, Sandor would visit one of his former lovers. In a night of intense erotics he would come out of the past and provide a lover with a vivid visitation of former gratifications. As he left early in the morning, his partner would feel she had been inside an intense erotic dream, in which the past had been relived. On these rare occasions, the lovers share not just the memory of eros, but the eros of memory. It is in **that** psychic place that the trisexual lives and functions, as the imagined **keeper** of memory.

II   Moods

6   *Moods and the conservative process*

I have found that when certain analysands establish crucial states of being in the transference they often do this by living through a mood. These patients can articulate their internal states of mind and ordinarily provide me with a narrative of their life, but important elements of their self experience are only expressed through moods. Although I will focus on the clinical situation and restrict myself to a study of those moods that are characterological – those that are repeated forms of being states – I first want to make a few observations on moods in general.

A person is often described as being 'in' a mood, giving those of us who are not in such a condition the sense that the one in a mood is 'inside' some special state. How far inside the mood is someone? How long will it last? Spatial and temporal metaphors register something of the special nature of this phenomenon. 'Don't worry,' a friend may say of another, 'he will come out of it sooner or later.'

A curious feature of being in a mood is that it does not totally restrict one's ability to communicate with the other. A person can be both in a mood and capable of dealing with phenomena outside the mood space. Yet to an onlooker it is clear that the person who is inside a mood is also not present in some private and fundamental way and this absence marks out the territory of mood space. The space in which a person experiences a mood is created, in my view, both by the territorial implications of the individual's difference in being and by the other's recognition of such a state as a legitimate area in which self experiencing has limited priority over self-other relating. It is a space, therefore, that is often licensed by a recognition of its necessity.

We need to experience moods.

Recognition of the need for moods is shown by the fact that

when a friend is clearly inside this special temporal and spatial dimension, our sense may be that he needs to remain within this territory for self experiencing without our commenting on it; our absence of comment may contribute to the boundaries of mood space.

As a person goes to sleep, he may have a dream. When a person goes into a mood, he may be some former self. Going into a mood is an essential condition for the creation of a being state that, like the dream state, may represent some child element in contemporary life. Time must pass before a person emerges from a mood, and when he does the space created for the experiencing of a mood disappears with the act of temporal emergence. If someone has 'gone' to sleep, he undergoes a particular psychic experience which is universally recognized. If a person enters a mood, he approximates in this form of psychic activity another means of establishing and elaborating elements of the infant-child self: sleep creates the dream, some moods establish fragments of former self states.

GENERATIVE AND MALIGNANT MOODS

Certain moods may be psychic phenomena that are as necessary to the well-being of the person as is the dream. While in a mood, a part of the individual's total self withdraws into a generative autistic state so that a complex internal task is allowed time and space to work itself through. By virtue of the person's psychosomatic identity during a mood experience, a special territory is usually marked out to ensure that this experiencing is not mistaken for object-directed communicating, even though it would be incorrect to assume that the person who is having a mood has no potential effect upon the other. In my view, what differentiates a generative from a malignant mood is the nature of the mood's function and the quality of that boundary that preserves a space for mood experiencing. If we feel, let's say, that a person's withdrawn imperviousness is a means of coercing another into serving some self function, then such a mood would constitute a malignant interpersonal process, one which I would like to differentiate from a generative withdrawal, when we do not feel that the

person's mood is fundamentally aimed to force us into some capitulative activity. To be sure, it
is not always possible to draw a hard and fast line
here, as almost all moods are invested with object-relational implications. A malignant mood,

MOODS
AND THE
CONSERVATIVE
PROCESS

from a functional point of view, would be one, however, that is
primarily aimed at some other. A person who sulks, for example,
would be using mood experience in order to effect some significant other. In a generative mood the person goes into himself to
contact the mute, unknown child self and thus has a greater
chance of generating some knowing of what has been part of the
unthought known.

The quality of the boundary that marks the territory for
mood experiencing must also be considered in assessing whether a
mood is generative or malignant. If a person emerges from sleep
and cannot distinguish his dreams from his wakeful perceptions,
we think in terms of a potential psychotic process. At the very
least the dream will have lost its generative potential as the awakened person, unable to distinguish it from reality, will no longer
have that perceptual differentiation necessary to reflect upon the
dream as an object (Pontalis, 1974). The boundary between the
self asleep who is dreaming and the awake self who is perceiving is
essential to the preservation of these two domains of distinct self
experience. Similarly, for a mood to be generative a person must
be able to emerge from a mood in such a way that he can reflect
upon the mood as an object without feeling the migratory effects
of mood experiencing overlapping into ordinary affects.

THE MNEMIC ENVIRONMENT

Musing on the often-heard comment 'I am not myself today'
Ralph Greenson (1954) stated that such a comment pointed out
the 'close connection between the questions "How are you?" and
"Who are you?" ' He wrote that: 'One can describe moods in
terms of objects. Patients do not just become depressed, but they
become the rejected little boy they once were in childhood. The
anxious patient is not just a frightened adult, but is the scared
little child of the past.' He concludes: 'Moods are not only derived
from the internal representatives of external objects, but are

often the representatives of one's own past state of mind; one's conception of oneself in the past' (pp. 73–4).

Moods are complex self states that may establish a mnemic environment in which the individual re-experiences and recreates former infant-child experiences and states of being. Just as the dream allows for the unconscious experience of child parts of the self, in elaborating and negotiating with adult life, so, too, does mood experience allow for previously lived self states to reappear in the ongoing negotiation with reality. When we become in our being that which we recollect from former self states, the psychic accomplishment of the mood may be as valuable as the work of the dream.

Indeed, because of the particular features of the analytic setting and process (Winnicott, 1965; Khan, 1974), the analysand's mood life may be particularly responsive to the nature of psychoanalysis itself, rather like a dream is a response to sleep. Analysands create environments within the clinical setting and the living through of a mood is one of the idioms for the establishment of an environment.

Who is it that emerges from within the mood? Since a special being state is established, what is the total self's relation to this part of the self? In what way may we be able to learn something of the person's relation to himself as an object through mood experience? An otherwise dour person, for example, might on occasion become rather inexplicably happy, even though such happiness might appear strangely incongruous with the person's ordinary self system. Every so often he might become rather silly and mildly vulnerable. It may well be that such an individual's 'happiness' – which might puzzle those who know the person as being oddly 'unlike him' – is a temporary regression to a former self state that prevailed in his childhood. In other words, the child self is still present in the person's total self functioning, but it appears to be an oddity relative to the person's more usual self. If so, the person has possibly internalized a lifeless parenting environment and the mood of infrequent silliness is an unconscious re-creation of the occasionally happy child self who is nonetheless dissociated from a lifeless parenting environment that failed the child's libidinal and ego needs. The 'usual self' of such an individual personifies and sustains the lifeless parenting environment, whilst the 'oddly' silly and happy self that emerges amidst a mood actually represents the former child self, still refused recognition by the depriving parental element.

An otherwise rather superficial person, who seems almost perversely content about everything, on occasion stumbles into inertness and something close to sadness. Such a mood could be the remembering of moments in childhood when the other than happy child – happiness being a parental need complied with by the child – registered other aspects of life. But the individual's mood of awkward sadness may, in his relation to himself as an object, re-create this person's experience of the way in which the parents disposed themselves towards sadness or vulnerability.

In order to clarify why I think that some moods may represent a breakdown in the individual's self development, in such a way that self states released in a mood are acts of conservation and protest, I will present three cases which illustrate my point.

CLINICAL EXAMPLES / I

David is a fretful man. Always involved in more than he can possibly accomplish, his dreamy ambitiousness is inevitably complemented by an intense frustration with his inability to complete even the simplest of tasks. Were he not quite intelligent and genuinely creative, he would only be hopeless, and yet his situation is compounded by the fact that, even while leaving many of his tasks undone, he has managed to receive recognition in his field and to get on somehow. He is modestly successful in three distinctly different professions which he maintains simultaneously. However much he might plan to fulfil the obligations of one of the professions he is no sooner embarked on such work than he is compelled to attend to a crisis in another area of his work life. Indeed, crises seem to punctuate his grandiose dreaming, as one dream after another is interrupted by a crisis that demands immediate attention.

Now and then, while ensconced in his study, he is able to feel a kind of sublime rapport with the intellectual aspect of one of his professions. In such moments, he feels quite enraptured by the aesthetic dimension of his task, but such experiences are painfully short-lived. A telephone call from a rather irate client might jolt him back to a recognition that he has not actually attended to some ordinary but essential task in one of the other professions.

As a child he was quite a daydreamer. Both of his parents, however, seemed to have supported his phantasizing as a dissociated alternative to living. They read him an uncommonly excessive amount of stories – sometimes for hours on end – whilst virtually all the other moments of the parents' lives were spent bickering with one another. With their child, however, they seemed to create rare moments of tranquillity; each night, for example, they regularly gathered in his room for the ceremonial storytelling, which somehow managed to abate their intense unhappiness with one another.

David's parents divorced when he was eleven, and he was completely deserted by his father, who waited a further nine years before he tried to see his son again. Although the parents had argued quite a lot, both were self-styled liberals, and it was contrary to their self image to debase themselves in unsavoury rows; they nit-picked and withdrew, or scored points over each other. It was a terrible shock for David when they divorced, and it was a catastrophe to be deserted by his father just as he needed paternal help in dealing with the shock of adolescence.

Whatever David's presenting material might be for any particular session it was often spoken against the background of a kind of character mood, although this mood was split off from the presentation of his narrative. As time passed, I became increasingly attentive to his mood, and I asked myself what sort of environment he was creating for himself, as his mood established a being state that was quite distinct.

How did he behave?

Often, when I opened the waiting-room door he would jump to his feet and race past me into the consulting room, rather like a professional entertainer called on to the stage. Once he had hurled himself into the clinical space, however, he would pause

for a second as if confused, almost as if he had
entered the wrong place. Whereupon he would
rearrange the analytic couch by taking off one of
the cushions, and he would move the couch a few
inches closer to me. All of this he did with the
grace of a lumberjack serving tea at a fundraising event; it was
so well done, even though odd, that it took me some time before
I saw it.

When he spoke, he would also rearrange his voice. That is the
only way I can describe what he did when he 'cleared' his throat
with guttural expulsions, as if this was a prerequisite to the material that followed. When he narrated life's events, he conveyed
his accounts with a kind of mournful urgency, rather like someone who feels he must describe a dreadful event that he has seen
as quickly as possible in anticipation of losing consciousness.
Crossing and then recrossing his feet, putting his hand under his
head to support himself, rubbing his face again and again, and
heaving and sighing were characteristics of his person in the
sessions. It amounted to a kind of emotive tidal activity, as he
would sigh in waves of released, but never resolved despair, and
his personal activity was never intrinsically linked to the material
presented. He would, however, stop this agitated activity as soon
as I spoke. The sighing would cease, his body would be at rest,
and he might report a dream or talk about material from another
session, all stated in a calm and serene manner. In fact, he was
dreamy, and sometimes he would slur his words or break off in
mid-sentence and lapse back into private thought.

By the time that I came to analyse this phenomenon, which I
regard as a character mood, I had already analysed his grandiosity as a need to be mirrored in the radiant light of an admirer,
something which he had lost through parental discord. The matter is further complicated by the fact that I think the parents denied their internal pain by treasuring their own split-off child
selves, acted out by them in relation to David, who in some ways
was overdosed with parental idolization. By preserving several
different professions he manages to sustain a boy's world, for reality is viewed as a kind of intrusive frustration of the life of daydreams.

The point at which I took up his mood was when I realized just how intent he was upon setting up an originating grandiose moment (as seen when he entered the consulting room) only to have that lovely possibility collapse into a kind of agitation (fretting at being inside himself) and then eventually a serenity that was occasioned usually when I spoke. Now what did all of this amount to?

One of the transference features of his mood was its mnemic singularity. He wanted to live inside this environment! Only through his mood of boyish ambition oblivious to true reality orientation could he preserve the last moments of family life. By living amongst grandiose dreams he remained in contact with his mother and father and their recognition of him as their child. His fretting did not register a frustration with reality: it was an expulsion of reality orientation. When I spoke, I was that mother or father telling him stories, whereupon he lapsed into reverential calm, knowing now that the parental objects were present. When I analysed the unconscious aim of his mood, there was intense resistance. Only well after a year of working this through did his resistance devolve into a desperate sense of loss. It was not simply that understanding what he was holding on to through his mood would mean separation from a delusion – that of being the boy with his family. It also meant that he had to mourn the loss of a compensatory future lived with his mother and father together. It is one thing to mourn the loss of an experience that has happened in one's past, it is quite another matter to lose the future, and David's registration of this loss was intense. To be a failure had been his greatest unconscious ambition. Not to succeed enabled him to remain 'at home' with his parents.

That mood which I have identified as a feature of David's character was in the nature of a mnemic environment. The unconscious aim of his fretting and his dreaminess was to create the familial atmosphere that prevailed at the moment when he suffered the loss of his family.

CLINICAL EXAMPLES / II

George contributes to the creation of his own personal environment through a recurring mood of anticipatory mourning. His mood is a suffusive expression of the certainty of grief. He knows he will be failed. Hence liveliness is only suffered by fools. Session upon session is characterized by a quiet but triumphant certainty that all will fail in life, and he certainly endeavoured for years to make the analysis fail, lest I come to the mistaken conclusion that analysis was a potentially life-enhancing process.

To some extent, it would be fair to say that George's mood was always the object of the analysis, but I felt I was able to analyse its unconscious function only when he turned to it as a phenomenon in its own right. This came about when he was involved with his first real girlfriend. She had promised him that she would leave her mother and come to live with him, but month after month she could not bring herself to make the move. For a long time he had been tirelessly supportive of her, but gradually a mood that I had often witnessed in the analysis began to prevail in his relation to her. Instead of telling her how he felt, something which he felt would reduce his potency, he used his personal withdrawal from her to compel her into anxious dependence on him. Although she could not move in with him, his withdrawal led her to telephone him more frequently and to ask him for reassurance. This he did not give. Quite the contrary. He addressed her as if the relationship was over and insinuated himself into her psychic life as a person who would both inflict and share the loss with her. At a certain point, however, this rather vengeful attack on his girlfriend seemed less predetermined. Indeed, he drew closer to her; now, he loved her the more intensely, but his expression of love was to withdraw from her and cause her a great deal of pain. Odd as it may sound, his libido declined in favour of a kind of grief orgasm. He would seek her out in order to undergo a form of intense mutual loss that would culminate in tears and agonizing pain upon separation. He characterized the ending of the relationship as fated. It was over, and there was nothing he could do. Yet he would remain with her to see her loss through to the end.

Something of this same phenomenon had been acted out by

him in the transference to me. His determined sense that we were all fated to mutual failure would be accomplished by his deft refusals to let me understand him. For the first years of his analysis he would change the version of his statements each time I tried to establish some understanding of him. I will describe the nature of my countertransference with George in some depth (see below, chapter 12) so I shall restrict my account here to the observation that I too was compelled to live in an environment of his creation, one in which the loss of the future was a daily certainty. I came to understand, however, that in many ways George's mood recreated an object setting. As an infant, he had been separated from his mother who left him in the care of different persons, and his father remained emotionally removed from him.

To a great extent, George and his parents mourned over a sense of mutual failure and of their collective fate. George knew that when he tried to talk to his father, his father would withdraw and change the conversation. Knowing this would happen, he often approached his father in a mournful manner that anticipated the outcome. The mother, a frequent witness to these occasions, would try to share the father's sense of failure and at the same time comfort her son.

I began to regard George's mood of anticipatory mourning as his way of recreating the family environment. Like David, he did not want to give it up, for it represented that little bit of intimacy that he had achieved with his family, and his sense of self was intricately featured in the collective mourning process. In the family environment each of the participants enacted a wistful hopefulness tinged with the knowledge of its inevitable and fated disappearance. They experienced loss together, they went off into separate and known corners of the house to sulk and slump into a desultory state, they tried to console and patch each other up. They knew this about one another very well indeed. They did not argue vigorously. They did not really try to engage one another. They used shared grieving and mutual loss as an alternative to all the other facets of living, and it was this mood that George

brought to the analysis, a special state in his
overall being that conserved his child self's relation to his mother and father.

109

MOODS
AND THE
CONSERVATIVE
PROCESS

CLINICAL EXAMPLES / III

Janet's moods seemed to vary. Indeed in the early years of her psychotherapy I never quite knew what mood would prevail in the sessions. One day she would be an intensely intellectual person. During such a state, she would try to engage me in conversation about different books she was reading or films she had seen; failing that, she would tell me how unscientific psychoanalysis was. Some days she would live inside the clinical space in a mood of serene absence. Her voice would be barely audible, and she seemed feather-like. Other days she would fairly burst into the consulting room and bubble over with a kind of diffuse excitement about the numerous exhilarating events that had taken place in her life since I had last seen her. This might be supplanted by a mood of sullen depression, when her voice deepened and words appeared like heavy weights that required the whole of her body movement to be released. Alternatively she might arrive in a passionate mood. She had met a sexy man, and the session would be taken up with a mood of erotic intensity as she narrated her partly conscious erotic fantasies about him.

It would be inaccurate to say that the presence of her moods established itself in my mind as an independent factor in her therapy, for she was fairly articulate and seemed to be working on important issues. She responded to transference interpretations about her changing experiences of me and often I commented on this. Even though some of this work was valuable, I was uneasy; something had not been properly analysed.

Gradually I realized that her moods were more like intense affect sensations that were substitutions for truly reflective and digestive thinking. She was in need of a 'happening' (Khan, 1974) in each session, a mood happening, in which the mood would dominate and transcend the content of her free associative material. The unconscious aim of this moodfulness was to create a level of being in which affect continued to function sensationally.

She resisted transforming her affect states into verbal representations which could be considered by the analyst and redigested by her.

Janet's aim, in creating the mood as a primary medium for being and relating within the analysis, was to preserve sensation as a way of life. Once I understood this the genetic consideration was not difficult, for she had been parented by people who were very hysterical characters and who had occasioned quite intense and varied affective experiences in her as their child. This kind of relating was favoured by the parents, so that, in her own way, Janet was preserving through diversity of mood that environment which allowed her some intimacy with her parents, conserving an identity and style of relationship that continued an unconscious and private relation to her parents.

THE CONSERVATIVE OBJECT

Moods typical of a person's character frequently conserve something that was but is no longer. I will call that experience-memory stored in the internal world a conservative object. A conservative object is a being state preserved intact within a person's internal world: it is not intended to change, and acts as a mnemic container of a particular self state conserved because it is linked to the child self's continuing negotiation with some aspect of the early parental environment.

A child not only stores his experiences of an object in that process we term internalization, but he also conserves self states which may eventually become permanent features of his character. Furthermore, the internal world is not simply composed of self and object representations; if it were, mental life would be restricted to whatever permits of symbolism. A child may endure an experience which is registered not through object representation but through an identity sense. Children do not simply cognize objects; they also experience shifting and evolving self states that may be biased by an object setting (a family, a school, a play scene) but are not necessarily identifiable with a particular object. A child may thus have a profound self experience without being able to link this being state with any one object. Such self states are nonetheless untranslatable into that symbolic order characteristic of object representation: they yield, instead, identity senses and they therefore conserve the child's sense of self or sense of being rather than his understanding of such being through fantasy or object representation.

A child may undergo an intensely private self experience that defies his representative capacity, so that the being state persists as a conserved rather than a transformed (symbolized) phenomenon. A child of two-and-a-half, for example, might be overwhelmed by a sense of worthlessness linked up with his more well defined psycho-motor aggressiveness. He might not be able to settle this experience in his being into any object representation that would enable him to work on the problem. The sense of being would be stored, however, as an 'object' in the internal world, but as a conservative object: the experience is stored rather than representations of the experience. The child will, however, know something even if this knowledge has not been elaborated through thought proper. The conservative object is another form of the unthought known.

When a child is, for one reason or another, left to work on a life problem that is beyond his capability, he often assumes the problem to be unresolvable and it therefore becomes an inevitable part of his sense of identity. If a child's father, for example, departs for a year, and if this separation is inadequately worked through with the mother and father, then a child may assume this loss (of the father and of the child self lost with the absent father) is a self-defining event. The concept of working through or of time's contribution to the resolution of life issues is unknown to the child, as **traumas are not experienced as events in life but as life defining.** It is my view that if the parents are unable, through perception and appropriate empathic understanding, to transform the particular fix that a child is in by virtue of some life problem, then such a fix becomes an identity sense that is conserved by the child as partly definitive of life itself. I am quite certain that some of the child's internal fixes are so private as to defy even the most empathic parent's perceptive care; all persons will, in my view, therefore, conserve rather than represent some states of self. The unthought known is a substantial part of each of us.

In the course of ontogenesis, the person will have an ongoing relation to these conserved states of self as much as to his represented objects. During that special state of being that allows for the release of the conservative object – in moods – the individual will remain in contact with that child self who endured and stored the unrepresentable aspects of life experience.

THE TRUE SELF AND THE
CONSERVATIVE OBJECT

When a mood serves to release a conservative object for experiencing, it differs from ordinary affect experience in that the true self is allowed an unusual freedom of expression precisely because of the dissociative feature of a mood as an allowed for, and therefore unintruded upon, right. Nonetheless, there is something vulnerable about a person caught in a mood. It is as if we are witness to an element of the 'kernel' (Winnicott, 1952) of the person being acted out in our presence.

The psychoanalyst may allow for a substantial period of time to elapse before analysing the patient's moods. The Winnicottian and Kohutian sense of the need to allow for the patient's prolonged transference usage of the analyst as a selfobject may be part of an implicit recognition that the analysand needs to establish a mood without premature challenge. Nonetheless, it will become necessary at some time to reach the person while he is 'inside' the mood. It is my view that this often means contacting part of the individual's true self, but a true self that may be frozen at a time when self experience was traumatically arrested, and which sustains the child's rapport with his parents and his loss of personal reality.

David's moods conserved his memory of the early psychic death of true self living, since his personal creativity was transformed into an insignia of loss due to the pathology of his parents' depression. Janet's moods were alternatives to symbolic communication, for she used moods to sensationalize her affect: she needed affective fixes to give herself a sense of personal reality. I

believe she recollects that moment in her early
childhood when the only contact she achieved
with her parents was through the sudden alternating effects the parents had on one another and
on her. With all three patients, I was aware that
each was preserving something very important – some essential
feature of the core of the self – and that this part of the self was
recurrently established through moods. My hunch was that when
I aimed to analyse the nature of this act of self preservation
through the conservative object I would meet with an intense
resistance. I was not wrong.

Some analysands feel that their moods are the most important
authentic memories of their childhood, often because through
mood the person feels in contact with a true self experience. A
conservative object frequently serves an important function in
analysis when it preserves a self state that prevailed in the child's
life just at the moment when the child felt he lost contact with the
parents. When this is the case, a conservative object preserves
the child's relation to the parents at the moment of a breakdown
in parent-child engagement. Adult analysands may form intense
resistances to psychoanalytical knowing of the conservative object, as they feel the analyst is endeavouring to remove their preserved relationship to the parents. David, Janet and George were
preserving through the conservative object a relation to the
parents of their childhood, a relationship that was periodically
recollected through that psychic enactment characteristic of
mood.

George, for example, found my analytical understanding of
his dense moodfulness very worrying because he not only felt that
his mood of negative intimacy was his only true relation to his
parents, but he believed that his sense of identity was inextricably
linked up with this particular recurrent mood. As I analysed his
resistance to my interpretations he flung himself deeply into
moods. It was clear that he experienced the analysis of his moods
as a challenge to his identity and as an attempt to refuse him the
right to continue a particular relation to his parents.

Some analysands use moods as a primary means of relating to
their internal objects precisely because the parents left the child

with a state of being as a kind of fated element in his total personality. This reflects a fault in the parents' ability to function sufficiently as transformational objects. It is the continual task of each parent, as a transformational object, to perceive and identify the nature of a child's ongoing needs and dilemmas, then to find some appropriate way of speaking up about the specific issue, and then to find some means of facilitating a negotiated solution which enables the child to develop. Transformational object functioning by no means implies that the parent must gratify a child, as the parent will often have to frustrate a child's wishes and find a solution that is less than totally acceptable to the child's omnipotent demands. When a parent refuses to perceive, identify, address in speech and facilitate through attitude or action an element presented by the child to the parent, then this aspect of the child's self may be left in isolation: apparently unnoticed, uncommented upon and with no facilitative resolution. If so, the child is stuck with a self state that registers not simply an arrest in his personal development, but an arrest in the parent's parenting as well. No child, in my view, develops a point of fixation all by himself: one must speak of a family point of arrest and fixation. The parents' refusal to address a part of a child to some extent amounts to an implicit 'let it be' or 'he is just that way' which later on becomes the nature of mood experience: let's just let him be while he is like this.

The conservative object has enormous therapeutic potential, precisely because of its essential character of preserving some disowned aspect of the child's true self, the moment of breakdown of the relationship with his parents and the fault in the parents' functioning as transformational objects. In the mood state the patient is available for potential transformation of what has primarily been mood experiencing into sentient knowing. As the analyst gradually perceives, identifies and addresses the mood, he is already functioning where the parents did not – as a transformational object. When I talked to George about how his moods represented his intense anguish both over his place in their lives and at being restricted in his knowing of his parents, and when we discovered how his mood of mournfulness was an act of unconscious complicity with the parents' breakdown, I was already functioning as that transformational object.

No analyst becomes a parent to the analysand. Good analytic work is part of a tradition of transformational object functioning, and in that sense alone it bears some relation to mothering, fathering, and even possibly brothering or sistering. Therefore, although we do not become the mother or the father, we do possess generative paradigmatic skills that reach the child element in the adult analysand. We do this within the clinical setting when the patient is regressed to such an extent that we are a transference object, so we tend to utilize the same complex range of skills that typify parenting. Thus we may, through holding and interpretation, provide a limited transformation in the patient's being state that amounts to a more skilled and appropriate intervention than prevailed when the analysand was a child and presented the same being state to one or another of the parents, who were unable to respond empathically because of their own developmental arrest. Just as the child's ego takes over the parents' function as transformational object, so does the patient, in his handling of himself as an object of need, interest, facilitation, knowing and analysis, inherit the analyst's transformational object functioning.

SUMMARY

In brief, moods are psychic phenomena which serve important unconscious functions. Like the dream, a mood has a kind of necessary autistic structure to it: people who are in a mood, like persons who are asleep, are inside a special state where a temporal element is at play. They will emerge, like the dreamer, after the spell is over. Some moods, particularly those that form part of a person's character, are occasions for the expression of a conservative object – that disowned internal self state that has been preserved intact during childhood. When a person goes 'into' a mood, he becomes that child self who was refused expression in relation to his parents for one reason or another. Consequently moods are often the existential registers of the moment of a breakdown between a child and his parents, and they partly indicate the parent's own developmental arrest, in that the parent was unable to deal appropriately with the child's particular maturational needs. What had been a self experience in the child, one that could have been integrated into the child's continuing self development, was rejected by the parents, who failed to perform adequately as ordinary 'transformational objects', so that a self state was destined to be frozen by the child into what I have called a conservative object – subsequently represented only through moods.

7   *Loving hate*

I N Freud's early theory of instincts, love and hate were conceived of as nonidentical twins. Love aimed to acquire pleasure and pleasurable objects, and hate expelled the unpleasurable into the outside world. 'The ego hates, abhors and pursues with intent to destroy all objects which are a source of unpleasurable feeling for it,' wrote Freud (1915, p.138), equating hate with destruction. After a partial reworking of his instinct theory in 'Beyond the pleasure principle' (1920), Freud incorporated love among the life instincts and placed hate in the service of the death instinct. At this point, therefore, hate had two potential functions: it could serve a mnemic purpose ('to restore an earlier state of things' (p. 36)) if considered a facet of the death instinct, or it could fulfil a purely expulsive-destructive function if conceived according to the earlier instinct theory.

Psychoanalytic theory is not shy of references to destructive hate. Indeed, if we consider hate in object-relations theory, we assume a complex process whereby an internal object is damaged or destroyed and the ego is faced with the exceedingly daunting task of renegotiating internal reality in the wake of such hate. An internal object that is damaged by hate may lead to phobic withdrawal from the external representations of the object, or it may lead to an addictively depressive state that is a compromise formation between the wish to damage the object further and the dread of being attacked from within for such destructiveness. If the internal object is psychologically destroyed, it may be expelled into fragmented objects which assume a bizarre quality (Bion, 1962).

When a person hates, is it always true to say that he wishes to destroy? I am sure that most clinicians can find an exception to the rule of destructive hate in their clinical work, and I will examine certain nondestructive forms of hate. It is my view that in some cases a person hates an object not in order to destroy it, but to do precisely the opposite: to conserve the object. Such hate is fundamentally nondestructive in intent and, although it may have destructive consequences, its aim may be to act out an unconscious form of love. I am inclined to term this 'loving hate', by which I mean a situation where an individual preserves a relationship by sustaining a passionate negative cathexis of it. If the person cannot do so by hating the object he may accomplish this passionate cathexis by being hateful and inspiring the other to hate him. A state of reciprocal hate may prevail, but in the persons whom I shall be describing, such hate is singular, not genuinely mutual. The subject finds that only through hating or being hateful can he compel an object into passionate relating. Therefore, although two people in such circumstances may seem to have accomplished a reciprocity of hate, it is illusory, as the object is never assumed to be capable of genuine mutual action: even one of hating.

Viewed this way, hate is not the opposite of, but a substitute for love. A person who hates with loving passion does not dread retaliation by the object; on the contrary, he welcomes it. What he does live in fear of is indifference, of not being noticed or seen by the other. Passionate hate is generated as an alternative to love, which is assumed to be unavailable.

The literature on the positive function of hate, or fundamentally nondestructive hate, is sparse. In Europe, Winnicott was one of the first analysts to emphasize its positive functions. In an early paper on aggression, he argues that 'aggression is part of the primitive expression of love' (1936, p. 205); he further stresses that, in the course of his ruthlessness, an infant 'does not appreciate the fact that what he destroys when excited is the same as that which he values in quiet intervals between excitements. His excited love includes an imaginative attack on the mother's body. Here is aggression as a part of love' (p. 206). Winnicott always saw aggression as a positive factor in human growth, frequently equating it with motility, and he would never have made it equivalent to hate. But in his work on the transitional object, he

makes it possible for us to imagine a form of hate
which is positive; that intensely concentrated,
aggressive use of a transitional object, which is
founded on the infant's knowledge and gratitude
that the object will survive. The infant needs the
object of his hate to survive attacks against it and this object,
which is itself the trace of the mother's capacity to survive the
infant's attack, is carefully and jealously guarded by the infant
against true destruction (against loss or actual change of state).
Winnicott realized that each child needs to hate a safe object,
since in so doing he can see the total experience of a certain kind
of hate through to its completion. In attacking the object, the infant brings to bear, in reality, a self state which up to that point
has been primarily internal, and as the object allows for this mis-
use of it, its capacity to survive is appreciated by the infant, who
needs to externalize and to actualize his hate.

In 1940 Fairbairn wrote a profoundly insightful paper about
the schizoid individual who, because of his early experiences as
an infant in relation to a particular kind of mother, regarded his
love as destructive. Some schizoid defences therefore aimed to
isolate the individual from others; more significantly, they were
developed to prevent the schizoid person from either loving or
being loved. Such an individual 'may quarrel with people, be ob-
jectionable, be rude. In so doing, he not only substitutes hate for
love in his relationships with his objects, but also induces them to
hate, instead of loving him' (p. 26). By using hate in this manner,
the schizoid acts in a curiously 'moral' manner. According to
Fairbairn, 'the moral motive is determined by the consideration
that, if loving involves destroying, it is better to destroy by hate,
which is overtly destructive and bad, than to destroy by love,
which is by rights creative and good' (p. 27).

Balint (1951) regarded hate as a defence against primitive object love and archaic dependence, and Searles (1956) argued that
vengefulness was both a defence against repressed grief and a
covert means of maintaining an object tie. Pao (1965) said that
one of the 'ego syntonic uses of hatred' is that it allows the person
to feel something, so that eventually 'hatred may become an essential element from which one derives a sense of self-sameness

and upon which one formulates one's identity' (p. 260). Stolorow (1972) added that there are certain patients who use hate as a defence against the 'possibility of forgiveness' (p. 220) because to forgive would be to destabilize the person's object world, one presumably constructed through hate.

Other analysts indicate in their work a sophisticated understanding of the ways in which hate serves specific, and potentially positive, functions of the self. But I do not want to review the literature, I am only suggesting the outline of a tradition of looking at hate in a different way: associating hate more closely with love rather than assuming it to be the direct opposite.

There is no one particular family idiom that sponsors a loving hate. I do not claim that the pathological family situations that I shall discuss are the only pathways to loving hate: I am sure there are many. Furthermore, it is worth bearing in mind that a discussion of pathology often precludes consideration of more 'ordinary' forms of a phenomenon. In the natural course of affairs, children hate their parents with a passion, lasting a few minutes or even hours, and this hate aims to conserve the parental object, not to destroy it, so that the child can have the full course of pleasure in hating. There is an ordinary need to hate the loved object, one essential to the child's cumulative expression of self states that further enables him to feel a sense of personal reality in his lived life.

In the following clinical vignettes, however, I will illustrate how loving hate emerged as a major dynamic in the development of different persons, and I will discuss what pathological purposes it served. It bears repeating that when I use the word 'loving' I mean to suggest a passionate cathexis of an object, a 'falling' into hate that constitutes a profoundly intense experience in which the subject feels merged with the object and attempts to maintain an object relation through the terms of this fusion.

'WELL, HE'S A PAIN IN THE NECK, BUT WE DO LOVE HIM.'

We are all aware of that person who fashions for himself a rather unique aesthetic in his character by being an irritant, whom we can predict will almost always prove to be difficult in a social situation and whom we are quite content to hate for a brief moment. And yet it would be untrue to say that we continue to hate this person; paradoxically, we may feel quite an affection for him. I can think, for example, of a friend who in many respects is a pain in the neck. If my wife and I invite him to dinner, he will almost inevitably try to irritate at least one of us. After a journey to an exotic country where he basked in tropical luxury and returned to our English world with a magnificent tan, he said to my wife: 'The problem with men who have been living in England for a long time is that they no longer know how to be attractive to women. And look at his shape. He's fat and he doesn't stand like a man.' Now, most of the time this comment would not bother me – coming from him – but it just so happened that for the two weeks prior to seeing my friend, I had been trying to lose weight, and I had been taking some exercise. This I had to do on an exercise bicycle which I could 'ride' between patients. Ten minutes is not much, but it's better than nothing. Still, I do recall that during these rather pathetic 'journeys' on my bike I felt a bit foolish and depressed that at mid-life things should have come to this. I had, nonetheless, tried valiantly to convince myself that the results – being fit and trim – would compensate me for a newly acquired sense of the absurd. As it was, however, when I saw my friend, I was feeling rather handsome. This was not the moment when I wanted to hear about how I had degenerated, even if the jab was put in his ridiculous manner, yet I am convinced that one of his talents is knowing when people feel vulnerable, and choosing that moment to wade in and say something that makes one want to kill him. However, in the moments that follow such an irritating encounter, it is possible to feel something like affection for him, a sort of 'well, he sure has proved to be in good form!'. Furthermore, he does know something about oneself that borders on intimacy and, since he tends to express affection through negative charm, one often knows his irksomeness for what it is. To be sure, now and then I do find myself asking why I keep seeing him, since he really can be maddeningly abrasive: at the last dinner party he 'ruined' a convivial discussion by informing us that we were all bourgeois dilettantes incapable of a genuine discussion of the very topics that we ourselves had raised. Of course, at that moment he was accurate, and we could have killed him!

It was therefore with some additional interest that I discovered Paula, one of my patients, to be just such a person. She had a reputation among her friends for being outrageous, and in fact she was capable of setting one friend against another and gossiping in a way that was moderately scandalous. I knew this about her from her accounts of her life, but for the first years of her analysis no meaningful aspect of this emerged within the clinical space. Looking back, I can see that her somewhat gigglish barks ('Ohhhhhh! You've got it all wrong! Oh, forget it. I'm just being bitchy. You are right, and I don't like the fact that you know so much about me.') were designed to move me towards a more combative relation to her and expressed a need on her part to be allowed unreasonable and troublesome behaviour in the sessions.

She found it frustratingly difficult to be a troublemaker in the sessions because she was an analysable person, was genuinely motivated to understand herself, and so, in an odd sort of way, being understood mitigated a full expression of a segment of herself. I understood her rather too well, or prematurely, and thereby denied her sufficient room in which to become a 'bad character'. But in the third year of her analysis, she went through a series of personal crises in her private life that made her really quite dependent on me. Up until then, she had always kept an almost exact emotional distance from me, and I was aware that she was keeping quite a bit of her internal life to herself. Now, as she became more dependent on me, she also became argumentative, loud, combative, and 'unanalysable'. I was never in any doubt, however, that her bad behaviour was an expression of loving hate. It became clear that as she began to fall in love with the other, she felt in considerable danger and protected herself against this anxiety by developing her love along the lines of a negative intimacy. 'Oh, you, you would say that'; 'Oh, that's typical of you'; 'On the way here, I was telling you about myself, but then, of course, you said to me . . .'; 'What did you mean last week when you said. . . ? I suppose you meant the same thing you told me last year, which is just what you would say, isn't it! Why are you like this?': all of these 'protests' revealed an intense preoccupation with me, a positive transference only partly, and ineffectively, negated by her use of hate.

Both of Paula's parents were greedy in needing to give to their infant a certain kind of love. As a child she had feared the intensity of parental affection, praise and facilitative eagerness. Eventually it seemed to us both that her difficult character was a defence against the fear of being consumed by her parents' love. So long as she was irascible – 'Oh, you are a wretchedly uncooperative child!' – she could mitigate the intense need of her parents to have a wonderfully lovable offspring. To be difficult within the context of her family was a great relief. It was reassuring to find that she could be hateful, and she very carefully ensured that she would develop into something of an eccentric, taking respite in her mother's warnings to friends – 'Oh, don't expect Paula to warm to you, she's a rather nasty sort of little girl, aren't you Paula?' – because she was insured against the parental need to extol her virtues and draw her into the depersonalized space of their idealized daughter. We can see how being hateful, if only in this modest 'pain-in-the-neck' way, may be a defence against the destructive valency of certain forms of love. Being hateful allowed Paula to conserve a sense of self, whereas being lovable would have jeopardized the integrity of her own identity.

It is also possible to see how in the transference Paula spoke to me rather like her mother spoke to her. It is not without irony that this seemingly rejecting mother was the safer object, while the all-embracing mother was worrying. In being the hateful object, Paula identified with the rejecting element in the mother's character, a part of the mother that she could actually use and rely upon: the mother who does accept and cognize rejection and has some capacity for differentiated living. By being a difficult child, Paula brought out certain latent features of the mother's personality, in particular her narcissistic anger: 'Oh, the hell with you, if you don't want me, then just be difficult.' It is this mother that Paula can love. It is this mother with whom Paula can identify, so that we can see how her eccentric character, in which she cultivates being a pain in the neck to her friends, is both a reflection of what she brought out in the mother and that part of the mother with which she was able to identify. This is a positive use of hate, if we take into consideration the peculiar circumstances of this family's idiom. It allows in this instance for a child to enjoy qualified love of the partly differentiated mother.

'OH, THANK GOD WE HATE EACH OTHER. I FEEL SO FREE.'

From Jane I have learned of another form of loving hate. Not content to be a pain in the neck, she has sought out a partner who will reciprocate her passion for destructive activity. She and Charles typically enjoy a few days of quite intense affection for one another. He brings her flowers, she cooks him wonderful meals, they have a lazy Sunday reading through the day's newspapers, they go to the movies and enjoy discussing the film, and they make love with considerable passion. After a few days of this, each of them seems to feel slightly uncomfortable with the way things are going. 'Too good to be true' shifts imperceptibly into 'it's not true to be so good'. Jane feels a sense of oppression after a spell of getting on well with Charles. She has a sense of reliving that destiny set for her in her childhood when she was the family's 'nice' girl who would, according to her mother's oft-verbalized dream, 'marry a nice man'. For a substantial period of her childhood, she was oppressed by her own premature ego development (James, 1960), which had evolved into a false-self disorder by latency. As a model child, she cannot recall ever having been a problem to either parent, and in adolescence she would either have become suddenly delinquent or had a breakdown were it not for the fact that both parents (as we shall see) acted this out for her.

Jane was never in any doubt about why she needed to hate Charles. If everything was too good to be true from her point of view, then she would undo the sense of impending doom by be-

coming outrageously contentious and inspiring
an almighty row with her partner. By hating
Charles with a passion and by being hateful in
turn, Jane felt more fully established as a person
and more fully exhibited. It was as if she were
saying: 'Here I am, mother: look at me! Look!' And watching the
externalization of hate was a significant feature of Jane and
Charles' festivals of black passion. Standing in the kitchen,
Charles would watch as she would pick up a dish and with careful
and deliberate aim throw it at him. She would watch as he, in
turn, would fill a cup full of water and with equally measured
accuracy pitch it at her. Sometimes crying, sometimes screaming,
and often laughing, in a short period of time they would almost
destroy their flat. Exhausted, they would collapse on the bed or
on the floor, leave each other alone for a period of time (it varied
from a few minutes to a few hours), and then make up.

When she first reported these incidents to me, Jane did so
with considerable embarrassment. She expected that I would dis-
approve. Instead I said on first hearing about this, 'It seems that
you enjoy these fights'; and, in great relief, she said: 'I do. I don't
know what I would do if he couldn't hate me the way he does. It's
such a relief! And he is so sweet. Even when he throws things at
me, I love him. But I love hating him too. I need to do it. I couldn't
stand it otherwise.'

Jane came from a family which prided itself on its calm and
rational approach to life. Each member of this rather large family
was quite an apparent extrovert and, as a group, they threw
themselves into shared interests, hobbies and adventures (such as
moving from one country to the next). Their ostensible individual
strength and their collective heartiness were sufficient for quite
some time to conceal an underlying inability to achieve intimacy.
If any member of the family was in distress or trouble, the difficulty would be known only through the report of persons outside
the group. Jane can remember feeling terribly oppressed by the
family's nature, and when the entire system collapsed, she experienced the family breakdown with mixed feelings. When the
parents had a ferocious row and the children felt a collective paralysis as they heard accusations being thrown back and forth

between mother and father, Jane can recall feeling both terrified and relieved. A sense of 'my God, what is happening, and how are we going to survive this?' was countered with another feeling: 'Thank God, I am not the only one who feels this whole system stinks. They do too!'

In a very brief period of time, the father left and married a person totally different from his previous wife, and Jane's mother changed from being an energetic, outgoing woman to a frenzied, vengeful person who was determined to get even with 'that son of a bitch'. In some ways both parents acted out and expelled a family false-self system, but Jane could not participate in this primitive actualization of other parts of the self, since she was then absorbed in looking after her mother, who continuously asserted, 'You children, God bless you, are all that I have in this world'.

In her parents' homes, Jane is still a model person. She cannot get angry with her mother or father, and she fails to establish any of her own privately developed interests if they meet with parental opposition. It is only in her relation to Charles and in the clinical space that she can express the primitive parts of herself.

Her occasional need to love Charles with passionate hate amounts to an unsuccessful attempt to fuse love and hate, and to bring unintegrated areas of the self into greater proximity to another. She dreads being captured into becoming that false self of her childhood to which she reverts when she is with her family of origin. Passionately expressed hate reassures her that she isn't capitulating into being a compliant self, and Charles' participation in loving hate safeguards the infant self's right to be heard and expressed within the adult world. Thus loving hate can both conserve the integrity of the self and keep object relating alive and true.

'AT LEAST I CAN HATE YOU –
YOU'RE ALL I'VE GOT.'

George's hate is comprised of an intensely nourished feeling that he is neglected by people. He records each moment of slight with meticulous care and takes considerable pleasure in storing up the evidence to use against the offending object in some imagined eventual confrontation. At the same time, his microscopic observation of the other's disposition towards him does give him a certain knowledge of the other's personality and, at times, he is aware of the non-malignant, even good, portions of the other's being. Such recognitions are distressing to him, and he often attempts to rid himself of such perceptions.

In the course of his analysis, it became clear that his intimate knowing of a hated other, often giving rise to feelings of déjà vu, was of course composed of his own projections. This other has to be made up of split-off parts of George's self, because his mother's absence in his early life did not give him sufficient sense of the other to facilitate generative introjections. A generative introjection is one in which the infant takes in a part of the mother, so that when it is linked up internally with a drive, and when the infant re-projects the introject, it matches up with the intrinsic characteristics of the mother, thus enabling the child to feel in some form of harmony with the outside world. George had to construct the mother out of a vacuum – rather than introject that which was there – and as her absences were so frequent, that which George tended to project into the mental space of 'mother' were those moods in himself that were created by her absences. We can say that if a mother is an insufficient selfobject – and in George's case the mother was a withdrawn and depressed woman who avoided maternal care by immersing herself in her professional life – then the child must form some kind of alternate selfobject that is most likely to be composed of projected self states, such as isolation, despair, helplessness, frustration and rage. In forming an object that contains these affects (Bion, 1962), the child constructs an object through loving hate. He dreads desertion, and although he may feel intense hatred for the mother, he also treasures her, as she is all he has.

In that loving hate that characterizes George's contemporary object relations, he aims to make the object indebted to him forever. He looks forward to that day when the other acknowledges wrongdoing. The wish is not for justice, but for a confession that gives him unconditional licence to regress into dependency upon the other. As I have suggested, the ultimate aim of this form of hate, therefore, is a kind of loving merger with the object. This is why the hated object must not be destroyed – indeed, why it must be protected against true harm. George was in fact a staunch defender and protector of his mother, and he rarely talked about her except in glowing terms during the first year of his analysis. Nevertheless these positive feelings suddenly collapsed quite dramatically, revealing a very private and secretive hateful relation to her. He really knew very little about her, but insisted upon maintaining a sense of intimacy through detailed observations of her, which filled him with private loathing. Not a courtly love. A courtly hate.

THE NEGATIVE SELF-OBJECT

In addition to the examples I have given above, it is possible to talk about one other exceedingly common expression of loving hate in the clinical setting. I will not give a case example, but instead I will discuss the intent of that person who seeks to be an irritant to the analyst – to get under the analyst's skin – in order to compel the analyst to hate him. There are certain persons who feel that until the analyst can hate them, and until they can see evidence of such hate, there is a risk that they will never have been known. It is through hate evoked in the analyst that this kind of person seeks to achieve his sort of intimacy with the clinician. It is when the clinician's steady state of mind and even temper break down under the weight of the patient's negativity that the analysand takes hope; for it is there, in that moment when he sees the analyst's hesitation or senses his frustration, that he feels himself in rapport with the analyst. In that state there is a sense of merging with the analyst, whose even-mindedness until then – even when he is being empathic and sympathetic – has felt like a refusal, a rebuff.

This person wants to convert the analyst into a negative object. He aims to find his double in the analyst's frame of mind, and has constructed a negative self-object, that is, an object not differentiated from himself but carrying his projections and iden-

tifications. Although as far as I know Kohut intended his term 'selfobject' to be used for those
psychic situations in which no differentiation
exists between self and object, the sort of person
I am describing does recognize difference. It is
more accurate to say, perhaps, that these people seek to convert a
differentiated object into a non-differentiated one, and this is accomplished through loving hate. Each is in fact split according to
corresponding splits in the ego: one part of the individual recognizes the object's independence, while another part of the ego
assumes self and object to be fused. It is only when negative self-
objects are formed that the person feels in rapport with the other.
A differentiated object is in some ways a lost object or a non-
object.

People of this type are object seekers, even if that which they
find or create is a negative self-object. It is my view that the concept of the death instinct, insofar as hate is concerned, should be
reserved for those individuals who seek to destroy objects in order to live in an objectless world. I do think a form of hate can be
identified which is in the service of a death instinct, and I am of
the view that certain forms of autism in children reflect this wish
to annihilate the object world in order to be returned to the pre-
object world.

Some families are fundamentally cold and unloving. For
varying reasons the parents find it next to impossible either to
love their children, or more to the point, to demonstrate their
love and also their lovableness. A child who is raised in a milieu of
this kind discovers that his loving impulses and gestures are not
mirrored in a positive way by the parent. The child's ordinary
positive aggression and love are not validated by the parent. Instead such parents may interpret the child's aggressive libidinal
cathexis of themselves as an insult or as an indication of a moral
defect. These people may be exceedingly rigid, or very religious,
or particularly sour in their being. Whatever the reason for the
nature of their own family style, such parents refuse to celebrate
their children, and are instead constantly finding fault with them
and in some cases seem drawn to conflict. Gradually, the child
loses his belief in love and in loving. Instead, ordinary hate

establishes itself as the fundamental truth of life. The child experiences the parents' refusal of love and their constant aloofness or harshness as hate, and he or she in turn finds his or her most intense private cathexis of the parents to be imbued with hate.

To some extent, these children sense the parents' need to hate. Disinclined, perhaps, to tamper with a system, and curiously reassured by being the object of intense feeling, such children may become consistently hateful. To be cathected by a parent, even to the point of becoming a reliable negative self-object for him or her, is a primary aim for children, as their true dread is that of being unnoticed and left for dead.

When a person's hate is destructive of his internal objects, we know that the emptiness he feels is due to his destructive activity. With his internal objects mangled or useless, there is nothing of value left, and he will feel only the deadness of the annihilated objects or the emptiness of an evacuated space. The precise opposite is true, however, of those persons I am discussing. Children who are reared by cold and unloving parents find that hate is a form of object relation, and they hate the object in order not to destroy it, but to preserve and maintain it. Hate emerges not as a result of the destruction of internal objects, but as a defence against emptiness. Indeed, it represents an effort to emerge from this vacuum into object relating.

These children may suffer from a kind of vacuum anxiety, a state created by intense isolation. Affective life is so meagre that objects are only dimly cathected. Such a person has a sense of losing the remnants of psychic life, of fearing the termination of affective existence altogether. Although this anxiety may have different causes and may evolve in different ways according to varying ego defences, such an individual finds that by annoying someone or by inspiring hate in the other he has been provisionally guaranteed a psychic life.

RETROSPECTIVE MIRRORING

There is another form of family idiom that sponsors a particular kind of hate. Some families are emotionally shallow. The parents

may be unusally concerned with creating a
'happy family'. A certain kind of superficial support is provided, but core emotional issues are
avoided and channelled through a kind of
pseudo-sublimation. If a child is acting out some

distress, a parent might typically say, 'that's not done here', or
'cut it out right now'. Since there is no effort to investigate why
the child is misbehaving, the behaviour is never allowed a symbolic elaboration, for example by means of explanation to the
mother. Instead the families rely upon stereotypical speech patterns to control the children. As such, these patients report family clichés as if they were life-defining categories, and they are
unusually impoverished in their own relation to themselves as objects of perception and interest. They cannot elaborate an
internal experience. If asked how they feel they are surprisingly
inarticulate and will resort to a cluster of clichés, such as, 'uh, I
dunno, I'm kind of down' or 'I've had it, you know, I'm going to
be number one now'. Although the clinicians know what the person means, or at least can make a fairly good guess, language does
not serve to communicate, but instead to discharge the self of tension. Thus an effort to inquire why someone doesn't feel himself
to be 'number one' any more yields only further substitutive
clichés.

Such people may also resort to sudden action. If angered by a
friend, they may 'write him off'. If a love relation goes wrong they
can find another partner with comparative ease, and they can do
so amid a culture that supports the replacement of an old
part(ner) with a new one. One does not get the impression that
they have the ego ability to cope with their own narcissistic injury
and aggression.

True love was never a real possibility for such people given
the nature of their family life. In subtle ways the parents did not
provide enough characterological presence for the child to settle
his loving feelings. As curiosity about oneself or the other is not
encouraged, the children become deficient in techniques of ordinary insight and self-reflection.

It is curious, then, that parental anger and the sudden emergence of hate may be the only deep experiences in which parent

and child are mutually engaged. They rarely take place during childhood, but are exceedingly commonplace in adolescence, when conflict with a parent can create an atmosphere of fear and violence. Typically, the family atmosphere, which has previously been superficially harmonious, breaks down. An early adolescent discovers that his mother has become furious with him. An overly constrained mother or exceptionally composed father might all of a sudden, when angry, say things otherwise deleted from the family vocabulary and the family's sense of its own being. In order to feel increased contact with the parent, the child may cultivate hate. For in doing so, he discovers that the parents will give signals about their private and often confused experience of their offspring.

In one case, for example, an eleven-year-old girl angered her mother by being rebellious. This led the mother to call her a self-ish little bitch, an outburst which surprised the girl, but which also excited her. In this instance she had caught mother out of her ordinary self. She knew that to push mother more would yield both more of mother and more of mother's experience of herself as daughter. Using the veil of innocence by appearing oblivious to mother's reason for being cross, the child inspired the mother to recall many previous occasions when the child had annoyed her. Again the child experienced this interchange with mixed feelings. The mother's response was rather frightening, but it was also ex-citing, and beyond that it was interesting. For in mother's enu-meration of all the times when she felt internally critical of her daughter, her child found images of herself within the mother.

This recollection of the child is a form of retrospective mirror-ing, which is an ordinary form of object relation. Reflecting with a child on his or her past (selves) gives a child a chance to see how he was and to keep in touch with this phenomenon we call 'self'. But retrospective mirroring may be the primary form of feedback that a child gets from a parent about his specific nature; when a parent lists observations about the child, a child has the sense of having been seen by the parent, which may be an unusual and gratifying experience. This need to feel seen may be so compelling that a child continues to provoke parental hate just to have negative intimacy and retrospective mirroring.

Erikson's concept of 'negative identity' (1968) is not unrelated to the formation of a negative self-object and the abuse of retrospective mirroring. He claims that negative identity is 'perversely based on all those identifications and roles which, at critical stages of development, had been presented to them as most undesirable or dangerous and yet also most real' (p. 174). It is not difficult to see how a late adolescent may assume a negative identity in order to be what his parents have dissociated from human life, and he may compel the parent to act out aspects of his own negative identity. In so doing he urges the parent to become a negative self-object, one in which there is little psychological differentiation between the teenager's hate and the parent's. In such an interaction the teenager may feel strangely closer to his parent than ever before, and the parent may wish to rid himself of the adolescent not because he cannot bear his behaviour, but because he cannot bear the intimacy of the relationship and refuses the claim being made by the child for this closeness.

LOVING HATE: A PERVERSION?

Those persons who are drawn towards being hateful and who cultivate the passion of hate alert us to the possibility of a perverse object relation. Stoller (1976) has argued convincingly that perversion is the erotic form of hate and that, in assessing whether an object relation is perverse or not, one must ascertain whether or not the subject desires to harm the other. Is this the aim of loving hate: to harm the other? It certainly looks this way. We can add that, as loving hate appears to be a singular mode of cathecting the object, the range of affects is impoverished, thus alerting us to another feature typical of the perversions. Finally, we can point to the stereotypical and repetitive nature of loving hate; it seems that the person aims to create an object relation through an affect rather than find an other and develop affective life in harmony with increasing intimacy. Does this not suggest a dehumanization of the other, a point which Khan (1964) stresses in his definition of perversion as a drive to alienate the object from true contact with one's inner life?

In my view, we are once more called upon to ask whether the outcome of a psychic activity necessarily defines the intention, for it is true to say that the forms of hate I have discussed, and term 'loving hate', may harm the other or alienate the other. But Stoller and Khan are careful to define the perverse as the intention to harm or to distance the object, and it is my view that the primary aim of loving hate is to get closer to the object. Further, we know that in the perversions, the subject uses a scenario to close down the possibility of surrender to affective life, while in loving hate the person surrenders to affect.

8 *Normotic illness*

WHEN Winnicott wrote that 'it is creative apperception more than anything else that makes the individual feel that life is worth living' (1971, p. 71), he was aware that psychoanalysis focuses on those disturbances in human subjectivity that make creative living difficult. As if to gesture towards a different pathway of disturbance, he suggested another axis of illness.

> People may be leading satisfactory lives and may do work that is even of exceptional value and yet may be schizoid or schizophrenic. They may be ill in a psychiatric sense because of a weak reality sense. To balance this one would have to state that there are others who are so firmly anchored in objectively perceived reality that they are ill in the opposite direction of being out of touch with the subjective world and with the creative approach to fact. (1971, p. 78)

I believe that we are witness either to the emergence of a new emphasis within personal illness or we are just getting around to perceiving an element in personality that has always been with us. This element is a particular drive to be normal, one that is typified by the numbing and eventual erasure of subjectivity in favour of a self that is conceived as a material object among other man-made products in the object world.

We are attending an increasing number of disturbances in personality which may be characterized by partial deletions of the subjective factor. Therefore, we write of 'blank selves' (Giovacchini, 1972), 'blank psychoses' (Donnet and Green, 1973), and an 'organizing personality' (Hedges, 1983). The effort to explore selected features of these personalities can be found in the work of Masud Khan (1974, 1979), André Green (1973), Donnet and Green (1986) and Robert Stoller (1973, 1976). Such persons are often unsuccessful in their effort to be rid of an intrapsychic life, since they are unable to resolve that psychic pain which derives from the annulment of internal life. They are usually aware of feeling empty or without a sense of self, and they seek analytic help in order to find some way to feel real or to symbolize a pain that may only be experienced as a void or an ache.

There is a certain kind of person, however, who has been successful in neutralizing the subjective element in personality. As Winnicott suggested, some people have annihilated the creative element by developing an alternative mentality, one that aims to be objective, a mind that is characterized less by the psychic (by the representational symbolization of feelings, sensations and intersubjective perceptions) than by the objective. This mentality is not determined to represent the object, but to be the echo of thingness inherent in material objects, to be a commodity object in the world of human production.

In the following account a particular kind of person will be described, one who has for the most part escaped our attention, although Joyce McDougall's intelligent and searching account of what she calls the 'antianalysand' (1980) may very well be a description of the person I term a 'normotic'.

A normotic person is someone who is abnormally normal. He is too stable, secure, comfortable and socially extrovert. He is fundamentally disinterested in subjective life and he is inclined to reflect on the thingness of objects, on their material reality, or on 'data' that relates to material phenomena.

We may speak of a common normotic element when we identify any mental activity that constitutes a transfer of a subjective state of mind into a material external object that results in the de-symbolization of the mental content. If this element is over-utilized, if it is a means towards the evacuation of subjective states of mind, then the person may be subtly moving towards normotic illness. If the normotic element is ordinary, then normotic illness develops when the subjective meaning is lodged in an external object, remains there and is not re-introjected, and over time loses its symbolic function as a signifier. Normotically disturbed persons successfully house varied parts and functions of their internal world in material objects, and even though they use these objects and collect them into a familiar space, they serve no symbolic purpose. Such an individual is alive in a world of meaningless plenty.

NORMOTIC PERSONALITY

The fundamental identifying feature of this individual is a disinclination to entertain the subjective element in life, whether it exists inside himself or in the other. The introspective capacity has rarely been used. Such a person appears genuinely naive if asked to comment on issues that require either looking into oneself or the other in any depth. Instead, if the evolution towards becoming a normotic personality is successful, he lives contentedly among material objects and phenomena.

By the subjective element, I mean the internal play of affects and ideas that generates and authorizes our private imaginations, creatively informs our work and gives continuing resource to our interpersonal relations. The subjective ability amounts to a particular kind of internal space (Stewart, 1985) that facilitates the reception of unconscious affects, memories and perceptions.

The normotic seems unable to experience evolving subjective states within himself. Without moods he may appear unusually steady or sound. If he is forced by circumstance into a complex situation in which the subjective element is called into play (such as being part of a family quarrel, or discussing a film, or hearing of tragic events), he betrays the absence of a subjective world. He may speak of a phenomenon as an object in its own right, laden with known laws, and thus understandable. A quarrel might lead him to say 'you people are just being unreasonable', or *Hamlet* might inspire him to say 'an unhappy young fellah', or more often than not, he lapses into respectful silence.

This is not to suggest that he does not go to the theatre or the cinema. But he stresses that he is **going** to a play or that he is in possession of season tickets. He avoids discussing the content of the play by emphasizing the play as something to go to or to possess. He is sincerely incapable of reading and commenting on a poem. The capacity to consider a poem is a sophisticated mental accomplishment and requires a subjective ability which eludes this individual.

Instead, the normotic is interested in facts. But he does not have a passion for factual data in order to establish a common knowledge that sponsors a group's creativity (as in the scientific community). Facts are collected and stored because this activity is reassuring. It is part of a personal evolution in which he unconsciously attempts to become an object in the object world. To collect facts is ultimately to be identified with that which is collected: to become a fact in one's person. It is truly reassuring to become part of the machinery of production. He likes being part of an institution because it enables him to be identified with the life or the existence of the impersonal: the workings of an institution or the products of a corporation. He is part of the team, he is at home in a committee, he is secure in social groups that offer in pseudo-intimacy an alternative to getting to know someone.

The normotic takes refuge in material objects. He is possessed of an urge to define contentedness through the acquisition of objects, and he measures human worth by means of collections of acquired objects. But this kind of appropriation is not passionate, unlike, for example, when a person buys a boat and cherishes it, working on it during weekends and learning about sailing lore. Material objects are accumulated in a wishless manner. They appear in this person's life as if they were logical outcomes and signatures of his personality.

It would be untrue to say that the normotic person is not in possession of a sense of identity. This is not an as-if person or a false self, as defined by Winnicott. It is not easy to describe the nature of his identity, other than to say that an observer may feel that it seems to be an artificial acquisition, as if **no mental work** has been employed in the historical fashioning of this identity.

It would also be untrue to say that the normotic person cannot fall in love or form a relationship. He is attracted, however, to those of like mind and, since love can come close to some of the

addictions, he can be in love with someone without this ever making a claim on his subjectivity.

Is his affect impoverished? Not in the sense
that he is affectless. He may have a sense of
humour, he enjoys a good laugh, and seems fun-
loving. But rather than experience sadness, he slows down.
Action is the quality of life for him, so depressions or anxiety
states do not appear in a mentally elaborated form: they only slow
him down in his otherwise 'faultless' pursuit of happiness. In extreme form, he would strike us as appallingly empty, but this observation is all the more remarkable given that he would appear
so only to us, whilst in himself he would seem to be without want.
In this sense, the presence in contemporary literature and film of
the human who is revealed to be a robot is a recognition of this
personality type emerging in our culture. Such representations
are less descriptive of the future of robots than they are accurate
prognostications of a personality disorder that is already with
us.

This person may be a workaholic. He thrives on the structure
of life and constructs his future through revised agendas. He
often knows what he will be doing every hour of each day. Spaces
are appropriated into rituals, thus obviating the possibility of
spontaneous choice. He knows where he will eat lunch, or that on
Thursday evenings he will be playing cards, or that on every
Monday he will have dinner with his wife. Recreation lacks playfulness and is pursued with the same zealousness as any chore.

It is striking that such a person does achieve something of a
state of reverie. A female patient wanders from one store to
another in the course of her day. She might find herself in a
supermarket for an hour or more, not because she is in particular
need of any food or other items but because the material aesthetic
of the supermarket, resplendent with its vegetables, cereals and
canned goods, is soothing.

From the supermarket to the pet shop; from the sportsware
store to the large hardware shop; from a lunch with friends in
which there is an itemization of actions lived out by each, to the
home for a listless cleansing of the kitchen; from a tennis match to

the jacuzzi: this person *can* live a life without ever blinking an eye. If his mother or father is dying the normotic does not feel grief, but instead engages in a detailed examination of the nature of the disease, the technology of the hospital treating the person and the articulation of clichés that are meant to contain and launder the experience of death: 'Well, she's very old you know, and we've all got to go some time!'

This person is by no means friendless. Indeed, he may be exceptionally adept at organizing dinners and parties. Topics that require a capacity to tolerate the subjective element in life, however, are rarely raised, and the friendships are characterized by mutual chronicling of life's events, rather than by intersubjective exchanges in which the increasing intimacy that allows for a true sense of knowing one's friend is established. The capacity to speak frankly about one's self, about one's personality and one's feelings, is unknown. While many people **need** to engage the other in mutual knowing, aware that such intimacy involves both parties in the precarious balance of ambivalence, no such requirement appears in the normotic.

This is not a person without conviction or standards, but both seem to be inherited from somewhere other than the self. Little thought or subjective drive seems to have gone into the **workings** of the mind. Such a person is in possession of a curious alternative to guilt. He does believe in right and wrong, yet instead of that kind of inner dialogue which takes place in the interchange between ego and superego, a dialogue that is often the articulation of guilt, there is a kind of teutonic legal introject. There are many rules or paradigms that suggest right and wrong behaviour. On careful examination, however, such rules are not really responsive to changing circumstances in life, and they are less reflective of critical acts of judgement than photographic feats of mnemonic recall.

THE UNBORN

It is striking how this person seems to be unborn. It is as if the final stages of psychological birth were not achieved, and one is

left with a deficiency. Or, at least this is how it
seems, when one is working with such a person
who appears to be content and happy, and yet is
so like the infant for whom the breast will always
be the ultimate solution to distress and the fulfilment of need.

What is lacking is that originating subjectivity which informs
our use of the symbolic. The normotic does not see himself other
than as an object (ideally smart and spruced up, productive and
sociable) among all the objects of the material world. Since he
does not perceive himself as a subject, he does not ask to be seen
by the other, nor does he look into the other.

Having no interest in subjective states and seeking material
objects as things-in-themselves — for functional rather than symbolic purposes — the normotic has only partly developed the
capacity to symbolize the self. In Bion's language,[5] there is an impoverished production of 'alpha elements', a term which he uses
to represent that mental transformation whereby emotional experiences become a possibility in the first place. 'Alpha elements
are produced from the impressions of the experience; these are
thus made storeable and available for dream thoughts and for
unconscious waking thinking' (1977, p. 8). This underlying flaw
in the person's mental life means that he registers and communicates his being through 'beta elements', which for Bion represent
'undigested facts' or facts in existential life that do not evolve into
subjective states of mind. Although I do not believe that the
absence of alpha function in the normotic is solely due to hate or
envy, Bion's description of the person whose alpha function is
chronically deficient comes close to defining the nature of the
normotic, and I shall quote it in full:

Attacks on alpha-function, stimulated by hate or envy,
destroy the possibility of the patient's conscious contact
either with himself or another as live objects. Accordingly
we hear of inanimate objects, and even of places, when we
would normally expect to hear of people. These, though described verbally, are felt to be represented by their names.
This state contrasts with animism in that live objects are

endowed with the qualities of death. (1977, p. 9)

The attack on alpha function means that the person never really comes alive, and is therefore only partially born. Unable to find alpha function, stuck in a primitive communicative exchange characterized by beta thinking and functioning, the normotic solves psychological problems by medicating himself (usually by overdrinking) and living among material objects.

AETIOLOGICAL CONSIDERATIONS

I can make sense of the evolution of normotic illness only by considering such a development within the life of a family. At the most fundamental level the normotic was only partly seen by the mother and the father, mirrored by parents whose reflective ability was dulled, yielding only the glimmer of an outline of self to a child. In spite of his profound study of the nature of mental functioning, Bion places the attack on alpha functioning only within the infant: hence the references to hate or envy. It is a source of puzzlement to me why madness within the mother or the father, or between the parents, or in that atmosphere that is created by all participants in the child–parent interaction, should be eliminated as one of the potential sources of disturbance in the child's development of alpha function. This is all the more bewildering because Bion does acknowledge the vital function of the parent as a container for the infant's psychic life. If so, is it not conceivable that a parent, through projective identification, can lodge an unwanted and destructive part of himself in the infant, leaving the child possessed of a certain confusion and overwhelmed with destructive feelings?

I do not understand why some children give in to such a family atmosphere and become normotic, and why others do not. I am not arguing that normotic adults inevitably produce normotic children. Although those persons who become normotic must have come from normotic families, some children raised in such an atmosphere manage to discover and sustain a private subjective world in striking contrast to the parents' lives. Others be-

come perpetually delinquent, registering subjective life through continual feats of acting out, a
testimony to their rebellion against normotic
mentality. Perhaps the difference between normotic children and those who emerge into health
(or neurosis) is that some children find a way to be mirrored even
if the parents are not providing this. By finding their reflection
elsewhere they internalize a mirroring function and utilize intrasubjective dialogues as alternatives to interpersonal play. They
develop an introspective capacity, and life for them will be meaningful even if incomplete.

Although the subject will have to be studied further and in
greater depth, I think it is highly likely that the children who give
in to the normotic element perceive in the parents' way of being a
form of hate that we might conceptualize as a death instinct. Such
a hate does not focus on the personality of the child, so it would be
untrue to say that the child feels hated by the parent. It may be
more accurate to say that the child experiences the parents' attack on life itself, and that such a parent is trying to squeeze the
life out of existence.

It may be, however, that the child's disposition to be emptied
of self reflects his own death drive, an activity which can only be
successful, in my view, if the parents wish it to be. Parent and
child organize a foreclosure of the human mentality. They find a
certain intimacy in shutting down life together, and in mastering
existence with the unconscious skill of a military operation. Because the normotic person fails to symbolize in language his subjective states of mind, it is difficult to point to the violence in this
person's being, yet it is there, not in his utterances, but in his way
of shutting life out.

Normotic parents wish to become objects among objects. This
striving implicates the child in the evolution towards a certain
mentality that could correspond to the child's own death instinct.
The drive **not to be** (human) but to master being facilitates the
movement towards the inorganic state of constancy that Freud
(1920) considered when writing of the death instinct. The accomplishment of this drive (not to be but to have been) is to rid
the psyche of the tensions of being and to transfer the self into

external objects which become alternatives to self awareness. This is why the normotic transforms intrapsychic and cultural experience into mnemic excreta: a holiday snap is more important than the actual experience of visiting a new place, a subscription to the opera is more significant than going to see the opera.

If there is a dialectic of 'death work' (Pontalis, 1981) in which parent and child develop a reciprocal preference for maintaining an unborn self, the partnership develops into the child's personality disorder by virtue of the parent's adamant refusal to be alive to the child's inner reality. This is the death work of a certain family 'life', as the child gradually internalizes this partnership and transforms its terms into his relation to himself as an object (see above, chapter 3), which results in his refusal to entertain the inner life of the self.

As the parents of the normotic person were not sufficiently alive to his inner reality, they did not facilitate the creative expression of the inner core of the self. We could say that they were responsive to the child's false self development, in that they responded to the child's adaptation to convention with praise and material reward. It is my view that the parents' transformational object function (see above, chapter 1) was of a particular kind.[6]

I do not believe that anything remarkable takes place in the history of the normotic person. These children are reared in structured settings by parents and are provided with toys and playthings, and certainly do not suffer deprivations of a material kind. But neither of the parents is inclined towards the celebration of the child's imaginative life. If they do enter into play I think it is often designed to terminate the playing, to subtly turn the child towards reality. Above all, they are concerned that their children be normal and they do not wish them to act in a way that could be construed as inappropriate or odd. So the child is rewarded for being good, where good means ordinary, and he is ignored or threatened for being imaginative, particularly if this is expressed in social settings.

It is important to bear in mind that as these parents disown the imaginative element in their child, they offer instead some

kind of ritual in its place. An empty structure re-
places creative lack of structure. For example,
the child who is wanting to play murder with his
father is pushed into watching TV. Programme
follows programme, day after day, in a predictable manner.

The child might perhaps be encouraged to become an athlete,
and the father could decide that throwing a football is the way to
go about it. Exercising such ritualized and available activities is
another example of the child accommodating to a pre-existing
form set up by others. They do not depend on the child's imaginative life, although children may still endeavour to imagine themselves being football heroes, or the like. Such children, although
they may engage in sundry outdoor activities, all of which are
quite physically and educationally stirring, participate in a life
that becomes an alternative to living from the core of the self. In
their continuing transformational object function, the parents
direct the child's psychological life **outward** into physical activity
or into some structured and ritualized container, such as a tele-
vision set or a video game. The child's creative invention of life is
not encouraged.

Withholding response to the creative element in the child
amounts in some ways to a **negative hallucination,** since important parts of the child's personality are not noticed. As the child
lives on, these parts of the self are **the not-there elements** and, as
each of us inherits those basic paradigms generated by the
parent's transformational object functioning in our own way of
looking after our self as an object, the not-there elements of parental negative hallucination join the child's own intrinsic
defences (such as denial) to become the not-there particles of this
person's intrasubjective life. When a child enters adolescence, if
he does suffer from too much psychological pain, he is in the
horrifying dilemma of being unable to symbolize his pain. Instead, he experiences the negative hallucination, which is only a
kind of blank, an ellipsis that forms a continuing amnesia. This
may be all the more agonizing as the child may appear to have all
that he should want, and the parents may be vigorously indifferent to idiomatic behaviour.

If psychotic illness is characterized by a break in
reality orientation and a loss of contact with the
real world, then normotic illness is typified by a
radical break with subjectivity and by a profound absence of the subjective element in everyday life. As
psychotic illness is marked by a turning inward into the world of
fantasy and hallucination, normotic illness is distinctive as a
turning outward into concrete objects and towards conventional
behaviour. The normotic flees from dream life, subjective states
of mind, imaginative living and aggressive differentiated play
with the other. Discharges of mental life are favoured over articulated elaborations that require symbolic processes and real communication. We could say that if the psychotic has 'gone off at the
deep end', the normotic has 'gone off at the shallow end'.

A normotic family may be successful for quite some time, depending on material comfort and the availability of personal
wealth. As they need a supply of material objects to enrich their
personal happiness, they are far more dependent than other sorts
of people on the flux of economic life. For example, if one of the
parents becomes unemployed, this amounts to more than redun-
dancy: it threatens the breakdown of a mentality. It does not lead
to reflection or to affective states that deepen the family members' understanding of themselves and of their life. A father may
become absent, either literally, by going off and staying away
from home, or he may sit before the TV for long periods of time.
We would say that there is a depression there, but from inside the
family; it is the experience of 'leave your father alone' whose mental equivalent is 'leave that part of your mind concerned with
your father alone'. Such statements abound, and in this way the
mind is gradually shut down.

A mother may convert the house into an object that must be
exhaustively cleaned. Her somewhat lifeless and compulsive activity would be striking to us, but inside the family this might be
described as 'your mother is helping out' whose mental equivalent is 'when you believe you see signs of distress in us, cancel
this idea, and replace it with an observation of the action you see
before you'. If the father finds work again, this entire episode will

be negated and probably only referred to in cliches: 'boy, that was really tough' or 'well, you have your downs as well as your ups'. If matters do not improve, however, strain begins to enter the picture in such a way that a normotic defence cannot successfully endure.

The most common form of breakdown is alcohol abuse. When this person feels psychic pain or when he is invited by fortune to undergo incremental subjective experiences, he refuses to do so and drinks himself into an anaesthetized state. Alternatively, he may throw himself even more exuberantly into his work, staying at the office for inhumanly long hours. He might, along with other activities, become an exercise fanatic, jogging for ten miles a day. If he becomes depressed and is incapable of work or exercise, he will characterize himself in mechanical metaphors. He is just 'shot', or 'kaput', or 'in bad working order'. He may seek a chemotherapeutic solution to his state of being.

Certain psychosomatic disorders and eating disturbances may be forms of normotic breakdown in which the person tries to elude introspective examination of the subjective origins of distress, preferring the focus of a concrete breakdown, such as a pain or dysfunction of part of the body or a preoccupation with taking in food and monitoring the shape of the body.

The above processes are all syntonic with the normotic personality. They are endeavours to remain within the normotic personality and its assumptions. Some homosexual disturbances, however, may be understood as anti-normotic personality formations. The homosexual's adornment in exaggerated representations of the subjective element can be a defiance of the normotic way of life. Where the normotic parent may have stressed 'reasonable' thinking, the homosexual may espouse the superiority of anti-reason. Where the normotic parent never tolerated the controversial, the homosexual may become perversely addicted to collecting controversies. This defence against the normotic element (rather like the compulsive defence against schizophrenic illness) nonetheless contains the trace of its intended antithesis. For the homosexual's creativity may only be artifice: the subjective appropriated for the purposes of adornment. The homosexual may become the material object, as if he is endeavouring to retrieve desire from his past by being that which is compulsively collected. Sexual promiscuity amongst homosexuals has the character of a material phenomenon, and is in part an inverted representation of the normotic illness.

The most fragile period in a normotic person's life is during adolescence. It is my view that we can often observe how a child raised in such an atmosphere feels unbearable strain and turns to either drugs or suicide as an alternative to life in the family. We can also witness the family dynamic more clearly, as normotic parents often exorcise themselves of their adolescent child as if they are cleaning house.

TOM

Some time ago I was invited to interview a patient in front of the members of a department of psychiatry in a large hospital. I was not accustomed to this experience and looked forward to it with some reservation and anxiety.

Before the patient entered the room of roughly thirty people, we were told by the family therapist that the patient was an adolescent who had attempted suicide by cutting his arm from the wrist to the elbow. This event had followed a disappointment in school when he felt he had failed people. For several days after the disappointment he had become 'dreamy', a change which had been observable to his friends and apparently to the members of his family, although no one said anything to him about it nor investigated his mood. He then attempted suicide and would certainly have died had he not been discovered. After several weeks in a hospital he seemed much better. He had become attached to a young psychiatrist who was enthusiastic and empathic, if a bit unsophisticated. It was clear that he cared deeply for the boy.

We learned that Tom had been placed on antidepressants, as his dreamy state, which was typical of him at times in the hospital, was deemed evidence of a clinical depression. After less than a month, he was released from the hospital. Within a few days he was re-admitted following another serious suicide attempt. He resumed his relation to the psychiatrist, and we were to discuss

particularly in the mind of the hospital adminis-
trators, was the fact that he was about to over-
stay his allotted time.

Before seeing the patient, I imagined him to be a rather depressed looking and hopeless chap, and I thought the interview would be difficult: how would I be able to get him to speak about himself? I was quite surprised when he entered the room and strode confidently to his chair. Sitting next to me was a handsome, athletic, wholesome looking lad, neatly dressed in cotton trousers, tennis shoes and stylish short-sleeved shirt. He opened the meeting with some appropriately humorous comment about the rather unusual nature of this event. Clearly he knew me for what I was and he meant to be up to any skill on my part.

I think it is accurate to say that although I did interview him, I never overcame the shock of meeting him. This became somewhat apparent in the consultation. For Tom behaved as if nothing was at all unusual in his immediate history. Although he had a ferocious scar visible on his arm, he did not relate to this suicide attempt. After five minutes of chat, I said to him that obviously he must be in great pain or else he would not have attempted to kill himself. He handled this comment as if I had not meant what I said. He politely rebuffed me with an 'OK'. He did respond to those questions I put to him about the events leading up to his suicide attempt, and it was clear that he had felt terribly isolated since moving to his new school, and had entered into athletics in an effort to find friendship. He had never been allowed to mourn the loss of his friends from the previous school, for his father led the family with clichés about how strong people put things behind them. As the interview progressed, we were all moved by the utter failure of Tom's family to **think** about what they had all been through. Since they had not engaged in any mental work to deal with the distress of such an upheaval, needless to say they did not discuss it with one another.

When I tried to discuss Tom's experience of the move with him, he would inevitably refer me to one or another of his father's remarks: 'It will all turn out for the best' or 'If you want to get ahead in life, you have to get on with life'.

We knew from the family therapist's report that Tom's father was a genial but shallow man who worked as an engineer. He was not oppressive or heavy handed, and spent quite a lot of time with his children, inevitably engaged in outdoor activities: football, water skiing, basketball. He never gave the impression, however, of having sat down with one of his children to discuss any of their problems.

Tom's family, like many such people, appeared ideal. They were civic minded and took part in many local social events. No doubt they were regarded by their friends as steady people with their feet firmly planted on the ground. When Tom tried to kill himself, the response amongst his friends must have been similar to his family's reaction: it was beyond belief and outside the purview of common sense. It was therefore something that could not be considered and should be labelled as an unfortunate event, a 'real shame', which would no doubt end when Tom snapped out of it.

While sitting with Tom, I felt I was confronted with a mentality that admitted of no inquiry or reflection. It was clear after a while that it would be fairly useless to question him further, since he was unable at this point to speak of himself to another person. So I decided to tell him a bit about adolescence as I had experienced it. I said that I had felt dreadfully uncertain at times about how things would turn out in my life. I reminisced about high school sports and recalled how dreadful I felt if I did not do well in competitive games, but how much worse it was if I let the team down, which, I said, I inevitably did. After going on in this vein for a while, I then said that I could not get over how little of the uncertainty and doubt and anger about being an adolescent seemed to be expressed in him. With humour, I said that he reminded me more of one of his father's fifty-year-old colleagues than he did a sixteen-year-old. I said that I reckoned that he was trying to live up to some impossible standard, which made him feel furious and incompetent at times, and that he must be figuring that if this is what he is to be stuck with in life that he might as well do himself in.

When I started to talk about myself, he seemed more

interested, but also more anxious and uncertain,

as no doubt he was unaccustomed to hearing an
adult talk to him about the ordinary fears and
uncertainties of adolescence. He remained composed and polite throughout the interview, in
contrast to myself. I now realize looking back that I was rather
more slovenly than I usually am (I was slouching in my chair,
whilst he was sitting quite properly), and I was at a loss for words
(while he had an answer for every question). In other words, I was
closer to the adolescent experience than Tom was, while he, in
turn, was closer to emulating the businesslike orientation to life
that he believed characterized normal behaviour.

It is my view that Tom's breakdown constitutes a mute refusal
to live within normotic culture, even though at the point of his
suicide attempt he had not discovered other avenues for the expression of his feelings. Hopefully that will come with his psychotherapy.

DEFLECTING THE SELF

As has been argued, the normotic person is nurtured in an environment in which the parent avoids responsiveness to the core
of the child's self. In health, a child's play leads the parent to
elaborate on this experience through affective participation, imaginative mirroring and verbal comment, so that the child evolves
from playing to speaking, to feeling enhanced and enlarged by
language. In the normotic family, the child's play goes uncommented upon, except as an object, much as one might point to a
chair and say 'there is a chair'. The parent does not interact with
the child's imaginative inventions, he does not elaborate any of
the child's imaginings by commenting on them, and the child is
not reflected by the parent. Instead of being mirrored by the
parent, the child is **deflected**. This is accomplished by diverting
the child from the inner and the psychic towards the outer and the
material.

Normotic families develop a library of material objects. If a
child is working on some inner psychic problem or interest, the
family usually has an external concrete object available for the
transfer of the psychic into the material. Let us imagine that a

four-year-old child is on the verge of enacting in play his interest in his penis as a weapon in heterosexual intercourse. He invents a space game in which he invites a boy or a girl to be his victim while he imprisons them in a capsule which he is determined to preside over with a sword. I say that he is on the verge of this activity because, by the time he begins to set this game up, a normotic parent would already have intervened to direct him elsewhere. He would be told that if he wants to play he should throw the ball or ride his bicycle and that he should be nice to his friends and not act like a monster. He might be told to sit down nicely with his friends and watch TV. This example illustrates the concept of a deflected self, a self that is transferred elsewhere. This is fundamentally different from the act of dissociation that Winnicott (1960a) refers to when writing of the schizoid character, for in this case there is a private inner self that goes on living a secret life, hidden and protected by a false self. Schizoid persons do have complex, possibly even rich, inner fantasy lives, but suffer from a lack of spontaneity and liveliness. The normotic person is almost exactly the opposite. He may be quite extrovert (although not truly spontaneous) and a past master at utilizing material objects, but he would have very little inner psychic life.

It is difficult to characterize the atmosphere that prevails in the normotic person's inner world. Indeed, I am well aware that by discussing this issue removed from a particular clinical example, I run the risk of lumping complex phenomena together in a way that can be oversimplistic. Nonetheless, I believe it is possible to discuss certain characteristics of these persons' inner lives.

Because the normotic individual is not known and reflected by the other, he is deficient in his own techniques of insight. He is also relatively unable to introject an object and is therefore both unable to identify with an other and hampered in the ability to empathize. His inner object world is strangely objectless. This individual does not think about others. He does not delineate the nature of an other to himself. One patient seen in analysis rarely spoke of any person, or any distinguishing traits of such a person.

Instead she listed her daily happenings, all of
which seemed to take place in a void. As she

chortled on session after session about what had
happened that day, I struggled to define the
quality of her inner life. She was not empty, that
was for sure. She bubbled over with accounts of events, often
striking for their sheer meaninglessness. If I was unable to define
the quality of her inner life, I was nonetheless able to characterize
it, as it reminded me of certain radio talk-ins, when we find ourselves listening to the host and someone on the end of the telephone engaging in animated meaninglessness, artfully trivializing
complex and significant issues. My patient's inner world seemed
like a background noise, full of trivial observations and listings.

If such a person really does not introject objects, nor indeed
project herself into objects, what mental mechanisms do characterize her internal life? In my view, she incorporates rather than
introjects, and excorporates (Green, 1981) rather than projects.
If for the moment we think of the difference between incorporation and introjection in the clinical setting, this distinction as it
is used here should be clear. If a patient takes in the analyst
through the senses, he is incorporating the analyst not introjecting him. The sight of the analyst and his consulting room is diet
enough for such a person, as is the smell of the analyst and the
room, as is the feel of the couch and the sound of the analyst's
voice and other sounds that characterize the consulting room. Incorporation in and of itself is non-representational, and the analyst as an internal object is relatively meaningless. If a patient
thinks about what the analyst has said, if he imagines his analyst
and develops an internal relation to him, then we can speak of
introjection. As the term is used here, introjection refers to the
internalization of the object's personality (or part of it) in a dynamic relation to some part of the patient's self. The patient who
incorporates takes in only sense presentations and keeps them at
a non-representational level. This is the equivalent of Bion's beta
level of functioning.

An excorporation is an act of expulsion of an object that is
roughly equivalent to the terms of incorporation. Again, it is useful to consider Bion's formulations, in particular his concept of

the 'reversal of function' (1958). We not only take in an object through the eyes, we also eject objects through the eyes. The same is true of hearing, of smelling, of touching. In the clinical situation, some of the more common forms of ex-corporation are the occasions when a patient coughs, or yawns, or taps the couch or sighs.

What is the nature of normotic communication? I do not think that it follows the laws of Bion's theory of beta functioning – specifically, objects are not manipulated via projective identification. Almost the opposite happens. It is as if language 'transformers' are used that launder a communication of all meaning, thus enabling the person to vaporize conflict and appear perfectly normal. This takes place by incorporating phrases that are in themselves meaningful, but that are used so repetitively that they eventually lose their originating subjectivity. I am referring to the use of familiar phrases by a person, indeed to the constriction of vocabulary, a foreclosure of language that would be observable only over time in the knowing of any one individual. So, for example, a person who has a normotic personality disorder would be found to use a vocabulary of phrases that laundered the self of meaning; phrases such as 'that's tragic' or 'uh huh' or 'yeah' or 'wow' that nullify meaning whilst appearing to recognize significance. Or a person might have more complex phrases such as 'gosh, that's really amazing' or 'it's extraordinary what the world is coming to' which deflect meaning away from inter-subjective exchange.

The function of transformation from potential meaning into meaninglessness reflects a process derived from the parents that is installed in the ego to form part of its procedure. This ego function is in the nature of a memory of the early mother and father, who in their functions as transformational objects constantly denuded the child's gestures of their meaning function. This interactional paradigm becomes one of the many laws of the child's character.

As has been suggested, the outcome of such a situation is a person who appears really quite extroverted and able. He seems to be without conflict, even in a troubled world. He manages dis-

tress through the use of 'language transformers'
that alter significance into insignificance by virtue of the use of a vocabulary of phrases that
function as evacuators of meaning.

155

NORMOTIC
ILLNESS

FROM SUBJECT TO OBJECT

Normotic children conceive of themselves as objects. Becoming a good object for someone is a worthy enterprise. Nurtured by parents who approve of their behaviour, they, like the parents, develop a concern to appear perfectly normal. This does not result in a schizoid split, at least as we have commonly understood it, because in such children the development along false self lines is materially rewarded, and as children these people are really very pleased to contribute to the population of the norm.

Family members wish to be placed in each other's minds as solid and friendly objects similar to the position of the material objects they all value. These families pride themselves on their articulation of a known and familiar identity (such as being American or English), and they take pleasure in seeing the other recognize himself in them. A normotic person is concerned with being 'a good guy' or a person 'people would like to have around'. The self is conceived of as a material object, much the way any common object is imagined. And valuing the self is determined only by the external functioning of the self, as it appears to the norm: the person's treatment of the self as an object has a quality similar to a quality control department's concern with the functioning quality of a product.

In the person who maintains a normotic personality successfully, a sense of isolation is mitigated by virtue of his ability to mingle with objects and to feel identified with the commodity object world. For instance, driving a car that one is proud of may be an unconscious act of marriage. In this way, products become part of one's family, and the normotic's family of objects extends itself throughout the material object world. The sense of 'family' is revealed when the normotic is in a strange environment. When travelling, the normotic may be quite unhappy because he cannot find any common or family object. In such a world of alien objects there is an increased strain to maintain his familiar internal sense

of self and of well-being, so that the simple discovery of a familiar object, such as Coca-Cola,
can be greeted with an affection and celebration
that other people reserve only for human beings.

CONCLUSION

There is a personality type that we psychoanalysts have tended to
neglect in our writings, because, as Winnicott has suggested, this
disturbance lies along the axis of the normal. Yet, if we look
closely, we can observe that some persons are abnormally normal. They are unusually rooted in being objective, both in their
thinking and in their desire. They achieve a state of abnormal
normality by eradicating the self of subjective life, as they strive
to become an object in their own being.

In his cultivation of material phenomena the normotic has become an object, both for himself and for his others: an object with
no subject, an object alive and happy in a material world. Such a
person suggests that mind itself, in particular the unconscious, is
an archaism, a thing to be abandoned in the interests of human
progress.

9   *Extractive introjection*

G ENERATIVE mutuality in human relations depends, amongst other things, on an assumption that the elements of psychic life and their different functions are held in common. If **A** talks to **B** about his grief over the loss of a parent, then he should be able to assume that **B** knows what grief is and will 'share' **A**'s problem with him. If **A** confides in **B** about her sexual frustration with her husband who is no longer interested in her, then **A** should assume that **B** knows about the need for sexual gratification and can understand what frustration would be like.

In an ordinary life, if it is possible to speak of such, couples and families share the elements of psychic life and their functions through a division of labour. In a marriage, a wife may tend to process the element of comforting physical care in relation to her children, while the husband may process the element of 'management' of the outside world. In contemporary life, partners pass the functions of these elements back and forth between themselves. The healthy wife and husband value and understand the elements being processed by the other.

In the modern child-guidance clinics, psychiatric hospitals, and in the secluded space of a psychoanalysis, however, the psychoanalyst is more likely to be aware of failures in mutuality, particularly breakdowns in the sharing and understanding of the common psychic elements and their functions.

Kleinian psychoanalysts, in particular, have focused on one way in which a person may rid himself of a particular element of psychic life. He does so by putting it into someone else. If a father feels guilty over impulse buying or the pressure created internally by the urge to be impulsive, he may break psychological contact with this impulse and its inspired guilt by criticizing his child's ordinary impulsiveness. As the parent unconsciously rids himself of this unwanted part of himself, his overly censorious relation to the child's impulsiveness creates the 'desired' effect. Unable to bear the father's censorious approach, the child becomes even more impulsive. In studying human relations, whenever we note that one person compels another to 'carry' an unwanted portion of himself, then we speak of 'projective identification'.

I believe there is a process that can be as destructive as projective identification in its violation of the spirit of mutual relating. Indeed, I am thinking of an intersubjective procedure that is almost exactly its reverse, a process that I propose to call **extractive introjection**. Extractive introjection occurs when one person steals for a certain period of time (from a few seconds or minutes, to a lifetime) an element of another individual's psychic life. Such an intersubjective violence takes place when the violator (henceforth A) automatically assumes that the violated (henceforth B) has no internal experience of the psychic element that A represents. At the moment of this assumption, an act of theft takes place, and B may be temporarily anaesthetized and unable to 'gain back' the stolen part of the self. If such extraction is conducted by a parent upon a child it may take many years of an analysis before B will ever recover the stolen part of the self.

SOME EXAMPLES

A common event. B is a five-year-old child and is seated at a table with his parents. He reaches for his glass of milk and spills it on the floor. A parent yells: 'You stupid idiot, why don't you watch what you are doing!' In the fraction of a second prior to that comment, B has felt the shock of his mistake and has been cross and upset with himself. But A's comment steals from B the expression of shock, of self-criticism and of reparation to the group. These elements have in a sense been stolen by A. At this point B is likely to be further stunned by the parent, who assumes furthermore that B is not upset, critical or wishing to make it up to the family. It is this **assumption** and its expression that represents the violence against B and constitutes an extractive introjection, as A

arrogates to himself alone the elements of shock,
criticism and reparation. These can, of course,
be quickly restored to **B** if **A** were to say something like, 'oh, I'm sorry, **B**, I know this is upsetting to you, and we all do this sort of thing, so
don't worry: here, have another glass of milk'; whereupon **B**
might then say, with relief and also in contact with himself, 'I'm
sorry, **A**, for being clumsy', having in that moment processed the
elements of shock, criticism and reparation. Later I will explore
how extractive introjection which is maintained alters the intrasubjective function of a psychic element. The victim could rad-
ically dissociate himself from the element of criticism because its
function is to isolate him from the family world. He might willingly allow himself in such a circumstance to be the family fool in
order to be part of the group, thus giving up his own contact with
important psychic elements.

    B is a four-year-old at play. He is moving small figures about
and is engaged in a private drama that is nonetheless realized
through actual objects. The space is entered by **A**, who creates
such distraction that **B** loses his **playfulness**. This is a common
enough occurrence, particularly if we say that **A** is also four. But
let's imagine that **A** is the mother or father, and that each time **B**
sets up a small group of objects to play with, the parent enters the
scene and appropriates the playing by telling the child what the
play is about and then prematurely engages in playfulness. **B**
might continue to play, but a sense of spontaneity would diminish
and be replaced by expectant gamefulness. If every time **B** is
spontaneously playful the mother or father takes over the play
and embellishes it with their own 'play', the child will come to
experience an extraction of that element of himself: his **capacity
to play**.

    B is a student in a class. This can be as either a five-year-old
or a twenty-five-year-old. The teacher, **A**, is knowledgeable and
intense. Ordinarily, **B** is quite capable of representing his views
coherently. But **A** does not permit this. He continually finds flaws
in **B**'s arguments and attempts to present a coherent point of
view. **B** becomes rather confused and perplexed. He is less

late. The less articulate **B** is, the more aggressively coherent and knowledgeable **A** is. Gradually **A** assumes the total function of critical thought, as **B** simply provides the material for **A**'s superior thinking. This procedure is in the nature of an extractive introjection, since **A** takes into himself what was partly **B**'s ability, the capacity to think clearly and to put thoughts into words.

B is an adult working in a setting with quite a few colleagues. One day he says something that is rather insensitive – in effect, he is overly critical of a colleague. He has felt privately unhappy with this and in the course of the hour or two after the event he empathizes with his colleague (**C**). He feels true sorrow, realizes that his colleague's view is actually essential to the overall view of things, and he plans to apologize. At lunch that day **B** anticipates that he will apologize to his colleague, but before he has the opportunity to do so **A** enters the situation and upbraids **B** for his aggression. **B** nods and at first agrees that yes, he was too thoughtless. **A** goes on. He proceeds to go over the situation as if **B** had not acknowledged what **A** had said. Indeed, **A** proceeds to praise the offended colleague, **C**, and in so doing suggests that **C** has been wronged. **B** may have an internal experience of feeling that his own private feelings, recognitions, appreciations and reparations towards **C** have been extracted from him by **A** who uses the situation to presume himself the only party capable of such capacities. Again, it is **A**'s assumption and its violent delivery that extracts from **B** what had been present.

B is alone in his room mulling over certain private internal issues. **A** arrives in a euphoric mood. What is the matter, **A** inquires of **B**. **B** tells **A** something of what is on his mind. **A** extracts the elements of **B**'s concerns and with great speed and intensity organizes **B**'s private concerns into a false coherence. The more **A** organizes **B**'s state of mind into 'meaning' the less **B** feels in contact with himself and, if **A** is a manic personality, **B** may gradually begin to feel dulled and inert, since he is left to carry the split-off deadness that typifies the other aspect of **A**'s personality. In this example, we can see how extractive introjection and projective identification may work together. As **A**

extracts **B**'s sense of inner workings, he deposits

in its place a split-off element of his own person-

ality: a deadness.

It is a community meeting in a psychiatric
hospital. Some thirty people are in the room
together with a rather loose agenda that permits enough space for
the introduction of feelings and thoughts as they arise. One of the
unconscious issues of each community meeting is the feeling that
no one person will ever have enough time to feel personally attended to. Thus, to some extent, each person is feeling neglected and
irritated by the inevitable failure of the meeting. But **A** will not
tolerate this. In a moment of fury, while getting out of his chair, **A**
screams, 'you people don't know what it is to feel frustrated and
angry', and he stomps out of the room, banging the door behind
him. In that moment **A** may have successfully extracted from the
group the individual experience of irritation, frustration and
anger. Through a violent fit of temper he has left the group
shocked and speechless. Only much later will individual members
compete to have the right of fury returned to them.

Another meeting. This time the executives of a corporation
are gathered together to work on a difficult problem. As the members of the group express different views and try to think their
way through to a creative solution to the problem, **A**, who has
been silent and perhaps envious of the creative capacities of his
colleagues, makes the following speech: 'I think we must take this
problem seriously. This is not a matter to be taken lightly, and we
have to act with great responsibility and caution.' Up until that
moment the group has indeed been approaching the problem with
seriousness of thought. No levity or lack of seriousness is present
and people are obviously thinking responsibly. By making his
morally narcissistic speech, however, **A** appropriates for himself
the elements of seriousness, responsibility and caution. It may be
very difficult at this point for any other person to express an idea,
as **A**'s position suggests that all ideas up until his speech have been
somehow irresponsible. Indeed, it is quite possible – largely depending on **A**'s power in such a group – that the group will become
silent or overly cautious in its thinking.

By utilizing a combination of curiosity, charm and quiet

persistence, **A** manages to get **B** to give intimate details from **B**'s life, so **B** betrays important feelings, self states and historical material. The necessity of solitude is destroyed. **A** then organizes **B**'s life and self into a coherent account, assuming a narrative authority and power, dispossessing **B** of his relation to himself as an object (see above, chapter 3). **A**'s narrative grasp of **B** is 'greater'; that is to say, more organized, intense, comprehensive, certain. **A** has violently extracted **B**'s relation to himself as an object. This sort of intersubjective violence is common in so-called encounter groups conducted by leaders who extract patients' relations to themselves as an object.

A and **B** have recently decided to live together. **A** is actually quite ambivalent about this because he does not like to share his space with anyone else and, although he quite likes **B** and is sexually attracted to her, she also infuriates him. A self-styled moralist, **A** is not comfortable with his irritations over **B**'s existence. He aims to transcend this. One of the most irksome irritations in **A**'s life are **B**'s pets, which **B** has brought into their shared life together because she loves animals and is a very caring person. Indeed, we can say that one of the reasons why **A** has persuaded himself to live with **B** is that she is loving and nurturing. In a short time, **A** can no longer bear the pets and discovers a device for their removal. He is affectionate and shows intense interest in them, but, after a while and with apparent heavy heart, he tells **B** that he finds it personally unbearable that such lovely pets should have to be confined to the small flat. Both **A** and **B** work during the day, and the pets are alone. This has bothered **B**. **A** suggests that if one really loves one's pets this kind of treatment cannot be allowed, and he tells **B** that he cannot stand it any longer: the pets must be sent to someone who has the time to look after them. As **A** assumes the function of loving concern, **B**, who has loved the animals very much, now feels guilt (not love) and anxiety (as she knows something will happen to them). She gives up the animals, now believing that all along she has been cruel, when in fact she has been loving. **A** has extractively introjected the elements of love and care and appropriated them into himself, leaving **B** to feel dreadful.

I hope the examples given clarify the intersubjective process which I have termed extractive
introjection, a procedure in which one person
invades another person's mind and appropriates
certain elements of mental life. The victim of extractive introjection will feel denuded of parts of the self. When this process
occurs in childhood, the victim will not have a clear idea why certain elements of mental life seem not to be his right. For example,
a child who is constantly attacked by a critical parent for the
child's mistakes will in adult life discount the value of his guilt. He
may expect punishment or harsh treatment since the healing
value of the structure of guilt has been removed by the harsh
parent. The said structure generates a mental process that mod-
erates a potentially destructive error by means of the self-
arresting affect of sorrow which leads to identification with the
harmed other and sponsors the capacity to repair the damage.
When the structure of guilt is removed by a critical parent, the
person will feel anxiety but will have little sense of sorrow, empathy and reparation. He will never be able 'to make good'.

When we analyse our patients' projective identifications, we
should simultaneously consider both the effects of extractive
introjection as an alternative explanation and the interplay of
these two defence mechanisms. For example, a patient may be
internally damaged because he has evacuated parts of the self via
projective identification, leaving him with a certain hollow or
empty state of mind. The analyst will eventually come under considerable pressure to bear all the evacuations, as this patient tries
to split off and project the psychic contents and mental structures
that involve the elements of destruction. There might also be a
very different kind of patient who is also rather empty, but who is
not emptied by virtue of projective identifications. I refer to the
person who has been emptied by the active violation of the other,
his internal life having been extracted from him. In an analysis,
the analyst will not come under pressure to take this analysand's
unwanted parts into himself. On the contrary, this analysand will
seem almost incapable of projecting into the analyst. More likely,
the analysand will develop a parasitical transference in which he

assumes that all that is life-enhancing (including destruction) is inside the analyst, thus inspiring him to live as close to the analyst as possible.

It should eventually be possible for us to differentiate kinds of illness by considering the effects of pathological intersubjectivity. For example, a mother and father who projectively identify unwanted split-off elements of their own self into their child will burden this child with a highly complex and chaotic internal world. In adult life this person might be an unintegrated collation of parts of his intrinsic self and unwanted parental introjects. This is true of the borderline personality. Another mother and father may extract mental content and structure from a child, denuding the child of the contents and structure necessary to the processing of mental conflict. In this case the adult would seem mentally impaired or impoverished rather than overburdened with mental conflict. It may be that the person I have described in the previous chapter – the 'normotic' individual – suffers from a form of extractive introjection. If so, I do not think the normotic child is witness to the parents' extraction and identification (by assumption) of the stolen mental element, but is the participant-victim of a process of extraction followed by vaporization of the psychic structure.

Undoubtedly, each extractive introjection is accompanied by some corresponding projective identification. As a person takes from another person's psyche, he leaves a gap, or a vacuum, in its place. There he deposits despair or emptiness in exchange for what he has stolen. The situation is further complicated by the fact that a child who is the victim of consistent extractive introjection may choose to identify with the aggressive parent and install in his personality this identification, which then functions as a false self. He may then act in a similarly aggressive and greedy manner, subsequently extracting elements of psychic life from others. But this false self is just that: a false act, an empty theft. This person does not truly appropriate the stolen elements, he just acts as if he does. One can think here of certain psychopaths who violate other people's states of mind, but who do not over time use what they steal to dominate or control a person. The theft is quick, fleeting and empty.

I believe we can differentiate between four types 165
of extractive introjection: the theft of mental con- EXTRACTIVE
tent, the theft of the affective process, the theft of INTROJECTION
mental structure, and the theft of self.

Theft of mental content. We have our own
ideas and mental representations. In a sense they are our creations, even though we hold ideas and representations in common
with others. These are subject, of course, to correction and alteration, both by ourself and by others. The theft of ideas is one of
the forms of extractive introjection and is often characterized by
an act of assumption. B tells A about his latest thinking on a topic
and A replies 'Yes, of course' or 'exactly' or 'naturally', and then
A proceeds to say 'and furthermore', as if A has already thought
B's ideas and adds many more of his own. This exchange is quite
common, and its effect often relatively harmless, although B is
likely to feel some irritation and perhaps a disinclination to talk
much further with A.

Theft of affective process. If a person commits an error he is
likely to feel the following emotional sequence: surprise/shock,
anger with the self, sorrow, a sense of guilt and responsibility,
reparation, and restoration of peace of mind. This affective process is an essential feature of the individual subject's experience
in life. But it can be interfered with by another so that the process
is interrupted and altered. The subject who has had the affective
process interrupted has instead the following emotional experience: surprise, shock, acute anxiety and fear, humiliation, con-
cealment and dread. If A extracts the elements of this process
from B, thereby altering the course of the emotional experience,
then the character of B's emotional life may be permanently
shifted. The damage here is more serious than with the theft of
mental content.

Theft of mental structure. A can assume the function of the
structure of that part of the mind we term the superego, so de-
structuring B's mind in such a way that B, instead of feeling re-
proached from within, expects to be humiliated from without and
eventually ceases to reproach himself, for he concerns himself
with either pleasing or deceiving (or both) the external superego.
If this occurs, then there has been an important loss of a mental

structure. If **A** denigrates **B**'s capacity to think issues through for himself and arrogates to himself the function of thinking, then the mental structure that generates rational thought and problem-solving will be dismantled, and **B** will not feel himself capable of solving a problem. Indeed, he may be left in a stupor with little confidence in thought itself, since he has come to regard thinking as a dangerous enterprise in which he feels anxious and threatened. **B** may give up secondary-process thinking and instead speak from the primary process, as a kind of fool or idiot savant who utilizes the licence of madness to engage in covert thinking.

Theft of the self. The parts of the self are multifold and, understandably, differ between people. I shall not outline them here. But each of us has a unique and idiomatic history. This sponsors the culture of the self, which is composed of many selves, and is perhaps our most valuable possession. The loss of a part of the self means not only a loss of content, function and process, but also a loss of one's sense of one's own person. A loss of this nature constitutes a deconstruction of one's history; the loss of one's personal history is a catastrophe, from which there may well be no recovery.

LOSS, UNCONSCIOUS GRIEF
AND VIOLENCE

The person who has consistently had important elements and functions of his psyche extracted during childhood will experience a certain kind of loss. He will feel that a primary injustice has occurred, that he has been harmed by something, and like Captain Ahab he may seek a vengeful solution. Indeed, vengefulness of this kind is a bitter and agitated despair that constitutes a form of unconscious mourning, as if the loss can only be undone by the law of talion: an eye for an eye, a leg for a leg. In this respect, the law of talion is an unconscious act intended to recover the lost part of the self by violent intrusion into the other – to recover what has been stolen from oneself.

We may observe how some children can develop relevant patterns of bahaviour if they have been violated by parents who have

stolen important parts of their psychic life. A   167
man who burgles may be violating a home to steal   EXTRACTIVE
the internal objects of a family, and in that mo-   INTROJECTION
ment his act may mirror his own experiences as a
child, compulsively reversing his life pattern
through violent redress.

When one person invades another's psychic territory he not
only deposits an unwanted part of himself, as in projective identification, but in some respect he also takes something. At the very
least he steals the recipient's peace of mind. That indeed is one of
the functions of projective identification. By putting unwanted
parts of oneself into another person the projector enjoys limited
peace of mind, a psychic state that is extracted from the recipient
who is left in confusion.

NECESSARY PARANOIA

One of the most important differential assessments a psychoanalyst can make in working with a severely disturbed person is
to determine whether the individual's loss of mind is due fundamentally to projective identifications, that is, acts of expulsion
which may reflect defensive manoeuvres against primitive anxieties over annihilation, or whether such a loss is due to the
absence of internal integrity because of the other's violent extraction of the essentials of psychic life.

Because the child who has had his mind extracted by the other
will have little ability to process the experience of being the victim
of extractive introjection, he will in some fundamental way know
very little of what has happened to him. Know, that is, in the
sense of being able to represent mentally the nature of the intersubjective phenomenon he has experienced. As I have examined
above, in chapter 6, the loss of mind may be stored in the individual's memory only as a life-defining event that is beyond comprehension. He may be either remarkably empty and indifferent
to his existence, or he may be quite the opposite: angry, depressed
and paranoid. But the paranoid process in this person differs
from paranoia that represents the individual's projection of unwanted elements into others, a paranoia that precipitates anxiety
in the person's relation to the outside world. For the victim of

extractive introjections, the paranoid state is an attitude of mourning, of loss over the 'gone', and constitutes a belief that something hostile 'out there' has taken something valuable from within.

Such a person does not live in hiding from paranoid objects, but quite the opposite – like Ahab, he seeks the other. He travels towards it in an effort to bring it back to him, or him to it. He does not identify it in order to expel it, but rather to continue the extractive process.

We may distinguish the paranoia that develops as a result of parental extractions of the child's psyche from the dynamically projective paranoia by examining the nature of the transference and the countertransference. The analysand whose paranoia is a form of anguished grief seeks a repatriation with the elements of the psyche. In the transference he believes that the analyst contains important psychic processes and he is determined to gain these talents for himself. Although the analyst will come under pressure to give the elements of psychic life back to the analysand – this will be the patient's unconscious concept of the transaction – the analyst will not find himself persecuted by the dynamic qualities of the more ordinary paranoid process. Namely, he will not have to carry or to bear unwanted sections of the patient's mind. Quite the contrary. The patient seeks to recover his mind and, as the analyst helps him to think and to repossess affects, mental processes and ultimately psychic structure, the analysand responds to the analyst's transformational function with something like object hunger, and eventually love.

My aim in this chapter has been to explore what I mean by the concept of extractive introjection and to provide vignettes to make the concept clear. I have not considered why some people are more vulnerable to extractive introjection than others, nor have I distinguished between its ordinary and pathological forms. It should be clear, however, that I believe extractive introjection to be a common and indispensable part of intersubjective processes.

I shall also have to postpone a more extensive examination of the interplay between projective identification and extractive introjection, as well as a full discussion of the implications for psychoanalytic technique of working with a patient whose inner emptiness is determined by the other's extraction of mind rather than the subject's projective identifications.

III Countertransference

10   *The liar*

A scene one of my patients, Jonathan, presents to me frequently is typical of the phenomenon I will be addressing in this chapter. Jonathan is late for work because of an argument with his wife. His employer asks about his absence. He replies that his employer will hardly believe what has happened to him that morning. He left his house as usual, with plenty of time to get to the office, when he was pulled to the side of the road by a police car. The policeman radioed for assistance, and soon there were several police vans surrounding his car. He was paralysed with fear but the occasion did not fail to inspire an indignant curiosity over this bizarre event. His querulous impulse was muted by the grotesque logic of events. He was shoved into a police van and handcuffed. Wordless, the police took him to the local precinct where he was placed in solitary confinement. After what seemed an eternity, but could only have been about one hour, a smartly dressed detective entered the cell. The detective apologized; a mistake had been made and he was free to go. He was escorted to an unmarked police vehicle and returned to his own car which remained at the scene of his unofficial arrest, and then drove to work. As he narrates this lie to me, he says that he can hardly believe that his employer was so gullible that he accepted this account for the truth. 'This story is like a cheap cops and robbers movie, or a poor man's version of Kafka. I don't know why I said what I did. I could easily have said I had a flat tyre. But instead I chose this outlandish story. And the poor fool believed me. He believed me. You see, as long as I can do this and get away with it, then I have no worries whatsoever. What is reality if I can do this? I needn't trouble with what I don't like.'

Is this the function of the psychopathic liar's lie, to negate reality? If the psychopath, who lies as often as he tells the truth, if not more so, uses the presence of apparent sanity in his relation to the lie, what is mad about his activity? Where is the madness to be found? In the content of the lie? In the liar's relation to his lie as an object? In the liar's relation to the other, to whom he tells his lie?

With Jonathan we psychoanalysts face, as we do with any psychopathic liar, something of an ironic dilemma. As the liar's lie is an expression of his psychic reality, then the lie becomes an articulation of that truth that we value so highly. Jonathan has certainly lied about what has happened to him in reality, but has he lied about his psychic reality? Knowing that he was late for work because his wife has threatened to leave him, his lie expresses some dread about his reaction to her threat. The threat might arouse in him an impulse to murder her and thereby retain possession of their children, a thought that has occurred to him on numerous occasions. He could be arrested and tried for murder. But in the lie he is freed. His innocence is established. Nothing has happened. It is more than possible that the well-dressed detective who frees him from potential imprisonment may be a personification of a transference perception, as he has often viewed me as someone who, firmly situated in reality, may be able to free him from his madness.

THE LIE AS METAPHOR

Jonathan says that his lies emerge in an unpremeditated manner; they are being told before he, as a conscious subject, has any apparent influence over them. He also claims that he feels a certain indebtedness to this capacity to lie, even though he is, of course, aware of the potential danger to which such lying exposes him. He believes that it is only through the lie that he can feel a sense of personal reality. It is only through the lie that feelings about reality can emerge.

In this way, the liar's lie (and henceforth I will be strictly referring to the psychopathic liar's lying) is a metaphor. A conventional truth and the conventional attitude towards speaking the truth is violated by the revolutionary logic of metaphor. A simple comparison between simile and metaphor establishes how much

more disruptive and evocative metaphorical representation is than simile. Had Jonathan said
that his trip to work was like a terrible incarcera-
tion by the police, he would have been drawing
an overt comparison between the events in re-
ality and the corresponding feelings and thoughts derived from
psychic reality. But the omission in metaphorical logic of the 'as-
if' linkage provided by simile erases ordinary ways of expressing
truths that have been constituted in relation to reality.

Metaphor is an evocative mode. An unusual image or an impossible juxtaposition is used to speak some truth that is difficult
to set in realistic or descriptive prose. It is misguided to separate
the logic of metaphor from its evocative function: it jolts or sur-
prises the object. So does the liar's lie. It also provides the subject
who speaks through the logic of metaphor or the subject who
articulates his truth through the lie with a curious sensation. The
unruly defiance of metaphorical representation releases both unconscious significance and the affect linked with the meaning.
The psychopathic liar's lie allows him to believe that he is actually
telling the truth, as what he says feels to him to be so much more
truthful than events as they have been lived in reality that he is
almost powerless to prevent the lie from being told.

REORDERING REALITY

It is through the lie that Jonathan changes his relation to reality.
In either lying about what has happened to him or in falsifying
what will happen to him, he sustains an illusion that past and future realities are expressive of his omnipotent manipulation of
the object world. He continually tests this out by lying to see if the
other is taken in. As he lies very effectively, he is continually confirmed in his belief that he can make of reality what he wishes. It
is not simply a question of finding safety through the lie. He feels
protected, certainly, but the essence of his lie is that it provides
him with an affective and imaginative relation to the outside
world that he cannot otherwise achieve. It is as if he needs the lie
in order to actualize dissociated self experience. It is not the content of the lie which allows this, but the process of lying itself,
since in the act of reordering reality he is released from what he

experiences as a terrible bondage. He is free to be
expressive.

But why not tell the truth? Why not be imaginative in terms of one's experience of the truth? Telling the truth does not mean one is fated to empty
and compliant narration. Critical positions are possible, aren't
they? Not for Jonathan, nor for most psychopathic liars. Expressing the truth seems an act of madness, an utter impossibility
in those situations where telling the truth is crucial to an actual
expression of the subject's feelings and thoughts. The fact is,
however, that Jonathan maintains sufficient phobic distance
from persons so that he is rarely pushed to the point where he
must lie in order to avoid a specific truth that he feels would be
catastrophic. Most of his lies seem absolutely unnecessary. How
can we explain this oddity?

There seem to be two orders of lie. He lies on occasions when
he feels himself to be trapped and imagines that the truth would
be devastating. Though these experiences are always very intense, his relation to this kind of lie is qualitatively different from
his relation to the unnecessary lie. The lie told to prevent some
ghastly truth from emerging does not seem liberating; he does not
feel he has come alive through the lie. He usually feels terribly
anxious and is very worried that his lie has been ineffective. For
days he lives in fear that something dreadful will happen. Only
after a very long time does he finally recover and promise himself,
as consolation, that he will never allow himself to be put in such a
position again.

The second order of lying, the apparently unnecessary lie, is
accompanied by a lively sense of triumph and confidence. This
lying is incessant; he lies several times a day, and on some occasions the lies are very complex and are kept up over long periods.

Once, for example, he said that on his way to the train station
he saw a young boy approached by a slightly older boy. They
seemed to be having an illicit rendezvous, but he thought little of
it. Then a few days later he saw both of these boys again, in
another area of town. This time he was sure he saw one of them
with a syringe. He has told this lie to two girls who work at his
office. They are drawn into the tale and spend a good deal of time

imagining what could have been happening. The

next day he tells them they will never believe
what he has seen. On the previous evening he was
sitting in a cinema when once again he saw the
two boys together. To his utter astonishment one
of them came over to him and asked him if he would join them.
Overwhelmed with respect for such a coincidental process, he
could hardly refuse. He joined them and after the cinema they
went to the elder boy's house. There the younger boy tried to seduce him, and he ran out of the house, jumped in his car and
drove home.

On hearing this the girls are astonished. They share his utter
shock. A week later he asks them if they recall the two boys. Yes,
of course they do, how could he believe they would forget it so
quickly. He then says that one of the boys telephoned him and
asked him if he would spend a weekend with him at his country
cottage. Again he did not refuse. He went to the cottage and would
you believe it, but there, at the cottage, was a high-level political
official who was showing blue movies to a group of women who
surpassed description. They were meta-decadent. On hearing
this, the girls are beside themselves with curiosity. What was happening, they asked? What happened after this? From this point
on, Jonathan spends much of his time answering their questions.
The genesis of the lie shifts from his subjectivity to theirs. They
ask the questions, and he fills in the answers. This particular lie
went on for some six weeks before it was supplanted by another
lie, one involving him in an imaginary political scandal. As he
works in several different places during the week, he is able to
sustain five or six such lies, all of which take up a very considerable amount of his time. In fact, on occasion he has very little else
to do other than lie.

REASON

What have we understood in the analysis about why he does this?
We know that he is the eldest child of a large family and that both
his parents are ambitious people who have achieved notoriety in
their work. Intellectuals and exceptional rationalists, they have
created a remarkable atmosphere in the home. It is designed in

such a way that the interior of the house seems to evolve quite naturally from the classical Greek temperament. It is sparse. The library is graced only with classical texts. The interior of the house is all white. It is from this space that the father, in particular, speaks as if he is specially delegated to do so from the ancient muses and philosophers. He is weighed down with an appropriate sense of history. Any problem is resolvable as long as those participating in its solution have patience and follow the logic of reason. Any irrational affect, such as a burst of temper, is regarded as a most unfortunate breakdown in the subject's communicative and rational potential, and he is brought back to reason as quickly as possible. That is not to say that the parents lack feeling. But all of their passion goes into their formidable intellectual powers. Thus they can become quite heated in their discourse, but only in defence of some rational point that is meeting with an irrational resistance.

It is within this frame of reference that we may look at this family's decision about how to raise Jonathan during his early years. Two months after his birth his mother left him for three weeks to attend a conference in another country. Both she and her husband regarded this as a perfectly rational thing to do. The child was born, was alive, was doing well and seemed happy. The mother had already passed him into the care of a full-time nanny and a housekeeper who assured her that her departure would have no effect on the baby. Little Jonathan seemed a model of tranquillity and contentedness.

The effect of the parents' division of the caretaking function amongst several people meant that during a typical day Jonathan was passed from one person to the other. Mother would say hello in the morning and then she would go to work. A housemaid looked after him until lunch time. Mother would make an appearance for some ten minutes to collect the mail and say a few kind words to him. In the afternoons he was looked after by his nanny who enjoyed teasing him, often bringing him to tears with what can only be described as highly sadistic behaviour. The father would arrive home in the early evening but was buried in his books and had little time for him. The closest moments with the

father were during the middle of the night, as it
was father, not mother, who came to his room
when he was in distress.

THE TWO OBJECTS

I infer, from the structure of Jonathan's personality, that as an
infant he had at least two distinct experiences of the object. The
first such experience is of the object objectively perceived. He
sees the mother. He sees the maid. He sees his father. The second
experience of the object is more complex and more important.
The **other** object is a phantastical one; it is the object derived
from reality but obeying the laws of Jonathan's needs and his desires. In particular, this second experience of the object fills the
many gaps left by the absence of actual lived experience with the
parental objects. It is only in phantasy that Jonathan can evolve
a completed experience with an object, as the continuous interruptions by the parents of their potential use as Jonathan's objects left him bewildered and compelled him to create an alternative world.

It is important to bear in mind that these two experiences of
the object alternate with one another and have an almost equal
existential status. It is from the second experience of the object
that Jonathan's lying derives. He lies psychopathically
(automatically) because lying functions as another order of self
and object experience, an order that consistently helped him to
recuperate from the actual absences of the parents. The recuper-
ative function of the phantastical relation to the parents became
far more significant to him than the actual relation to either of
them. Jonathan's lying is not just phantasizing. His lying constitutes an alternative relation to reality, one that he feels is quite
natural and essential to his existence. Indeed, the paradox is that
Jonathan believes to give up the lie would be equivalent to aban-
doning reality testing, as lying has become his way of relating to
the outside world; not only of testing it, but of using it and of
finding some elements of reality that bring comfort and joy.

THE FUNCTION OF THE LIE

The psychopath's lying has a different history and function from the ordinary person's lie. Ordinary lying is sometimes fairly innocent. A person lies in order to protect someone from a truth that is imagined to be painful. Or a person lies to protect himself from some embarrassing disclosure. Or someone lies to inflict cruelty. Jonathan's lying brings him to life and coheres him in a way in which his narration of actual lived events does not. He lies, he often tells me, because lying is living. It is only by lying that he remains alive. I believe we can understand this feeling as a derivative of the second experience of the object. To lie is to put life into a void.

It might appear, therefore, that Jonathan's lying has nothing to do with relating to the actual parental object **per se**. Have I not said that the lie functions, as phantasy did earlier, to constitute a phantastical object, one that can be controlled omnipotently? It is only in the liar's relation to the other that I think we can see the trace of the original experience of the primary object, of that real object that left the small baby to fend for itself through the compensatory solace of phantasy. It is here, in the liar's relation to the lied-to-object, that the madness of the psychopathic liar can be located.

Jonathan's lying is always preceded by a particular sensation. As he lies every day, this feeling is with him most of the time. He has an inkling that there is something ruthless in the environment. The sense of a ruthless presence cannot be located in any particular object, in any anticipated event, or in any place. Is this sense of a ruthless presence some projective identification of the very impulse to lie? No. It is this global affective sensation that is the source of Jonathan's feeling that he must lie, an activity that he believes will keep him alive and in touch with himself, rather than inert and in passive relation to some potentially hazardous but as yet unidentifiable presence. I believe that he is recollecting, through an affective sensation, the relation to that primary object that is just about to leave him. This anxiety therefore is a mood that conserves a self-other experience, and indicates the presence of a conservative object. In a recollection of the way he must have felt as a small infant, he believes that his very existence is somehow always in doubt.

Jonathan usually feels that something is just on
the verge of instituting a ghastly sequence of im-
peccable logic against him. I believe that he lies
not only to fool the other, but to humanize his
personal setting, since he feels that he is close to
an oppressive dehumanization. He must lie in order to block the
presence of a tyrannical reason. What joy he experiences is that
ecstasy which comes with the defeat of any oppressive force; he
feels he has won a battle fought with all the odds against him.

THE TRANSFERENCE

The experience of the primary object is, then, transferentially
present, in Jonathan's mood, in his sense that something ruthless
is nearby. His lying has a double function derived from the relation to the primary object. Firstly, it serves to counteract the
ominous presence of the primary object, recalled in the lying process as a sensation that surrounds him. Secondly, when he lies to
the other he also unconsciously recreates the very trauma that he
suffered constantly in relation to his parental objects. That is, he
presents to the other a version of reality which the other accepts
as true. In fact, the other is unknowingly engaged in an encapsulated hallucination à deux, a fact that does not emerge – if it
ever does – until the other discovers that all he has been told is a
lie. It is at that moment, when the liar's version of reality is
breached by the truth, that both liar and other share the madness of the lie together. What has been an unknowing hallucination à deux becomes a trauma à deux. Each member of this
folie à deux is confused. What is true? Has it all been made up?
The liar recuperates for a moment. Perhaps, after all, some of it
was true. But such hope yields little. The other usually remains in
a state of shock for some time. When Jonathan has been found
out by his friends, they invariably do not know what to say to
him.

THE SHOCKING DEPARTURE OF REALITY

If the experience of the primary object is transferentially existent
in the affective sense of a ruthless presence, it is also present in
that potential trauma that is always there when the liar lies.

When the liar creates a world for the other, he believes in that world himself, and he feels both more alive and closer to someone who shares the world with him. When the truth dispels the lie, it takes with it the world of self and object representations created by the liar. What is present is the trauma of a shocking departure of a shared reality. It is no comfort to know that the lie spoke a psychic reality, since both liar and other feel a terrible sense of betrayal.

I believe this sense of betrayal is actually a response to the loss of an animated, sentient, narrative presence, a 'voice' that brought liar and other close together. The lie, then, is not only a negation of reality. It is a denial of trauma which can explode into a re-enactment of that trauma. Indeed, the trauma that the lie attempts to undo is latent in the very lying process itself. It is the trauma of a mediated reality which suddenly disappears with no warning or notice. When the liar creates a lie for an other he transfers the baby's experience of the mother's function as both mediator and narrator of his existence, as each liar creates, mediates and transforms a world for the other. When this function disappears, the loss of the liar's narrative process re-creates, I believe, the liar's unconscious experience of the loss of his mother, who was known in the early months of life not as a discrete object, but as a transformational process.

In presenting a world to the other, a world that disappears from sight when found to be based on an untruth, Jonathan re-creates for the other an experience that is remarkably similar to his own as the baby of his absent parents.

THE PSYCHOANALYST'S
COUNTERTRANSFERENCE

In my work with Jonathan I have found my own countertransference useful and informative. Many times I have not known whether Jonathan was telling me the truth or whether he was lying. In such moments I am unable to distinguish between fact and fiction. Is what he is telling me true, or is it completely false? When this occurs I am unable to establish a link with his representational world. It is difficult to trust him.

I have come to realize that he is transferring an entire psychical environment; he imports into the analysis the total experience of his early relation to the primary object. In becoming a presence who fashions illusions but represents them as realities, Jonathan represents the mother in the analysis. His narrative is only illusory because that which it represents is never sustained long enough to be linked to any emotional reality. Another person, in this case myself, will be the victim of that illusory presence and feel those anxieties that arise due to the maddening unreliability of the object. Jonathan compels me to know what it is like to be in the presence of an experience that has no real existence. It is out of such an absence in relating that the liar must create the object from his own imagination and manipulate the actual object world to create the illusion of a life being lived.

Those feelings in the other that occur after the trauma of revelation are also dissociated fragments of the liar's experience of the primary object. In my countertransference, I have often felt frustrated and angry soon after the trauma of being lied to is overcome. I may subsequently have felt a sense of personal futility: Am I ever going to reach this patient? The analytical endeavour seems so hopeless. Then I have usually felt a personal sadness: Jonathan's lying is so poignant a picture of a young man trying to create a world for himself, yet alienating it in the very moment of its creation. My anger, my frustration, my sense of futility and my sadness are all, in part, countertransference affects. Living with Jonathan's re-creation of the activities of the mother, now as her object, I know what it is like to have been him: to feel the trauma of absence, the frustration of illusory relating, the anger of the betrayal, the futility which comes from resourcelessness, and the sadness of knowing that there is something in Jonathan (as he saw in his mother) that cannot stop what he is doing.

My contact with my countertransference constitutes something of a cure for the analyst, in working with such patients. Since I am at least able to identify my feelings, I recover from the madness of the liar's imposition as an enunciator of delusions. In knowing that, I also have learned that it is one of the several ways that this young man can also recover from the madness of his sensibility.

A COUNTERTRANSFERENCE PSYCHOSIS

In one particularly intense period in his analysis Jonathan quietly inquired about the nature of confidentiality in psychoanalysis. He wanted me to state whether what he told me was entirely confidential, or whether under certain circumstances I would disclose information. The question seemed to come out of the blue, as if the object of our thinking at this point bore no anxiety or no relation to what we had been discussing: an innocent question.

I asked him why he wished to know at this point in the analysis. He told me that he would prefer not to tell me now, but would inform me immediately upon my giving him an answer. We went back and forth over this, and as we did I began to feel uneasy. It was hard for me to assess the reality, the subjective basis in Jonathan, for presenting this to me. In all the sessions with him there was a certain playful impishness to his reports, and now that he put this issue to me, I was inclined to take it only half seriously. Yet I was not at ease.

Towards the end of the session he persisted and told me that he would like to tell me about something that was extremely important and had been on his mind. It did, however, involve a criminal act, and he wanted to be certain that he could tell me the truth, but only if I promised to him that I would not go to the police. I did the best I could under the circumstances to assure him that a psychoanalysis was designed to ensure that a person could say whatever came to his mind, but that I was not in a position to give promises about what I would or would not do. I said that I thought he was putting me in a position which I rather thought he enjoyed, since he delighted in putting many people in uncomfortable situations. He nodded.

In the next session he told me that he would say what was on his mind, in the hope that I would observe sacred oaths not to disclose patient information. Over the next weeks he elaborated in what at first seemed to me to be fanciful detail, but which be-

deed, I am not free to provide the details of this
planning, but it should be sufficient to say that he
seemed to be plotting in convincing detail a murder.

Over the weeks I became more anxious, and my interpretations that
this was a murder in the transference and that he was enjoying this
presentation had no seeming effect. He politely told me that, if anything, such comments helped him as he felt that I was so out of touch
with him that I was an innocent and that, when he had carried out
the murder, I could feel that I had not truly known what he was
doing, since I had always sincerely thought that it was transference.

After a while, I wondered. Possibly he really was planning to
kill this person. The more I pondered this situation, the less I
knew what to do. I decided to discuss matters with a colleague
who, in a helpful and matter of fact sort of way, simply said, 'tell
him that if he does kill this person, you most certainly will tell the
police'. She suggested that I would have to decide whether at some
point I should inform the potential victim so he could take safety.

Now, as I look back on this episode after the passage of time, it
does all seem rather extraordinary. How could I have come to
such a point of confusion? In fact I think that in this lie Jonathan
conveyed in the transference, and precipitated in the countertransference, the core of the liar's distress: some inability to distinguish between reality and phantasy. It is this psychotic quality
concealed in the omnipotence of lying that Jonathan brought into
the analysis through my countertransference, for I found I could
not distinguish between reality and phantasy.

Nonetheless, this understanding of the situation was not what
resolved the planned murder. I did tell him I would not preserve
analytic confidence if he did proceed to kill this person and, furthermore, that I would take whatever action I felt appropriate if I
thought he was proceeding to try to commit the murder.

Interestingly, it was this action on my part which converted
what might have been a psychotic action (murder) into a phantasy. For after I said what I did, the truly murderous intent and
the planning desisted. He did not reproach me for my inter-

vention as I thought he might, nor did he swear that he would not speak 'the truth' to me again.

THE TRUE AND FALSE SELF

Each liar obviously feels that the lie is essential for his self-protection. He elaborates fictions which he chooses to relate to as if they were real, and he brings along the other as an unknowing accomplice in the life of the lie. Some liars' lies are acts of omission, they leave out the truth. These persons live in a space like that of the negative hallucination, they choose not to see or narrate that which they know is true. In both types of lying, however, the liar uses deception to compensate for a severe lack in self formation. Jonathan's lying is so elaborate that it becomes a second skin, made up of the matrices of phantasy: the lie becomes a function of the false self.

We could not reply to the question: 'Who is the real Jonathan? Where is he to be found amongst his many versions of the self?' Jonathan has told me many times that all he has to lose is the inconsequential other. He says that the loss of such a person is meaningless to him. Though I believe this to be only a partial truth, what he emphasizes by means of such hyperbolization of feeling is his need to forget the other in order to live with his imagined objects. By living amongst false objects, generated by that aspect of himself that functions as a false self, he avoids violation of his true self. He cannot specify in phantasy how he believes he could lose his true self, and he says that the fact that he cannot justify this conviction is the only objective sign he knows of his madness. But he can point to the very real fact that every time he is close to being understood by someone (and this includes his own self understanding) he develops an acute sense of an imminent catastrophe.

Such a sensation is an unconsciously derived transference recreation of that madness and catastrophe that was present in reality yet completely unidentifiable at the time. This sensation constitutes the 'unthought known' (see below, chapter 15). It is in order to prevent this unphantasizable catastrophe from cohering into realization that the liar lies. On the one hand, he disappears from the scene of truth, just like the liar who omits it and destroys

that bit of himself in relation to the omitted truth
in order to avoid that trauma to the self linked
with the notion of expressing the truth in reality.
On the other, he spins out elaborate lies in order
to create a world totally different from the actual
world.

I believe we are mistaken if we regard the lie only as an act of secrecy. To be sure, every liar does have a secret – he knows the truth, and he knows the other is kept from it. Although this omnipotent relation to the truth may occasion some of the liar's lies, it is compensatory and not primary. Yes, the sense of secrecy derived from lying may sponsor sadistic impulses and cruel manipulations of the other. It may be accompanied by a slightly manic gleefulness. It may be encrusted in paranoid gloating (that the other has been fooled). These feelings and actions are ideational and affective compensations for the absence of an evolved sense of self and defend the liar against profound confusion about his safety and about the reliability and stability of the object world.

Implicit in the liar's lying is an assumption: the true self is unacceptable. Because inner reality is unacceptable, something that appears to be real but is not must take its place. Of course for the liar this is the lie, and lying constitutes a function of that false self that is hiding and protecting a true self. Jonathan believes, for example, that neither of his parents could possibly survive his true feelings. He is quite convinced of this. Is such a feeling a projective identification of compensatory omnipotence, or a mask disguising a sense of impotence, and reflecting his envy of the other's potency? I think neither. It is an axiom of his existence that his parents could not bear to hear his truth spoken to them. This conviction is not the derivative of an instinct, nor is it an anxiety sponsored by an instinct, but represents a belief that was a fact in his infantile life. It was a fact that neither parent, for different reasons, could identify with their child's needs. They could not deal with that guilt in themselves that might arise if they identified with the child's needs and recognized their callous disregard of his psychic, somatic and existential requirements. Caretaking of this sort is itself psychopathic, as the parents must escape their own inner realities in order to avoid psychic pain.

The essence of the psychopathic liar's madness, then, is implicit in his reflex-like avoidance of truthtelling, a diversion of the self and its others from speaking the truth because its articulation is equated with some unidentifiable personal annihilation. The liar's madness is made explicit, albeit unknowingly, in that traumatic moment when the other discovers that the world represented to him by the liar is not real. In that moment of madness, the other lives through the liar's deeply dissociated memory of being in the care of his traumatizing primary objects. To be with the mother, in reality, was to experience an intense overdose of a presence not sustained long enough for it to evolve transformationally into a shared reality, and equally devastating absences that retrospectively conferred upon the mother's objective reality a quality of hallucinatory ephemerality.

11 *The psychoanalyst and the hysteric*

IN a psychoanalysis each patient appropriates the analyst and subjects him to an idiom of object usage. If I am with an obsessional analysand, I may feel a sense of seemingly unresolvable frustration and irritation as a result of being the object of such a person's aseptic relating. With a manic patient I may feel frightened by the murderous quality of the patient's grandiosity. The borderline analysand's chaotic internal world may well preserve in me a prolonged sense of confusion and disorientation, while the narcissistic patient lulls me into the grip of the sleepmaker as I fight his obtuseness to remain alert.

It is an essential feature of clinical work for the analyst to reflect on his experience as the patient's object. Many psychoanalysts believe it is useful to employ the countertransference towards a reconstruction of the patient's early infantile object world. I might discover, for example, that the obsessional's sterile self narration is his transfer of a robotic maternal introject, a mental structure partly derived from lifeless parenting, and my position as the object of this transference may be similar to the patient's experience of the mother. In the grip of **an element** of this analysand's mother, my task is to inform the patient that I **am where he was**. I may discover that my countertransference with the manic patient re-enacts that person's registration of moments in his early life when he was cast off by a mother who could recuperate herself from depressions only by engaging in activities that enhanced her now depleted narcissism and led her to denigrate mothering and the mothered. My countertransference mood, in particular my fright and paralytic inability to believe I can communicate with a person so utterly transcendent and totally dismissive of me, may well re-present part of my patient's original experience with his disappearing and dismissive mother.

SO-G*

My struggles both to survive this patient's imprisonment of me in his history and to speak to his primary objects inevitably involve me in an alliance with the analysand's true self. Clinical work with borderline patients has taught me that my countertransference (here confusion and an inability to find a stable object in my patient) often re-creates the ambience of the parenting environment.

As we know, few patients enjoy the possession of an analyst quite like the hysteric. Freud experienced and registered the hysteric's theatre, in which the analyst is confronted with many others, and he also noted that she communicated through a forceful language of imagery which did not lead her towards reflection. Masud Khan (1975) has written that one aspect of hysterical enactment is the need to compel the other into becoming a witness-accomplice, a form of triangulation in which the hysteric compels the analyst to observe her introjects by means of a kind of performance art.

Why does the hysterical analysand so frequently dissolve herself into an event? What effect does this have upon the analyst? How can the analyst's countertransference both illuminate the nature of such a captivity in the comedic, and convert the force of dramaturgy into analytic reflection?

A DISCOURSE OF SENSES

Elegant, well-dressed, intelligent and informed rather than educated, Jane lives alone in a rather dingy flat and is quite restlessly depressed. When she first told me about herself, she did so with considerable dramatic flair, and the sessions were characterized by her vivid descriptions of what she had been doing in her life. I always felt a little uneasy when she suggested in her stories that she was capable of suddenly violent scenes designed to coerce someone into capitulating to her needs. I wondered when it would be my turn to be the object of such ferocity, and this led me to feel a private dread of her. She would often recount a day's event – one which was quite distressing and moved her to tears – and when she was collected, she would look at me coyly, laugh and bite her lip. She used analytic interpretation readily but with

such energy that I could sense her need to grasp it
before she flew into a rage over its meaning. After
the first few months she became despondent and,
although she used analytic insight intellectually,
she gave me warning that she was not happy with
the way things were turning out.

Neither was I. I became distressed by the self observation that
although I was easily moved by her narratives, I was reluctant to
take her seriously. I found it impossible not to laugh now and then
at her comedian-like representations, for I found her narration
of certain life episodes infectiously funny. Several times she
nearly moved me to tears with acutely sad tales about unfortunate moments in her life history. I became aware that she was
affecting me but not in any lasting way, since my laughter, or my
near-tearfulness, was so immediately evoked by her that I never
felt I was actually taking in what she was talking about.

I became increasingly aware that I found her attractive and,
as she is a sensually appealing person, I knew I was looking forward to seeing her for that sake alone. At times she could make me
quite angry, particularly when she would scream at me and de-
nounce me for not understanding her. I am sure that when she
said this I was cross with myself because I knew in some way that
she was absolutely correct. I was not understanding her, even
though now and then I assuaged my guilt by telling myself that I
was functioning analytically and, in any event, I could not proceed any more advantageously than I had. Now, since I was in the
grip of this patient's transference, in what ways did she possess
me?

Sensationally.

Jane communicated through the senses. She was attractive
and knew it. Her body-gesture syntax led me to view her as a spec-
tacle, luring me away from a thoughtful consideration of her
internal life. On occasion, I was less inclined to listen to the content of what she was saying than to be snared by the musicality of
her vocal delivery.

She possessed a remarkable comic presence, and sometimes I
could barely refrain from laughing at her stories. On occasion I
was touched by her utter destitution, and now and then I felt

tearful. She could suddenly alter her moods and would often accompany such changes with a different body ambience in the session, the total effect of which was to shock or alarm me.

It is important to stress how the hysteric communicates through the **senses**, particularly if we understand the specific intersubjective communication available in the clinical situation through the transference and countertransference. What are these senses?

We see her. Visually vivid, she punctuates her narrative with body gesture. At times her image competes with her narrative as if to split the other: do I attend to what she is saying, or do I witness her as a self-contained event?

The body is aroused.

We hear her. Whether the hysteric begins with a whisper compelling us to move closer to listen very intently or whether she moves into operatic speeches, shrieking so that seemingly half the world can hear her, it is very clear that one form of the impregnation of meaning will indeed be via the ear, as the hysteric enters us with a kind of acoustic acuity that is at times remarkable.

The body receives.

We laugh with her. Although such moments may be short-lived, the comedian-like element in this person brings the analyst to laughter – more often than not as a discharge in affect of the very sensation that is presented to the analyst through the hysteric's transference. As she transfers excitement and confusion via her eventfulness, the analyst discharges it in the laugh.

The body shakes.

We are angry with her. Too much is too much. Often her misbehaviour is so irksome, or her sudden shifts of mood so irritating, that whether we express our anger or not, we are in fact quite angry.

The body trembles.

We are moved to tears. Almost, if not quite. But the hysteric can bring us into sudden, Hollywood-type tearfulness, as she narrates pathetic episodes from her life. Indeed, her true helplessness, and the fated way in which she loses people, jobs and her own self regard is deeply moving.

The body aches.

But seeing is not knowing and hearing is not understanding. It is as if the sensational discourse undermines true communication, and indeed as if the language of the body is a substitute for mental representation and thinking.

THE MOTHER

I was aware of dreading Jane's intense need, and this recognition led me to realize that I wished to be rid of her. Her grip, therefore, was essential, for I was unconsciously refusing her admission to my internal world. How had this happened?

As though she had some foreboding of my potential mood, she told me about her mother. It became clear that her mother was an enormously self-preoccupied woman, desperate to achieve an ever-elusive social recognition, wedded to a material view of reality and therefore inclined to be interested primarily in those aspects of her daughter that would appear respectable. Jane recalls that she felt connected to her mother only when she was in states of acute distress, sobbing or very angry, or when she decided to entertain and amuse her mother. Otherwise, her mother was never really interested in what she felt or had to say, and she can recall her mother frequently walking away from her just as she was about to describe how she was feeling.

In her transference to me, she was re-creating aspects of this relation. As a child, she procured mother's attention by giving voice to her senses: she lured the mother to her by being spectacular, or she burrowed into her mother's mind by acoustically forced entry. One aspect of my countertransference was my representation of the transferred maternal introject, as I had become unwilling to be moved beyond the sensational to the cognitive and reflective. That is, I was in the grip of a person whose prevailing assumption – that I could only be related to through coercion – nearly realized itself, since I was forced into being the mother's outline.

By transforming sense-communication into language, however, and by thinking and reflecting within the texture of the transference relationship about what Jane was doing, I was introducing for potential use by my patient an ego function that derived from my continuous transformation of sense and affect into sentiently reflective thought. As I have said in chapter 1, it is my view that one of the mother's crucial functions is her role as the infant-child's transformational object. Each mother transforms the infant's syntax of sense and gesture into language, for she continuously comments on her baby in the baby's presence. As she comments on the baby's gesture, she also frequently alters the baby's environment in his favour, thus linking language with actual transformation of the environment. This provides the infant with a natural passage into speech, since speaking becomes associated with the transformation of the self and is partial compensation for the narcissistic losses implicit in the necessity to speak to the other about the self. It is unlikely that Jane's mother functioned as a good-enough transformational object. I think she was left as an infant to employ only very crude effects on the other, so that although she acquired language, words were used more for their effective coercion of the other – almost as sensory hold – than for communication as we ordinarily think of it.

Hysterics, therefore, do not believe in using language for the reciprocal exchange of feeling and meaning because the mother did not give the hysteric a continuous experience of finding through language adequate transformation of unintegrated affective and instinctual states.

THE AIMS OF EXTERNALIZATION

It is my view that one of the reasons why the hysteric becomes an event for our witnessing is the need to compensate for her mother's inability to internalize her. She must place her internal world outside herself through theatrical representation of feelings and thoughts in order to be recognized by the mother. Hysterical patients believe that the only way they will ever be known by anyone is if they can compel the other to witness them because of their unconscious conviction – based on cumulative experiences of the mother – that no one thinks about them. If

we realize that the hysteric's externalization of
psychic states occurs because of her adaptation
to the mother's failure to internalize her child,
then I think it becomes clearer to us why hysterical patients bring with them an urgent need to
become an event in our presence so that it is exceedingly difficult
to forget them. We are witnessing the infant's desperate effort to
implant an image of himself or herself inside the refusing mother.
Such people seem almost wholly concerned to grip the analyst in
order to create an unforgettable vision, and such an aim takes
priority over thinking, reflecting and understanding.

The hysteric's mother may often be a powerful woman whose
effect upon the child is more sensational than it is thoughtful.
Jane's mother taught Jane the language of hysteria, in that she
kept her children off guard by her unreliable yet vivid moods and
actions. She would move from a dark depression to a burst of
active involvement in life; she would linger thoughtfully for a moment with one of the children and then suddenly disappear without any idea of having abandoned her child; she would scrutinize
the children and with dramatic flair but little understanding – so
far as the children could make out – deliver some pithy comment
on their appearance or their personality. These children knew
this woman in many ways, but not the least was the way in which
the mother got inside the children through 'stirring them up'.

Whether the hysteric's mother was traumatizing by intruding
sensationally upon the child or whether the child exploited senses
to gain the parents' attention, the adult hysteric's innervation of
her senses can be seen as an act of freedom. At least it is her way of
refusing either to be stirred up or to stir herself up, and, as the
sensational discourse has always been at her expense, her attack
on the senses and the body becomes a means to force thoughtfulness. As if she must try to compel someone into a talking cure.

One of the unanswered questions for the hysteric in a session
is: 'Who is going to be stirred up here? You [analyst] or me
[patient]?' Will she move herself into an event, exploiting her
feelings and intelligence, or will she scrutinize the analyst, pum-
mel him with questions, shriek at him, and transfer her distress

and confusion into him: often, as Khan has suggested, to watch the analyst struggle?

THE ANALYST'S CONVERSION HYSTERIA

I have said that in the countertransference I was unconsciously endowed with elements of this patient's mother, an introject now in me as an ego-alien phenomenon transferred by my patient. The other side of the countertransference – that part of me compelled to become a bit of the patient's infant self – emerged through a subtle but persistent fear of my patient. I never knew what Jane would do, and yet, viewed rationally, I am sure that I had nothing to fear. My fear was an element of something being relived by my patient and me, some crucial feature of my patient's infantile self-and-object world. I understood this fear to be my paralysis in the face of an object to whom I could not relate through understanding and who moved so quickly and bewilderingly in the session that I was suffering from a form of trauma.

When reflecting on how we become possessed by our patients, on how they grip us, it is well to recognize the fact that although we provide the setting for the patient, it is the analyst who becomes the patient's object, not the other way round. Each patient handles us differently as the object of their transference. I gradually understood that my experience with Jane must certainly have partly re-created elements of her relation to her mother. In these moments, I think the patient handles us in the way that she unconsciously recalls being handled by her own primary objects, so my fear and confusion re-created Jane's fright with her unpredictable and dismissive mother.

Hysterical conversion still exists. The primary difference is that in the past the hysteric converted psychic content into a numbed object that was a part of her body, whereas now it is the analyst who suffers the effect of hysterical conversion. It is as if my mind (my capacity to be empathically analytic) were numbed by my analysand, and as if I (the analyst who should be intently devoted to understanding his patient) were oddly indifferent to the presence of pain in the patient.

This conversion is achieved when the hysteric embodies a

specific affect or thought in a representationally
grotesque manner, compelling me in the countertransference to become numb in that potential
space where I ordinarily receive and reflect on
the nature of a patient's thoughts and feelings.

For example, Jane began a session telling me of a sad event with
her boyfriend. She had arranged to meet him at an ice-skating
rink with two other couples. She had only met the couples recently but had taken quite a liking to them. Her boyfriend was
traditionally wary of her friends as he came from a different
social class than she did, and on this occasion she had taken great
pains to assuage his anxieties. Telling me in great detail about
how the events unfolded, she informs me that when the boyfriend
turned up at the rink, he became suddenly offensive towards her
for no apparent reason and stomped off into the distance, leaving
her feeling humiliated and bewildered. At this moment in her
story I felt very sorry for her, but she began to scrutinize me with
increasingly irritated expectancy, ultimately demanding from me
some kind of positive verdict on her performance: 'Well, how do
you feel about what I have just told you?' Instead of feeling in
touch with that anguish that is quite genuinely contained within
the story, I feel attacked and certain empathic areas of myself
close off as I become more vigilant and gear up for the now familiar assault. I am also aware of a nagging feeling of increased irritation with her, a sustained sense that is punctuated now and then
with quite intense hate. On reflection, I think I hid from my own
affect by hiding within the psychoanalytic silence.

As I understood it, Jane could not contemplate her genuine
hate towards her boyfriend. She reports the trauma and begins to
hate me. A conversion takes place inside me, as I experience a
kind of psychosomatic numbness after a slight registration of hate
towards her. Having re-presented the original scene of that
nascent affect (hate) which she cannot contemplate, she places me
before a traumatizing and hateful object (herself) that not only
elicits my hate but also forecloses empathic receptivity to her
genuine sadness, and I am aware of numb feelings. In a way, Jane
becomes the image of the grotesque, giving location and time to
that element in her boyfriend that traumatized her, while I am

situated, as was Jane, before the object of her now repressed rage. I become the ice-rink.

That which is repressed in Jane is now in me, although it has been converted from the cognitively held to the somatically enervated, as I am more aware of feeling numb than I am of hating my patient. **If the repressed is to return it must come from me, for in the hysteric's conversion states the return of the repressed emerges from the psychoanalyst's countertransference.** In my example, I had to struggle to make my affect repeatedly known to myself, thus undoing my internal numbness. Naturally, amongst other things, this involved dealing with my sense of guilt over feeling this way, but in a short time I was able to speak up for her converted affect and her murderous feelings towards her boyfriend.

Jane has another, more common effect upon me, and that is that frequently I go blank. Recounting again in great detail, and delivering with passionate dramatic presence, the events of her life, she looks at me with searching eyes towards the conclusion of her presentation, and suddenly I am puzzled by losing my train of thought. I had been listening with the third ear so to speak, but suddenly I am deaf. Bearing in mind that her sensational theatre does prevent thoughtfulness and is biased more towards the direct effect of instinctual derivatives upon the object, it seems to me that such sudden loss of cognition on my part is again due to a conversion in the countertransference. It inevitably occurs at that moment when sensational dramaturgy is to be supplanted by reflectiveness. At that moment I cannot think. And as I draw a blank at what seems to be a crucial moment, my patient becomes increasingly agitated. Whatever has been recounted in her story up to this point as tragic fate will now be given grotesque form. If, for example, Jane has felt a loss of confidence in her work life and during the previous week she has made a deliberate effort to develop a new sense of worth, at some point in the session she will shriek at me: 'Do you understand what I have been telling you? Do you know what an ordeal the last few days have been?' At this moment I find it exceedingly difficult to think, and I feel quite blank.

I am persuaded, then, that the hysteric still converts the libid-

inal to the somatically enervated, and that the
conversion takes place in the transference-
countertransference transactions so that the
analyst's countertransference (a complex registration of the psychical and the somatic) is the

location of the enervated. I am by now well aware of precisely how
I am affected in Jane's presence. I am also well aware of the
necessity to return that which is repressed to myself first, since
the return of the repressed must first occur in the form of a self
analysis taking place within me rather than through an analysis
of Jane's free associations. (I will deal later, in chapter 13, with
the process of self analysis.)

When the hysteric represents her state of mind through a dramatic use of self (first a sympathetic figure, then an anguished
person, finally an enraged presence), she conveys to the analyst a
particular impression: that of a **wretched self**. This is the representation of a person who seems **afflicted** by the incompat-
ability of the different parts of the self. In showing the analyst this
wretched picture she notifies him of her belief that to surrender to
feelings is to become mad. At this very moment the analyst may be
struggling with his own potential madness, sponsored by the
patient, so the analyst's enervation (a self state the hysteric also
uses) functions as a defence against madness. I believe that this
enervated position is that **stance** taken by the child of the hysterical mother, a child who freezes her self state to protect herself
from the contagious confusion of the mad mother.

Indeed, this contemporary form of conversion more accurately represents the hysteric's early infantile object world, in
that two objects relieve the conversion process instead of just one
person (as when the hysteric was compelled to use her own body
as the other), and this allows the analyst to come into contact
through his self analysis with the hysteric's primary objects. Hysteria is the creation of at least two persons – originally mother and
child[7] – and what was previously presented in hysterical symptomatology as a neurotic creation, the afflictions of one person,
now becomes the illness of two persons in the analytical situation.

12 *Expressive uses of the countertransference: notes to the patient from oneself*

LIKE many clinicians these days I believe that for differing reasons and in varied ways analysands re-create their infantile life in the transference in such a determined and unconsciously accomplished way that the analyst is compelled to relive elements of this infantile history through his countertransference, his internal response to the analysand. Patients may enact fragments of a parent, inviting us unconsciously to learn through experience how it felt to be the child of such a parent and, ironically, they may almost violently exaggerate the child they had been in the transference, tentatively looking to see if we become the mad parent.

In this chapter I will not focus, however, on how we organize our countertransference experience into object-relational and genetic perspectives. I believe we are almost too eager to translate our experience into analytic frames of reference. Indeed, if what we refer to by the concept of countertransference is not to lose its integrity, then we must acknowledge more frankly that in the midst of countertransference experiencing the analyst may for a very long time indeed exist in an unknowable region. To be sure, he may know that he is being cumulatively coerced by the patient's transference towards some interpersonal environment, but analyses rarely proceed with such clarity that the clinician knows in **statu nascendi** what and whom he is meant to become. That his internal life is the object of the analysand's intersubjective claim is known, however, to analyst and patient alike. Disturbed patients, or analysands in very distressed states of mind, know they are disturbing the analyst. Indeed it is as if they need to place their stress in the analyst.

I think it is crucial that the clinician should find a way to make his subjective states of mind available to the patient and to him-

self as objects of the analysis even when he does
not yet know what these states mean. I also believe that on rare but significant occasions the
analyst may analyse his experience as the object
of the patient's transference in the presence of
the patient (Tauber, 1954; Little, 1981; Ehrenberg, 1984; Coltart, 1986; Symington, 1983).

COUNTERTRANSFERENCE READINESS
Alongside the analyst's 'freely and evenly hovering attention
which enables the analyst to listen simultaneously on many
levels,' writes Paula Heimann, 'he needs a freely roused emotional sensibility so as to perceive and follow closely his patient's
emotional movements and unconscious phantasies' (1960, p. 10).
If the analyst regards the emergence within himself of feelings,
phantasies, passingly inappropriate and withheld interpretations, and inarticulate senses about the patient, as disturbing his evenly hovering attention or upsetting his neutrality, then,
from Heimann's point of view, the analyst ironically would terminate an analytic relation to the patient's unconscious life. No
less a person than the founder of psychoanalysis said that the
analyst 'must turn his own unconscious like a receptive organ
towards the transmitting unconscious of the patient' (Freud,
1912, p. 115).

The psychoanalyst's establishment of mental neutrality is
akin, in my view, to the creation of an internal potential space
(Winnicott, 1974), that functions as a frame (Milner, 1952)
through which the patient can live an infantile life anew without
the troublesome impingement of the clinician's judgements. The
psychoanalyst's neutrality functions as a dream screen (Lewin,
1946): it is there, but only as an area within the analyst which
registers non-neutral feelings, phantasies and thoughts, just as
the dream differs from that internal screen that bears it.

By cultivating a freely-roused emotional sensibility, the analyst welcomes news from within himself that is reported through
his own intuitions, feelings, passing images, phantasies and imagined interpretive interventions. It is a feature of our present-
day understanding of the transference that the other source of

the analysand's free association is the psychoanalyst's countertransference, so much so that in
order to find the patient we must look for him
within ourselves. This process inevitably points
to the fact that there are two 'patients' within the
session and therefore two complementary sources of free association.

ANALYST AS PATIENT TO HIMSELF

It is in keeping with the spirit of psychoanalysis, as that discipline
which uses human interaction to discover the nature of the
patient's unconscious life, for the analyst to approach himself in
a session as the other patient, which he can accomplish by facilitating his own internal mental processes that complement the
patient's free associations.

By establishing a countertransference readiness I am creating
an internal space which allows for a more complete and articulate
expression of the patient's transference speech than if I were to
close down this internal space and replace it with some ideal notion of absolute mental neutrality or scientific detachment. (I explore this further in the next chapter.) Indeed, by maintaining an
internal space for the reception of the patient's transference, the
analyst is more likely to fulfil the intention of Freud's concept of
the analyst's mirror function.[8]

What the analyst feels, imagines and thinks to himself while
with the patient may at any one moment be a specific element of
the patient's projectively-identified psychic life. I prefer, however, to use Giovacchini's (1979) concept of externalization to
classify that creation of a total environment in which both patient
and analyst pursue a 'life' together.

Patients create environments. Each environment is idiomatic
and therefore unique. The analyst is invited to fulfil differing and
changing object representations in the environment, but such observations on our part are the rare moments of clarity in the
countertransference. For a very long period of time, and perhaps
it never ends, we are being taken into the patient's environmental
idiom, and for considerable stretches of time we do not know who
we are, what function we are meant to fulfil, or our fate as his

object. Neither do we always know whether what
we might call our existence is due to that which
is projected into us or whether we are having
our own idiomatic responses to life within the
patient's environment. This inevitable, ever-
present, and **necessary** uncertainty about why we feel as we do
gives to our private ongoing consideration of the countertransference a certain humility and responsibility.

The most ordinary countertransference state is a not-
knowing-yet-experiencing one. I know that I am in the process of
experiencing something, but I do not as yet know what it is, and I
may have to sustain this not knowing for a long time. I do not
mean that I am unaware of discrete affects and thoughts while
with a patient – of course, such mental life continues and is clear
up to a point. Nevertheless, I find that to see where I am, what I
am, who I am, how I am meant to function and in what psychodevelopmental time of the patient I live takes months and years to
discover. The capacity to bear and value this necessary uncertainty defines one of our most important clinical responsibilities
to the patient; and it enhances our ability to become lost inside
the patient's evolving environment, **enabling the patient to manipulate us through transference usage into object identity.** If
our own sense of identity is certain, then its loss within the clinical
space is essential to the patient's discovery of himself.

I think the analyst is more able to achieve that necessary process of drawing an identity together, which allows him to receive
and register the patient's transferences, if he can tolerate the
necessary loss of his personal sense of identity within the clinical
situation. By permitting himself to be used as an object (Winnicott, 1968), the analyst is part of a process that facilitates the
eventual cohesion of the analysand's sense of self, but in order for
this procedure to work it is my view that the analyst must maxi-
mize his countertransference readiness, listening to the patient
who is using him. Object usage can be discovered through the effect of the use. To answer the question 'how does a patient at a
preoedipal level employ us?', we must turn to the countertransference and ask of ourself, 'how do we feel used?'.

More often than not we are made use of through our affects,

through the patient generating the required feeling within us. In many ways this is precisely how a baby 'speaks' to its mother. The baby evokes a feeling-perception in the mother that either inspires some action in her on the baby's behalf or leads her to put the baby's object usage into language, engaging the infant in the journey towards verbal representation of internal psychic states. The infant element in the adult patient speaks to the analyst through that sort of object usage that is best 'seen' through the analyst's countertransference. The infant within the adult person cannot find a voice, however, unless the clinician allows the patient to affect him, and this inevitably means that the analyst must become disturbed by the patient.

If an analyst is well analysed and possesses confidence in his own ego functioning and object relatedness then I think it is more likely that he will have the necessary capacity for generative countertransference regression (see below, chapter 14) within the session. We know that the analytic space and process facilitate regressive elements in analyst as well as in patient, so each analyst working with, rather than against, the countertransference must be prepared on occasion to become situationally ill. His receptivity to the reliving of the patient's transference will inevitably mean that the patient's representation of disturbed bits of the mother, father or infant self will be experienced in the transference usage of the analyst.

Like most analysts working with quite disturbed patients, I have evolved a kind of generative split in my own analytic ego. I am receptive to varying degrees of 'madness' in myself occasioned by life in the patient's environment. In another area of myself, however, I am constantly there as an analyst, observing, assessing and holding that part of me that is necessarily ill.

In moments such as these who is the patient? In my view, much of the work of analysis will have to take place within the analyst (Feiner, 1979), since it is the analyst who, through his situational illness, is the patient in greatest need. Indeed, in order to facilitate the analysand's cure, the analyst will often have occasion to treat his own situational illness first. To be sure, in treating myself I am also attending to the patient, for my own disturbance in some way reflects the patient's transference. Thus in turning to myself as that other patient, I am cognizant that I may be analysing something of the patient's mother or father, or some aspect of the patient's mind which he finds unbearable.

THE ANALYST'S USE OF THE SUBJECTIVE

Because the analyst is the other patient, sustaining in himself some intersubjective discourse with the analysand, it is essential to find some way to put forward for analytic investigation that which is occurring in the analyst as a purely subjective and private experience. It is essential to do this because in many patients the free associative process takes place within the analyst, and the clinician must find some way to report his internal processes to link the patient with something that he has lost in himself and enable him to engage more authentically with the free associative process.

One difficulty is how to make material available to the patient when the analyst may not as yet know the unconscious meaning. Were the analyst to wait until that time when he knew what the patient was communicating to him through the transference, it might well be months before he could speak. More likely, because he restricted his interpretation to that which he knew, the unconscious meaning might be lost.

The analyst must be prepared to be subjective in selected ways in the presence of the patient in order for the patient to use his own nascent subjective states. How does one do this? To some very considerable extent it is a question of the analyst's relation to his own feelings and thoughts. I think it is quite possible to be firm and interpretively vigorous without translating the patient to himself, unless such translation is put to the patient as an idea emerging from the analyst's subjectivity, rather than from his authority. As Winnicott said (1971), the analyst needs to play with the patient, to put forth an idea as an object that exists in that potential space between the patient and the analyst, an object that is meant to be passed back and forth between the two and, if it turns out to be of use to the patient, it will be stored away as that sort of objective object that has withstood a certain scrutiny. Any examination of Winnicott's clinical case presentations reveals a person who certainly worked in a highly idiomatic way, and yet he concerns himself in his clinical theory with the unintrusive function of the analyst, with the analyst as a facilitating environment. How is it possible to be so idiomatic in one's presentation of interpretations and not be traumatic to the patient? In my view, the answer lies in the way Winnicott regarded his own thoughts: they were for him subjective objects, and he put them to the patient as objects between patient and analyst rather than as official psychoanalytic decodings of the person's unconscious life. The effect of his attitude is crucial, as his interpretations were meant to be played with – kicked around, mulled over, torn to pieces – rather than regarded as the official version of the truth.

If the psychoanalyst has a particular kind of relation to his own interpretations as possible truth-bearing objects, and so possesses a capacity to release the patient for new self experiences, then it is possible to disclose his subjective states of mind to the analysand. The aim of releasing the subjective state of mind into play is to reach the patient and provide him with a scrap of material that facilitates the cumulative elaboration of his own internal states of being.

Like many an analyst I announce the subjective factor by saying 'what occurs to me', 'I am thinking that', 'I have an idea', or something of that kind. If I know that my interpretation is going to be somewhat upsetting to a patient, I may say, 'now I don't think you are going to like what occurs to me but,' and proceed to put forth my thought, or, if that which is going on in me is significantly out of context with the manifest content of what the patient is discussing, I might say, 'this may sound quite mad to you but,' and proceed to state what I think. Inevitably, I strive to put my thoughts to the patient in such a way that he does not feel himself to be cornered or given an official version of the psychoanalytic truth.

The analyst's use of his own subjectivity, which admittedly is only part of the total interpretive picture, increases the patient's trust in the value of seemingly unsupported statements. If such

interpreting is developed by the analyst responsibly and judiciously, the analysis is enhanced
because the analyst is able to release certain
countertransference states for elaboration, and
in so doing, he makes certain split-off elements of
the patient available for knowing and analysing. Since so much of
the psychic life in the clinical setting is within the analyst, one of
our emerging technical difficulties is how either to give back to the
patient what he has lost or bring to his attention those parts of
himself that he may never have known.

SELF RELATING IN THE ANALYST
Each one of us is perpetually engaged in a complex relationship to
the self as an object (see above, chapter 3), and the analyst
demonstrates his own form of self relating in the way he perceives
and relates to his own interpretations in the presence of the
patient. For example, when in the midst of an interpretation to a
patient I may suddenly realize that I am slightly off base, and I
will stop myself and say something like 'nope, that's not it, I can't
quite find what I want to say'. If I realize that I am wrong, I will
say so and state something like, 'no, I think what I have just said,
as plausible as it is, is just not right'. I am well aware that I live
out a form of self relating in the presence of the patient, with one
part of me functioning as the source of material – like the patient
in the analysis – and another part of me functioning as the analyst. I do this because I think it is very difficult to put into words
what I believe a patient's mood to be. This open struggle to put
forth verbal articulations of one's own subjective states is an important feature of my technique, especially with the more
severely disturbed patient, for, in my view, I am gradually
putting out into that potential space between us those associations
that are moving freely within me but are occasioned by the
patient, and I am making it possible for the patient to engage
meaningfully in this struggle. Time and time again when I am
working to describe the non-verbal transference, the patient will
join in and use his or her own verbal representations to speak
elements of himself. Furthermore, of course, part of the analysand's total recognition of this process is his being found

through the analyst's registration of him, which the patient gradually values as another feature of the psychoanalytic process.

This selective and occasional verbalization of my own subjective sense of the patient's mood or intent is a vital cumulative prerequisite for that relatively rare moment when I make a direct use of the countertransference. In verbalizing my own subjective states I am, of course, making aspects of my countertransference available for mutual scrutiny within the session, and over time I enable the patient to use such interventions as important sources of material.

SENSING

The gradual non-traumatic use of my own subjectivity is an essential element in my work especially with severely disturbed patients. As I am particularly concerned to work with the emotional core of the patient in each session, it is important to be able to signify what, amidst the patient's associations, seems to announce true self activity. By true self activity I mean that which seems to work from the core of the self outward as a spontaneous gesture.

I am here referring to those sorts of feelings an analyst has in working with a patient which can be described as intuitions, or more accurately as senses. By saying to a patient, 'you know, I really don't know whether what I am going to say is true, but I have a feeling that . . .', or 'I sense you have moved away from the completion of a feeling; you seem to be saying . . .', I am endeavouring to establish a neutral vocabulary for the identification of the analysand's affects and nascent ego developments which can, in my view, only be reached if the analyst can work from intuitive sensing. I have often found that when I say to a patient that it is my sense that x is true or that he has avoided y (x and y being words that struggle to express an unknown but present state of mood or mind), such communications have proved to be important facilitators, so the patient can complete the developing feeling, thought or ego capacity which had been lost, discarded, or perhaps unappreciated by him up until that point.

It is my view that this kind of therapeutic intervention constitutes an indirect use of the countertransference. The analyst uses his relation to
himself as an object to put his own subjective
state into words, and he may very well be speak-

ing up for x (for what it means) before he knows what x is. That
is, the analyst does not consciously understand what the patient
means, but he has a sense of a meaning that is present and which
requires his support in order to find its way towards articulation
and the all-important task of analysis. Such an intervention is
obviously more suitable to those self states in a patient that may
be non-verbal or pre-verbal, and for some time the analyst may
need to 'pick up' and 'work with' his own affects and subjective
states, all the while functioning visibly as transformational object
to himself, engaged in the task of developing the unspoken for
towards meaningful and sentient verbal articulation. Obviously
in so doing, the analyst takes on the historical-existential trace of
the mother's function in relation to the infant, seeking out and
relating to the patient's unconscious gestures or infant speech.

A baby may make a sound or create a spontaneous gesture
that is mirrored and transformed by the mother's own verbalization of the phenomenon. She might say 'ooooh' or 'mmmmmm'
and her articulation is somewhere between sound as gesture itself
and symbolic communication in the adult manner. In some ways,
when the analyst speaks up for a subjective state in himself, he
does so in order to reflect an infant element in the patient and to
transform this element by putting it into some kind of speech.

By finding a way to do this with a patient, I am deeply aware
that I am now able to work with an analysand from my own sense
of conviction about what is true, rather than solely as the interpreter of unconscious themes. It is my experience that patients
benefit from the analyst's responsible and comfortable rooted-
ness in subjective experience. The assessment of that which is
true in the patient springs not inevitably from the rather over-
intellectualized cullings of unconscious themes as read by both
patient and analyst, but instead from a mutual sense of having
touched upon a detail in the session that gives both analyst and

analysand a sense of appropriate conviction that the patient's true self has been found and registered.

FROM INDIRECT TO DIRECT USE OF COUNTERTRANSFERENCE

By now it should be clear how I make an indirect use of my countertransference, by putting verbal representations of my subjective states of mind to my patient for consideration. In so doing, I establish my subjectivity as a useful and consistent source of material in the psychoanalytic situation. This constitutes an other source of freely associated material. As long as the analyst is judicious and clinically responsible, then the use of such self observations in the presence of the patient will enable the analysand to develop increased trust in the value of expressing as yet unknowable subjective states. Ultimately, of course, the aim of this indirect use of the countertransference is to facilitate the articulation of heretofore inarticulate elements of psychic life, or what I term the unthought known. Once the patient's self state is verbally represented, then it can be analysed.

By direct use of the countertransference I mean that quite rare occasion, one which may be of exceptional value to the effectiveness of the analysis, when the analyst describes his experience as the object. To be sure, there may be moments when it is difficult to distinguish between the indirect and the direct use of the countertransference, as, for example, when a patient is so persecutory or unreachable that the analyst's expressed observation of his own feeling state or state of self is somewhere in between expressing the sense of the situation and declaring how he feels as the object of the patient's transference. In such a case, communicating what the analyst senses about the patient in the session is an indirect use of the countertransference, and describing how he feels about being her object is a direct use.

Before I proceed to illustrate my thinking with clinical examples, I must stress that I am not at any point here, in relation to either an indirect or a direct use of the countertransference, referring to the clinician's thoughtless discharge of affect. As in any analytic intervention, it is exceedingly important to consider

whether the patient can use an intervention, and
this is why I place so much emphasis on the gradual presentation over time of the analyst's sense
of the situation, as a prerequisite to any direct
expression of the countertransference. Any dis-

closure on the analyst's part of how he feels must be experienced
by the patient as a legitimate and natural part of the analytic
process. If it comes as a shock, then the analyst has failed in his
technique. Finally, however much it might relieve the analyst to
describe his state of mind to a patient, such an action should
never be undertaken solely for the purpose of the analyst's self
cure. There are some patients to whom one could not ever use-
fully express one's experience as their object, and this must be
accepted.

CLINICAL EXAMPLES / I

I found myself in a curious position when Helen, a woman in her
mid-twenties, started her analysis. She would begin to describe a
situation, such as going to meet a friend, and then she would stop
her account in mid-sentence. She would pause for a long time,
often as much as several minutes, and then she would resume her
account as if there had been no interruption. Initially I focused,
as I always do with someone new to analysis with me, on how difficult it was to speak to a stranger and how hard it was to entrust
the simplest things to him. Her anxiety about being in the analytic
situation was very apparent, and this interpretation of the transference was necessary and to some degree accurate. But nevertheless, her long pauses continued, and I knew I had not fully
understood the situation. It was not due simply to initial anxiety
in the transference, of the sort: 'Who is this man, and how do I
talk to him?'.

I knew that several years earlier she had had a spell of psychotherapy with a psychoanalyst who was exceedingly interpretive.
She told me that she was accustomed to saying just a bit about
something, and the analyst would translate her fragment into a
full interpretation about some aspect of her relation to him. I
therefore considered it a possibility that she paused because she
was waiting for me to translate her through a particular type of

interpretation, and so I said I thought she was waiting for me to intervene like her previous analyst. She agreed with this, and for some time I thought that perhaps this was the crux of the matter. I rather expected her to get on with telling me about herself without such disconcerting pauses.

No such luck. Instead I found the situation quite unchanged, so I knew that this feature of her character was much deeper than I had reckoned; it was not just either a situational reaction to myself or a residual reaction to her previous analyst. As I realized this, I knew I would have to settle into this situation and accept it as the sort of environment she creates in which both she and her objects live. Increasingly I asked myself how I felt as an object of such a transference.

I knew that I felt irritated on occasions, but equally I felt there was no way in which to utilize this irritation for some kind of alteration of the environment. As it was very difficult for me to follow her line of thinking, because of the many interruptions and long pauses, I was aware of being confused by her. I found as the months passed that I would 'wander off' during these pauses, and when she would resume talking it might be a few seconds before I had returned to listen. My sense of her as a person was also changing. I was aware of thinking of her less as a person with a life to live and to tell me about than as a kind of opaque and diffuse presence. I did not think of her as helpful in the way that patients commonly assist the analyst to consider them. Instead, knowing in advance how the sessions would go, I began to feel bored and sleepy.

To be sure, I took internal measures against sleepiness in the countertransference. I thought a lot about what this might all mean within the transference-countertransference idiom, and I entertained the idea that she might be transferring to the analytic situation the nature of her mother's idiom of maternal care, and that I – the infant-object of such a care system – was an existential witness to a very strange and absent mother. I decided that the material expressive of the patient's mental life was now in me, insofar as my countertransference began to dominate the clinical situation, at least in my mind. I knew I would have to find some

way to make the material available to her.
After several months of analysis, when I thought
the patient was ready to receive an indirect expression of my countertransference, I told her
that I was aware of something taking place in me
that I thought was of interest, and I wanted to put it to her for
reflection and ultimately for analysis. I proceeded to tell her that
her long pauses left me in a curious state, one in which I sometimes lost track of her, and it seemed to me that she was creating
some kind of absence that I was meant to experience. A bit later in
the session I said to her that she seemed to disappear and reappear without announcement of either action.

The patient was immediately relieved when I spoke up for my
own subjective state. She said that she had long known about this
habit, but did not understand it herself, since it was not occasioned by anxiety, and that she would often experience a kind of
despair about being inside this habit, frequently wondering
whether there was any point in continuing to talk.

In speaking up for the situation I found myself in, I was also
aware of my own personal relief. No analyst should only interpret
in order to relieve himself of the psychic pain he may be in, but
equally neither should he be ignorant of those interpretations
that cure him of the patient's effect. In making my experience
available to the patient, I put in the clinical potential space a subjective scrap of material that was created by the patient, and by
expressing myself I gave a bit of something of Helen's self back to
her.

In the first year of her analysis, Helen was extremely secretive
about her relation to her mother, and I did not push her. I sensed
that she was protecting both her mother and herself, and on one
or two occasions during this first year I told her I felt this to be the
case, but I did not urge her to take it up. After some time, when
she was clearly ready to do so, she told me how distracted and
otherworldly her mother was, and how the mother had only been
able to relate to a small portion of her as a child, leaving Helen to
live through her childhood in secrecy and in dread of her true
self. Her mother's impingement on her true self was her absence
from relating, just as, I suppose, I experienced Helen's silences
SO-H

and absences as impingements in the clinical situation. This was not the case of a daughter hating her mother or of a mother being a hateful person. She was a kindly and loving woman who, nevertheless, absented herself from her children's lives for a number of reasons and left each of her several children severely confused.

CLINICAL EXAMPLES / II

Paul, a man in his late twenties, sought analysis because he insisted that he had never been able to feel close to anyone, and his girlfriend was distraught over his remoteness. True to his self description, he told me about himself and his life in a cold and detached way, although I found it almost a caricature of rationality, that sort of exaggeration of a phenomenon that is almost an invitation for someone to challenge its veracity. I sensed that his remote behaviour in the sessions was not true of him.

Nevertheless, he traversed the analytic terrain taking delight in questioning the intellectual validity of psychoanalysis and scoffing at my interpretations. Often he would tell me that what I had said 'might' be possible, but even if it were true, wasn't it just part of a large sociological phenomenon. He would then lecture me on the nature of the class struggle and the evolution of personal character as a feature of the dialectics of misfortune. It appeared as if his moments of joy in sessions were seized whenever he could reduce one of my interpretations to its latent intellectual assumptions, and he would chortle on about the implicit logics of my analysis: class issues, cultural assumptions, feminist or antifeminist elements, residual Americanisms, and a multitude of bourgeois interests.

I never felt, however, really insulted or cross with him. Frustrated, yes, and irritated at his investment in some kind of false relating at a manifest level: at his insistence that I see him as a cold and scientific person. In fact, I liked him. I knew, therefore, that my affection for him was a countertransference state that provided some evidence of dissociated loving feelings in him. Indeed, although he did present himself to me in the sessions in the obsessional manner – excreting, as it were, his material to be col-

lected by me into an interpretation, so he could
have the pleasure of destroying it – I knew that
some of this obsessional behaviour was a tease
and that some of his unconscious love was being
expressed through homosexual libido.

These obsessional preoccupations and homosexual feelings of
his were taken up in the analysis and occupied much of the analytic work during his first year of treatment. Both were, however,
compensatory dispositions, alternative ways of gaining satisfaction due to some kind of trauma in his early object world that did
not allow for more mature forms of love to evolve.

I knew about his more mature capacity to love from the
nature of his transference. Each analyst has an experience of living within the patient's created environment and, although Paul
often scoffed at me, tore my interpretations into shreds, and insisted he was a hopeless and monstrous person, he took great care
to present me with details of his life. Whenever I had misunderstood something he said, he sensed I had gone astray and very
sensitively helped me to restore my understanding. This would
take place even when he was ostensibly disgusted by me and dismissive of my interpretations. I 'knew', therefore, through my
experience as his object, that in part I was being well looked after,
and it was this experience that led me to realize this was an expression of his unconscious love.

There came a point in his analysis when I considered it necessary to use my sense of him as important evidence, and to do so
knowing that he would scoff at me and insist that this kind of
knowledge has no place in an analysis or in any 'serious' epistemology. Early on, I had told him: 'You want me to see you as
monstrous. Well, I don't buy it. You are a bit of a monster, but
not nearly as much as you claim.' He would take delight in making
light of such a remark, and would often extol the virtues of
rational and objective thought, but in such an unbelievable way
that on occasion I would say to him, 'yes, of course, you are a
robot, I know', challenging his version of himself in a vigorous
and humorous way.

Sometimes he would reflect on some event in the world that
had caused people great concern, one such moment being an

assassination attempt. 'I can't for the life of me understand why people get so upset about something like this,' he said to me, 'I think I have to ask people about this so I can understand. Why do you think I don't understand?' He said this in a puzzled pseudo-quizzical way, but professionally delivered with the expertise of many years' practice in appearing to have no feelings. When he asked me this 'question', I replied very simply, 'nonsense'. He laughed and asked what I meant by 'nonsense'. I said he knew very well indeed what I meant and that it was, as we were discovering, part of his false self to appear as if he did not have feelings when in fact he did. Invariably in such encounters with him, I would introduce the affective element, as I did when I said 'nonsense'. This brought him out of his false-self coolness into relatedness; he would laugh and clearly be relieved in some part of himself that I saw through his pretences. When he snickered and asked me how I knew he was talking nonsense, I never attempted to explain my statement or engage in a long-winded exchange with him. I decided instead to state that I knew somewhere from my sense of him that he was fooling himself and trying to fool others and that I was content to speak from this area of knowing, even though it was not equivalent with other ways of knowing through the production of 'evidence'.

The trauma in Paul's early object world was soon clear in his analysis. His father had been an exceedingly remote man who had never been part of the family, and it was not difficult to see how Paul's homosexual urges were erotized efforts to find a father (and also to dismiss him). His coldly obsessional false self was his unconscious reconstruction of his father's character. I therefore knew that in standing up for feelings as legitimate factors in human life, I was already in the countertransference a different parent than his father and also a different child than he was, insofar as I was intent upon speaking up for and valuing subjective states as potentially valid. This view of Paul's father and Paul's coldness is only one of several 'correct' reconstructions. It is also true that Paul is so angry with the father that he projects this cold rage 'into' the paternal introject.

There came a point in the analysis, however, when Paul

needed in my view a more direct analysis of his unconscious love. I decided that there was a nontraumatic way of speaking to him about my experience as the object of such love. In the course of one session I said to him: 'Well, you will really enjoy scoffing at this; nonetheless, I am aware of your secret capacity to love and look after someone because I am aware of the care with which you help me to understand you in these sessions, and I am aware of your affection for me, all of which I take to be manifestations of those very feelings you insist you do not possess.'

He proceeded to scoff at my remark in a rather half-hearted way, but I could tell from his response that he wanted me to continue and that he was relieved. I said, 'well you crank up the old robot you, but I think you are relieved and pleased that I know what I do about you'.

For some months he would now and then resume for a moment the robot act but I would confront him and analyse how he was dosing me with that cold father he had and how I was in the place that he occupied for so many years. I was sure that he expected me to give in, as had he, and I think that one of the reasons he kept resurrecting his identification with his father was his very real uncertainty about whether I could withstand the situation.

CLINICAL EXAMPLES / III

Joyce is an attractive woman in her middle forties who came to analysis knowing quite a lot about psychoanalytic theory, as she has friends who are psychoanalysts and has also engaged in academic research in which she uses psychoanalytic theory to develop her work. In the first weeks of her analysis I was puzzled by the fact that there was little relation between her narrated version of herself and the person whom I saw and experienced before me. She told me that she was seriously depressed and could not cope with life. She stressed that she lived in a constant confused state, and she claimed that she had no sense of self; indeed, she wondered if she had ever had a legitimate moment in her life.

Of course I have analysed people who do quite rightly make such statements, but they tend to demonstrate this fact through their behaviour in sessions. Joyce was fairly radiant. She was animated and reflective. She seemed in touch with her affects and did not experience undue anxiety in the sessions, nor did what she described as a depression seem to be depression as such; I sensed that it was more like an enveloped sadness that she had carted around with her through her life. When she talked about living in chaos, not having a sense of self, and wondering where her true self was, I was a bit suspicious. More than once I have been sought out by patients who want what they think of as a Winnicottian analysis, and such people often come with a lament collated from his theory of the true and the false self.

Joyce presented herself in the sessions as a chronicle of confusion, despair and emptiness, and during the first weeks of her analysis I listened and said little except for the occasional clarification. I was, however, immediately presented with a dilemma, since I thought that to continue to analyse her material without conveying my sense that it was strangely untrue would be to sustain a false analysis. I therefore told her that I was puzzling over something and that, bearing in mind that I was making my sense of something available only to further understanding of her and that I might well be wrong, I felt that she just did not strike me as the wrecked person that she claimed to be. She met this comment with rather intense intellectual aggression and insisted that she was every bit as useless and inept as she claimed, so my comment became a part of the seemingly irrational affective element of the session and subsequent sessions: where did it come from, and what did this comment mean?

Meanwhile my sense of her did not change. It was not only that Joyce reported professional accomplishments which in themselves refuted her notion of incompetence, but her liveliness in the session was transference evidence, from my point of view, of the presence of true self activity. When she talked about other people in her life or certain situations, she did so with humour and mental acuity and I found that I enjoyed her. Whenever she would turn her narratives to herself as an object, however, she would lower her voice and lambast herself by listing her latest failures. All of this was in the context of her

wretched climate of living with no sense of self.
For reasons of space, I shall not list all of the psy-
chodynamic considerations and possible transference explanations I thought about during these
early months of her analysis. I did know from her
that her early relation to her father had been very good and that
he had fairly worshipped her, but that when she was about six
years old he withdrew because of ill health. She receded into herself, although she devoted quite a lot of time providing her father
with psychological support. It became clear that when she had
lost him, she also lost his relation (and her own) to herself as an
ideal object. I interpreted this and analysed her presentation
to me of the so-called depressed self and absence of self as forms
of contempt: if she could not be that princess she once knew herself to be, then she would accept nothing as valuable. Indeed, to
trash all of her objects – her work, her friendships and her own
self – expressed an unconscious demand that she knew she deserved better. In many ways she confirmed this interpretation
although she did not like it, but its effectiveness was often due to
my consistent refusal to believe her assertions that she really was
a wreck.

Of course I do not make light of her difficulties. Her unconscious grandiosity, itself the memory of a relation with her early
father, is expressed by her destruction of those things that are
valuable in her life, and this creates a depressed atmosphere
which re-creates the other relation to her father, as she nurses
those objects in her life (including herself) that she has devalued.
Indeed, by presenting me with a 'schizoid' patient or one suffering from a 'basic fault' (she knew Balint's work) she was giving me
a gift, as I was meant to have my narcissism enhanced by resurrecting this wreck of a person into the possession of self and
the actualization of true self states. I was meant to be a miracle
maker, and her transference was unconsciously designed to nurse
me into meaningfulness, in effect, to restore the father and herself
to a previous golden era.

As time went on, however, I was faced with a more difficult
problem than the initial puzzles. She accepted and worked with
the interpretations about her unconscious grandiosity and

understood how this was a kind of memory. She lived through a recognition that what she termed depression was a mixture of phenomena: the destruction of her objects, an inverted expression of her anger and the location of true sadness over the loss of her father. Increasingly, however, I felt that she was living at some very considerable remove from people, including myself in the transference. This 'fact' of her character was by no means obvious. Indeed, she appeared to be quite the reverse, and the matter was further complicated by the reality of her genuine health and ego capacity. But I continued to feel uneasy about the analysis. She was absenting herself in a most subtle manner, and I could not find evidence for this in her presented material.

Fortunately she missed several sessions in one month and came late for a few others. This acting out became a turning point in her treatment, as it enabled me to reach areas of her that had previously been unknowable. When she arrived late for one session, she apologized and told me that she had been late for everyone that day, and, unfortunately, for me as well. I asked, 'you mean we are all the same?'. This comment was mildly irritating to her, as she felt I was placing undue emphasis on her passing remark. I challenged her in this manner because I was determined to reach through her health, ego capacities and object relatedness (which I had originally 'fought' to validate in the analysis) in order to find out where she was and why she was internally removed.

In the course of the session, I decided that I would have to use something of my own experience of her in order to place what I considered essential material into some space where both of us could work on it. I said: 'You know, I want to put forth for mutual analysis a feeling I have, because I think it is essential to do so in order to find you. I have this sense that you are only partly here in this analysis and that you have resigned yourself to a failed therapy, even though it will have appeared on the surface to have been meaningful.' At this point she launched into vehement protest. 'Look,' she said, 'I make everyone feel this way. There is no reason why you should take it that way, that is personally.' I answered: 'Perhaps what I have said has made you feel guilty which was not my intention, and now you are working to relieve me of what you regard as my distress, but in fact I feel that in putting it to you as I have done I am at least getting to grips with something that ails you.' She said, 'well I am like that with everyone', and stressed this several times. I went on: 'Oddly enough, when you say that, I am aware of realizing where my feeling comes from; as long as all of your experiences are democratic ones, no one person would appear to have any individual significance.'

I was encouraged in making this later interpretation by her vehement protest to my first intervention. The protest was more an animated and provocative plea for me to take the issue up and follow it through; it was not that sort of irateness that constituted true despair over a misunderstanding on my part. Indeed, we were very much in the midst of a struggle, and the reader may not be so terribly surprised to discover that she was concealing a loving transference neurosis. In the months to come, she managed to fall in love and to speak from the painful position of such need and internally private intimacy. In the many months it took to work through the infantile components of this transference neurosis, she repeated on several occasions that she had never originally believed that analysis could really help her but that my refusal to accept her original accounts of herself as a desperately ill person had given her hope that perhaps she might be found after all. She regarded the firm yet non-traumatic way I asserted my sense of conviction about her as the most important factor in her eventually entrusting me with her love and with those loving memories of her father.

CLINICAL EXAMPLES / IV

It is utterly impossible to describe the course of George's analysis in the space I have allocated here, and I shall only say that he is an Irish manic depressive psychotic, who has had several hospitalizations for his illness, and who can be both terrified and terrifying at the same time. In his middle twenties, more than six feet four inches, he is something of a frightening character when he becomes enraged in the consulting room, particularly as he

SO-H*

dresses entirely in black. Over the years, however, I have managed to find a way to live inside
the environment he creates, and I have done so
by analysing him even when he threatened to
murder me if I didn't shut up. As time went on,
what had been violence in him transmuted into a more libidinally
aggressive situation, as I would stand up for myself when he told
me he would kill me. On one such occasion, when he instructed me
to shut up or he would have to shut me up, I said, 'look George,
killing me would be redundant, as you spend most of these
sessions insisting to yourself that I am not really here anyway'. I
delivered such comments with vigour and firmness but not hos-
tility, and over time he gradually began to need this kind of response from me in order to engage me aggressively, a process that
continued for years and that mitigated his violent thoughts and
his terror of actually encountering someone.

The issue I shall take up here, however, arose after some three
years of analysis. Of course I had had many occasions to analyse
his grandiosity, his omnipotence and his utilization of saint-like
innocence (denial), and to his credit he was able to survive analysis and make increasing use of it. There was one characteristic of
his transference, however, which did not budge, even though I
had brought it to his attention one way or another in every
session. This was his tendency to tell me something about himself
(let's say some observation of an action on the previous day) and
the moment I took it up with him, perhaps to interpret it, perhaps
simply to clarify it, he would always change his original version.
The degree of change varied. Sometimes he would simply correct
my syntax as I might have put it just a bit differently than he did.
Other times he might edit out adjectives and take out the essential
element of his remarks. On more unfortunate days (for me) he
would deny having said anything at all. My interpretations of this
also varied according to his ability to use understanding on any
one occasion, but I stressed his anxiety, his need to control the
situation and his despair that I did not live inside him, so that
having to tell me something about himself was very distressing,
for it implied my separateness. I won't comment further on
the differing interpretations, only that after some three years

of analysis he continued to do the same thing.
Then one week he was a shade different. On the
Monday he was able to bear my analysing something without changing the details, and I noticed
that the material he reported was more specific
and less of the abstract kind of lecture on himself he was prone to
furnish as a way of preserving his secrecy. On Tuesday I discovered that he remembered what I had said on the Monday and
indeed seemed to be making some analytical use of it, so I found
myself shifting a bit inside, as I knew that I was feeling that just
possibly he was changing. On Wednesday he completely re-edited
Monday's material, wiped out our Tuesday session and eradi-
cated the sense I had had that we were possibly beginning to work
together. I recall that for some fifteen minutes into the session I
was saying to myself: 'Oh what's the use? The son of a bitch is
hopeless. You can't do a thing. Just let him rattle on for the whole
goddamn session and don't bother to find a way through to him.'
My response shocked and bothered me, for, although I had often
felt futile and very angry with him, I had never reached this
point. In my countertransference I was clearly feeling some
rather dreadful loss.

I decided against proceeding along my ordinary analytic line
of interpreting and communicating what he was doing and why I
thought he was doing it. In my view this would have amounted to a
kind of collateral dissociation through analysis, with me simply
providing a process description of what he was doing, amounting
to a kind of musical score. Instead I knew that I must get through
to him and that I had to find some way to reach him, as otherwise,
despite his being an analytically interesting person, I thought he
would be one of those unfortunate sort of people who spend a lifetime in analysis but are no different for it.

I therefore opted to try to describe the position I found myself
in, and I am quite sure that the very way in which I began to speak
somehow drew his attention far more acutely than any of my previous interpretations, since I was clearly struggling to break
through to something in myself as well. I said, 'George. Stop talking for a minute. I want to say something to you. I am aware of
feeling utterly hopeless, and I have been wondering if it is at all

possible to get through to you.' He went very still on the couch. 'Let me tell you of my experience and, if you can bear it, I think that it might possibly help us to understand this situation a bit better.' As much as what I had said up to this point was effective, I think it was my tone of voice, which I find impossible to describe in retrospect, that reached him, and he seemed to relax. 'My experience is that just when I think I have understood you and when we have established a mutual recognition of something about you, you disappear.' He heaved a great sigh of relief on the couch and said 'yes' so very quietly that I didn't realize he had said anything at that moment until after the session was over. I waited a moment, trying to collect my thoughts together and aiming to put them in a manner which he could use, and then I said: 'You tell me something about yourself, I am just in the process of digesting it and storing it for further understanding of you, and then along you come – wham! – and tell me what I have digested and stored inside me did not come from you at all. The problem I find is how to live with this despair occasioned by your disappearances.' There was a pause of a few minutes, and George seemed very deeply relaxed. I felt an enormous relief in myself, as if at long last I had been able to speak the truth, to stand up against something, and yet at the same time I felt that I had also stood up for George as well.

By way of parenthesis, I should say that by this point in the analysis I of course knew a great deal about his early childhood. As an infant he had been separated from his mother on several occasions and she left him in the care of a series of people – not nannies – while she went off to work. She had to leave him not because she hated him, but because she was depressed and could find narcissistic replenishment only in her work as a volunteer. George had never established a relation to his father, who was kindly but remote and who disliked the role of father. George was sent to boarding school in Europe and that was, in effect, the last the family had to do with him.

After several minutes' pause in the session reported above, I decided that such a direct use of my countertransference had to be used analytically, so I told him that I thought that my own

experience was like that of an infant in relation to
a mother; suffering this disappearance was, in
my view, exactly the position that he must have
been in during the first years of his life. Now you
see mother and begin to internalize her, and now

you don't see her, but a new mother cropping up each time. I said
that the analyst was to some extent dependent on the patient, and
in this sense, his position could at times be like that of an infant
dependent on the analysand for 'feeding' or 'playing', and that
my sense of hopelessness and futility must reflect his own infant
self confronted by someone who would, it seems, have nothing to
do with him.

I was quite aware that the analytical comment was somewhat
intellectualized and that it was explanatory, but I was quite content that it should be so, as the patient had just received a direct
countertransference comment from me. I thought he needed some
kind of frame into which he could place countertransference interpretation.

It became clear from the follow-up sessions that George had
always known about the position in which I was meant to live a life
with him. My previous analysis of his anxiety and his defences
against anxiety, although correct, had never reached the core of
the issue, and later he told me that he despaired that I would ever
speak up for myself. When I did, this did not burden him with a
sense of guilt. Quite the opposite, since the fact that I had not
personally resisted his created environment had left him feeling
doomed and monstrous.

CLINICAL EXAMPLES / V

Jane is the sort of patient that clinicians often term a 'malignant
hysteric'. Over the years this East-European woman in her late
forties had managed to perfect a technique of exploiting all of
her nascent affects into strategic devices to coerce others into
some form of submission. If, for example, her boyfriend had
been unkind to her and she had felt quite legitimately hurt,
she would sense that such a position put her at an advantage
with him. She would then hyperbolize her pain into pseudo-
dementia compelling the boyfriend into a depersonalized sol-

icitousness. If she felt guilty in a session about something that she had done to someone, and if I clarified with her her sense of guilt, she would raise her voice and berate herself with incredible emotional violence, knowing that she now had a true affect around which to cohere a moment's personality.

I have written about some features of my countertransference with Jane (see above, chapter 11), particularly my awareness that early on in her therapy I tended just to look at her rather than listen to her. She sits across from me in psychotherapy, and I noticed that it was her gestural and visual presence that I was drawn towards, a phenomenon enhanced by the fact that she is strikingly beautiful. In considering this countertransference phenomenon, I gradually realized that, as is true with many hysterics, she did not believe that the other would internalize her (that is, think about and consider her), so she needed to affect the other in different ways. As time went on, however, I was also aware that my pleasure in the sight of her was a defence against her emotional life which I found quite paralysing. Indeed, such was the intensity of her representation of mad scenes in the consulting room that I became remote and tried to steer clear of the intensity of her transference. I became aware, that is, of the numbing of my self states while I was in her presence, a phenomenon common in clinicians who work with very hysterical patients. With the contemporary hysteric it is not her body and self that is innervated but the analyst who is innervated in his countertransference.

Often her actions in any one session were so unpredictable, her moods so varying, that I never had a sense of where she was. Once she leapt out of her chair and flung herself towards my window while at the same time turning herself around to face me, shrieking out: 'What is that nice little yellow flower out there in the patio. It is so dear and sweet. And it's so nice that you take care of flowers like that. Life is wonderful, don't you think? The birds, the flowers, the trees.' At these moments she was the personification of an unbelievably scatty woman, and when she suddenly screamed something out, she would fre-

quently get people in the surrounding area to
be concerned about what was happening.

Such was her expertise at distressing people
that I gather that her previous therapist was
greatly relieved when Jane left the analysis, and
the highly skilled and experienced psychiatrist who provides
me with medical cover telephoned me immediately after seeing
her, informing me she was not at all sure that she could provide
psychiatric cover since she found her extremely upsetting.

For quite some time I was interpretively firm. I would concentrate on how she felt she could only communicate with
someone if she could coerce him. Whenever she was attempting
this with me (which was almost constantly), I would calmly inform her of what I thought she was doing. Although this did
settle her a little, and eventually became the bread and butter
of our work, I was nonetheless aware that personally I found
her traumatizing and that I had withdrawn from my more ordinary analytical self, hiding somewhat behind a classical stance.
I would often privately regret having her as a patient and would
think of a way to get rid of her: maybe she would move away or
become disillusioned with me and want to go to someone else;
or, if I was lucky, she would have a real breakdown, and the
hospital would take her off my hands. I thought I would have to
tell her that unfortunately I was unable to continue with her,
that private practice has its limits, and so forth. I knew, however, that these feelings were the emergence of her primary objects. Clearly I was beginning to become the outline of the
mother who was rid of her when she was a small child, and my
fortitude in sticking my ground, interpreting the transference,
and placing her idiom in a genetic reconstruction began to have
some effect, and – to my disappointment, I can now confess –
she felt I was helping her.

Then one session she came and plunked herself in the chair,
a kind of silly grin playing on her face. When she leaned forward to look directly at me in what was meant to be a searching
inquiry, she said: 'Uh, Mr Bollas, uh, Mr Bollas, it sounds so
funny to say that [she laughs], don't you think it would be nice if
you could just be a teeny bit warmer [A gushing effusive laugh

follows this]. I mean, I wonder if you could just be a teeny bit warmer. Not much warmer. Just an insie bit. It's just that you are so cold.' It is impossible, I fear, to convey just how maddening this woman could be, as the unreality of her self presentations almost defies communication. When she first embarked on her scripted, searching comments, I thought, 'oh my god, here we go again'. I felt quite differently, however, when she said that she thought I was cold because, although her delivery of this feeling was hysterically conveyed, the essence of the message was correct. I knew that I had withdrawn from her and that I was always on the alert for her next use of herself as a kind of afflicting event.

I decided that this would be an appropriate moment to make my experience of her available for the analysis. I said: 'I am very glad that you have said this because, in a way, I think you are absolutely correct. I have become somewhat cold as you put it, and I am aware of being distanced in these sessions, something that I think you are well aware of. But let's wonder, shall we, about how this happened. You see, it's my view that if you could convince yourself to stop being so goddamned traumatic, then I could be quite a bit more at ease with you, and we could actually get down to the task of understanding you.' To my surprise and relief, she said 'uh-huh' and seemed to mean it. I felt she had come into a different region of herself through the interpretation, an area of the self that I had not seen up till then. I lost heart for a moment when she created a look of studious innocence and said, 'I traumatize people? I upset them? Hmm. Could you just tell me something about that, about how I do it?' I replied: 'What, and make it look as if I am the only one in this room who knows about this? I believe you know very well indeed what I am talking about. In fact I think you brought up my distance from you because you know this element in your life needs recognition and resolution.' She said in a mature voice, which up till then I had simply not heard: 'Yes [pause] I do know. I know all about it. No one has ever lasted me. I drive everyone away from me.' This statement was true. Friends, such as they were, had deserted her. Employers would only last a few weeks. Colleagues asked to be placed elsewhere. Flatmates threw her out. And she protected herself against the immediate loss of family members by only occasionally visiting them, in that way preserving them against her destructiveness.

My direct use of my countertransference, in which I told her how it felt to be one of the objects in her environment, proved to be the turning point in her psychotherapy and allowed me to analyse her false self. I was able to identify her unbelievable self, which was often announced by saccharine confessions. This false self was even more maddening when she delivered rehearsed replays of insight derived from the sessions: 'Oh, I just know that this is what you were saying to me last time, isn't it? Here is me, just little ole me, doing this kind of thing again, huh? Isn't that it, huh?' Wincing may not be a finer articulation of countertransference feelings but I found it effective, as it gave her notice of an interpretation, such as 'you haven't thrown enough sugar on your remarks'. Crass as it may sound, I made comments like these with a sense of relief; they enabled me to feel warmly towards her. She felt met by such comments and would say in a remarkably different and authentic voice, 'uh-huh, you mean the same old stuff', to which I would nod affirmatively.

I have no doubt, both from my own clinical experience and from the accounts of other analysts, that it is quite possible to conduct a more classical analysis with neurotics and some characterologically disturbed patients and to feel that one is real and that the analysis is real. Yet there are certain patients with whom one cannot do classical work and at the same time feel real; indeed, it becomes necessary first to restore one's sense of personal reality in work with such patients before a more classical analysis can be initiated. The occasional direct use of one's countertransference as the object of the patient may be what is needed to initiate analysis proper. Although it could never become a substitute for contemporary 'classical' analysis, it is my view that without such interventions, a patient may be analysed but never reached and, inevitably, never helped by the analytical process.

Patients convey their internal world through the establishment of an environment within the clinical situation, and they necessarily manipulate the analyst through object usage into assuming different functions and roles. Very often the location of freely associated ideas – of those thoughts that spontaneously register the content of psychic life – is in the psychoanalyst. This is so because the patient cannot express his conflict in words, so the full articulation of pre-verbal transference evolves in the analyst's countertransference. The transference-countertransference interaction, then, is an expression of the unthought known. The patient knows the object-setting through which he developed, and it is a part of him, but it has yet to be thought. The psychoanalytic understanding of the transference-countertransference discourse is a way of thinking the unthought known.

I believe that it can be valuable for the clinician to report selected subjective states to his patient for mutual observation and analysis. By disclosing some of his subjective states of mind, the analyst makes available to the patient certain freely associated states within himself, feelings or positions that he knows to be sponsored by some part of the patient. Even though the clinician may not know what the ultimate conscious meaning will be of a subjective state of mind, or of a position he will find himself in within the countertransference, he can put it to a patient so long as it is clear to the analysand that such disclosures are in the nature of reports from within the analyst in the overall interest of the psychoanalysis.

I do not think that most interpretations should be either statements of feelings or senses within the analyst or direct disclosures of the positions in which the analyst finds himself. Such is the near-phobic dread of this area of technique within psychoanalysis that I shall state that the analyst must use such interventions sparingly, and only to facilitate the analytic process. Furthermore, it is essential that the clinician analyse those responses in the analysand which are unconscious reactions to or unconscious comments on the phenomenon of the analyst using his subjective state or reporting his direct countertransference

experience. For example, the clinician may say,
'I think you believe I have said this because I am
fed up with you, and your response is a kind of
apology.' Or, 'I think you are worried and believe something has gone wrong with me. You
have decided that now I am the patient and you have a distressed
analyst on your hands, such is the worry occasioned by my
putting forth a feeling for consideration.' Alternatively: 'You
seem amused, and I wonder if it isn't because you are thinking
something like "Ah. He's done it! He has broken the rules and I
have found him out!" thus giving you a curious feeling of triumph.' Or: 'I think you are finding it very difficult to consider
what I have said, as you are, for the moment, excited by the way I
have said what I did.' In other words, each analyst must be
thoroughly tuned in to the patient's unconscious response to his
intervention, as Langs (1979) and Casement (1985) have stressed
in their writings. So long as this unconscious reaction or comment
is fully analysed, the analyst can proceed to elaborate the aim of
this disclosed subjective state, should that be necessary.

I have stressed that I do not believe the clinician should make
a direct use of his countertransference without establishing over
time meaningful precedents for the occasional examination of the
analyst's subjective states, a fairly unremarkable phenomenon in
that I am referring only to those kinds of intervention when the
analyst says 'I feel', or 'I have an idea', or 'I sense that'. Such
interventions, however, are countertransference-inspired and
indicate some aspect of the analyst's trust in his subjective states
of mind. Furthermore, by virtue of his own self relating in the
presence of the patient, the analyst can verbalize subjective
states and contemplate them openly, or he can correct himself in
the presence of the analysand, thus demonstrating his own
comfort with the subjective element by using the analytical
method to understand some of his own states of mind.

The analyst's disclosure of a selective subjective state of mind
is not equivalent to the expression of affect (for example, 'you
make me angry') or the revelation of an unanalysed feeling or
phantasy. When I disclose a subjective state to a patient, I do
so with more concentration than when I make a clarification or

present an interpretation. More mental work goes into the evolution of the statement 'I feel' or 'I sense' than I bring to interpretation proper, precisely because disclosures of subjective states process much that is still the unthought known, and one's **intelligence** here is an invaluable asset in articulating the unthought known. If one is **thinking** very carefully, then in the moment of saying to a patient 'I sense', the analyst conveys that such phrasing is both a thoughtful moment and an occasion for the unthought to be given its space for articulation, such as with immediate and often inspired associations of the analysand. Ironically, even though I say 'I sense' or 'I feel', the articulation in such a moment reflects thoughtfulness rather than affectivity or mystifying intuitiveness. The analysand understands that the psychoanalyst's relation to the unthought known is **thoughtful**, even though the core of significance has yet to be discovered. This relation of thought to the unthought is a useful one in our clinical work. It allows me to tell a patient that I am not convinced by his explanations of his state of mind, even if I don't yet know **what it is** that we have yet to understand.

I am aware that some clinicians who value countertransference believe that the analyst should only make private use of this information and then make transference interpretations. This is often accomplished by saying, 'I think you are telling me something by showing me how it feels', an intervention which may in some ways be correct, but which sidesteps the truth a bit. To be sure, analysts do learn from their countertransference experience, and it is often true that up to a point patients do have a sense that they are communicating with the analyst by forcing him into a certain position within a session. The patient and analyst may not know for a long time what the meaning is of a cumulative establishment of the transference, but by making certain subjective states known to the analysand, the analyst enables the transference-countertransference discourse to be analysed as it develops.

If I had said to Helen, for example, 'I think through your self interruptions you intend me to have some knowledge of what it means or feels like to be lost', I believe this would not have been entirely true, since the reliving of one's history – full of communi-

cative potential as it is – does not mean that the
sole unconscious aim of such a reliving is to inform the other about oneself. I do not pretend
that the originating subjectivity behind the need
to make the patient's transference known springs

from the analysand when, in fact, I know the genesis of such interpreting comes from myself. Many patients would be quite content to remain unconscious of their transference usage of the
analyst. Admittedly, I did say to Helen that I thought she was
creating absence and I suggested that she aimed for me to know
this, but my intention is to provide a potential space in which the
analysand can give consideration to the unconscious motives that
organize her character. In my view, an interpretation of projective identification would have been false. My interpretation was
only meaningful to her because the transference interpretation
followed my countertransference disclosure.

If I had merely interpreted to Paul that he intended to inform
me, through his transference idiom, what it is like to be cold-
shouldered by his father, I think that the ironic effect of such an
interpretation would have been the unfortunate maintenance of
an aseptic world, since my interpretations would only have
sounded like odd echoes of his remote father. Paul needed me to
use my own rapport with my subjective feelings in order to stand
up for his potential self. In speaking up for what I felt or sensed, I
was, of course, representing in the analysis a split-off position of
the analysand, but in my view, the only way I could authentically
reach this person was to speak for that which he had disowned.

When an analysand uses language on the cheap, it is not only
the case that the patient may be discharging himself of pain or
excitation, but also that the analyst's words are not valued as
symbolic representations of meaning. In the more classical situation the analyst used that silence which is the hallmark of most
analyses as a background from which speech expressed meaning,
and patient and analyst listened to the free associations. Susan
Sontag brilliantly states the uses of silence:

> Still another use for silence: furnishing or aiding speech to
> attain its maximum integrity or seriousness. Everyone has

experienced how, when punctuated by long silences, words weigh more; they become almost palpable. Or how, when one talks less one begins feeling more fully one's physical presence in a given space. Silence undermines 'bad speech', by which I mean dissociated speech – speech dissociated from the body (and therefore from feeling), speech not organically informed by the sensuous presence and concrete particularity of the speaker and by the individual occasion for using language. Unmoored from the body, speech deteriorates. It becomes false, inane, ignoble, weightless. Silence can inhibit or counteract this tendency, providing a kind of ballast, monitoring and even correcting language when it becomes inauthentic. (1966, p. 20)

However, silence in an analysis does not initially function in this manner with the less neurotic and the more severely disturbed character disorder. Words weigh for nothing. Some patients may, alternatively, not speak at all, except for lifeless mumblings, since they exist in a kind of listless inertness. The analytical task is difficult and challenging with such patients, as the analyst must find some way to give weight to language, to give it body. By using language to speak selected subjective states, and by struggling on occasion to find the right words to express my states of mind, I am trying to give to language its meaningful representational potential. What I am concerned with is close to Masud Khan's concept of interpretation following the 'vectors of being and experiencing' (1974). It is related to Bion's idea of the evolution from beta to alpha functioning and thinking (1977). It is also relevant to Langs' typology of transference communications (1979).

The clinician, that is to say, must function openly as a transformational object. He must indicate that he perceives something, even if the perception is only of an as-yet-inarticulate movement of a potential significance, registered through a feeling state or a sense in one's being. He must trust such a perceptual registration as a potential source of knowledge, and he must transform the inarticulate sense or feeling into some form of ver-

bal representation that can be put to the analysand for mutual consideration. This inarticulate element is the unthought known; the patient
knows something, but has as yet been unable to
think it. The analyst here performs much the

same function that the mother did with her infant who could not
speak but whose moods, gestures and needs were utterances of
some kind that needed maternal perception (often achieved
through a kind of instinctual knowing), reception (a willingness to
live with the infant utterance), transformation into some form of
representation, and possibly some resolution (the ending of distress).

I think it is necessary for the analyst to use himself more directly as an area of shared knowing through his experiencing, if
he is to reach many of his patients. From his own experiencing,
the analyst may not only establish the value of feeling states and
subjective states, but he may also find a way to use this form of
countertransference experiencing for eventual knowing. In this
way the unthought known, which can only be thought via the
subject's use of the object in the transference and countertransference, is given its place in the fields of analysis. The psychoanalyst's establishment of an intelligent subjectivity, in which he
works to put his self states into language, constitutes an important part of the work (of thought) of analysis. If he cannot find a
way to do this, it is my view that he may well preserve in the
patient a quiet belief that psychoanalysis turns away from very
significant areas of being, knowing and truth.

13 *Self analysis and the countertransference*

FOR a long time I have felt that something crucial to our lives as psychoanalysts has been missing. Some twenty years ago when I read psychoanalytic articles with a greater interest than I can afford to give them today, I was drawn to the work of the early group of analysts: to Ferenczi, Abraham, Rank, and Deutsch. In my view it is Lacan, Winnicott, and Bion who have now given representation to that very thing which I believe has been seriously missing from psychoanalysis since the 'early' days. I believe this to be the **self-analytic element** which I distinguish from self analysis proper.

When Freud engaged in his own self analysis, he embarked on a procedure for exploring the internal world of the self. At the same time he investigated and developed **the creation of a capacity,** namely that ability to receive news from the self. In this respect he is one of the contributors within the history of western civilization to the evolution of a part of the mind. We might say this is the capacity for introspection. One of the objects of such ongoing insight is the dream, a mental object that has preoccupied us and compelled us to consider our existence and our fate from the dawn of civilization.

The discovery of psychoanalysis added a new dimension to the capacity to receive news from within the self. When Freud discovered the phenomenon of **free association,** he understood – uncannily it seems to me – that news comes from within the self only on its own terms. He knew that it was only by accomplishing a generative split in the ego (in which one portion of the self gave up the wish to know in order to experience) that a space could be created for the spontaneous arrival of unconscious derivatives.

By becoming himself a patient, through accepting the on-goingness of his illness, Freud created space for the arrival of disturbed portions of himself. I believe (on the basis of the correspondence with Fliess) that Freud would find himself in dark and troubled moods which he eventually allowed to be, as if he understood that to know himself he had first to experience his being. The analytic side of his mind would not fail when needed.

Masud Khan's eloquent presentation of the function of interpretation following the establishment of experiencing can, in my view, be said of Freud's self analysis:

> It is only when the vectors of **being** and **experiencing** are reliably established in a patient's capacity and functioning in the analytic situation that one can begin to discuss the mutative role of interpretation towards facilitating **knowing** of all the conflictual areas of intrapsychic and interpersonal realities in the patient. Only thus can interpretation facilitate insight. (1969, p. 205, author's emphasis)

Behind the analyst's own acceptance of himself as patient is the recognition that being and experiencing are prior to the knowing of that which is there to be understood.

The arrival of news, from dreams, daydreams, passing incomplete thoughts, inspirations, observations of the other, and idiomatic acts in our lived life, belongs to the arena of **experiencing** oneself which follows recognition of our being, the latter in itself being the establishment of a capacity for the collecting and placing of the experiencing. The more active agent – interpretation – follows being and experiencing and is only a part of the self-analytic element.

Lest I be misunderstood, I wish to state that by the self-analytic element I mean the accomplishment of an intrasubjective state, not the knowledge derived from such a capacity. Many psychoanalysts work with unconscious derivatives that trickle through to them from dreams and fantasies, but do not fully develop the self-analytic element in their patients.

Why? How do I believe I know this?

I can simply point to Freud's matter of fact and non-exhibitionistic **way of writing** about himself in his treatise on dreams and in other works. Significantly, he likened the ego to an explorer, an adventurer and a conquistador, images that personify the very qualities – courage and curiosity – that describe Freud himself. He dared to be where we must be to experience news of the self, and his writing of the experience was an integral part of the receptive capacity he facilitated by the creation of self analysis.[9]

Can we honestly say that Freud's genius in writing or telling of himself is an act that cannot be followed? Are we truly meeting the Freudian challenge if we state that to speak of ourselves is an act of exhibitionism? I wonder.

What is it about a Winnicott, a Bion or a Lacan – beyond simply their genius – that is so inspiring these days? Why do we enjoy reading their works even if much of what is there to be read is elusive and strange? Can we simply say that such analytic writers appeal to us because they have acted out against a fundamental responsibility to remain psychoanalytically kosher, an acting out in which we slyly participate by proxy? I think not. It is my view that people are drawn to the works of such people because in them they find a daring, **a courage to be idiomatic** and to stay with the private creations of their analytic experience and life – a profoundly Freudian accomplishment on their part. If such figures are excessively idealized, as I think they are, is it not more a measure of our impoverishment, of our failure, than of their search for idealization?

Well, by now my view is no secret. For I think we have failed to allow ourselves the full development of a psychoanalytic sensibility, which means the inclusion of ourselves as animated objects within the field of the analysable. We have lost pleasure in being bewildering to ourselves and in using a state of mind to sustain a capacity that Freud developed when he began his self analysis. We have not written about ourselves in such a way as to communicate this accomplishment to the wider analytic community. If our lives with our patients are lived in necessary seclusion, isolated from public view by virtue of the necessity of confidentiality, we can still explore mental phenomena and the puzzlement of being human by using ourselves as objects of examination and, in so doing, earn the respect and consideration of the intellectual community in the sciences and the humanities.

THE RECEPTIVE CAPACITY

In the ordinary course of a psychoanalysis the analyst is receptive to the analysand's free associations. He takes in the details of the patient's narrative, mulls them over, and eventually organizes them into an interpretation. The analysand, by virtue of working with the analyst, and as a consequence of identifying with him, internalizes the analyst's receptive capacity in his own relation to himself as an object.

A condition for the self-analytic function is the maintenance of a receptive space for the arrival of news from within the self. This works in accordance with mental processes that we may have been neglecting. For example, when we think of mental life, we tend to do so in terms of projection and introjection, that is, we actively put 'out' into the object world parts of ourself. If the aim is to get rid of unwanted parts of the self, we speak of projective identification, a highly active unconscious activity aimed at keeping what we cannot bear to have in ourself inside the other. We speak of introjection when we discuss mental processes which involve the taking in of some external object, taking into account of course the distortions created by needs, desires and anxieties.

I am less than happy, however, with the concepts of projection, projective identification and introjection (and variations thereof) when addressing self analysis and one of the self-analytic functions: reception. For here lies a paradox: this aspect of mental life activates when tranquillity is achieved. Reception of news from within (in the form of dream, phantasy, or inspired self observation for instance) arrives through evocation, a mental action characterized by a relaxed, not a vigilant, state of mind.

'To evoke', from the Latin **evocare,** means to call forth or to summon. *The Oxford English Dictionary* states that in early usages it means 'to summon up (spirits, etc.) by use of magic charms', or 'to call (a feeling, faculty, manifestation, etc.) into being or activity. Also to call up (a memory) from the past.'

The *O.E.D.* definition suggests that the summons is the result of a magic charm. This attributes agency to the called up, and would therefore be in keeping with medieval and renaissance requirements to view the workings of the mind as sponsored by some external agent: a magician or the devil. Nascent self states, dreams and inspired reflections, however, are not phenomena which can be aggressively summoned. Freud learned this to his great dismay, and some of his black moods were the direct outcome of the failure to yield more news about himself through sheer will. He had to wait.

The evocative mental process occurs when the mind is receptive and at rest. Khan (1977) terms such rest 'lying fallow', an accomplishment which as a form of tranquillity is essential to the self-analytic function. If I dare to be there where I am to hear news from myself, and if I can maintain that wish without aggressively seeking its accomplishment, then dream recollections, memories and the like will be evoked by this receptivity.

THE PSYCHOANALYST'S RELATION TO
THE PATIENT'S SELF ANALYSIS

If a psychoanalyst is burdened with a diligent work ethic (and I refer here to some classical analysts who believe silence is a resistance to be 'overcome' by interpretation and by effort in the analysand), or if the psychoanalyst is particularly prone to dialogue (often involving the analysand in long and complex interpretations) then it is my view that the analysand will not develop his self-analytic capacity sufficiently.

Such a capacity can only occur if the analyst knows that there are certain times when the analysand needs to be left alone. Winnicott (1971) termed this function the 'uninterpretive' act of the analyst which was necessary to the development of the analysand's private and internal mental development and, as I shall explore in the next chapter, non-interpretation is essential to ordinary regression to dependence. Reception and evocation have to do with creating **conditions** for the arrival of an object. We may think of a potential dream waiting for the conditions necessary for its dreaming (Khan, 1974). Indeed we could say that, whereas projection has to do with the relocation of an internal

object and introjection to do with the taking in of
an external object, evocation involves the creation of an object. Before this calling forth, no
mental object exists (or no set of internal objects
exists) in the form necessary to the mental realization or processing of the called forth.

An analyst who is too eager to put his patient's inner experiences into words, or who warmly pushes the analysand into
overcoming silence, in my view subtly erodes the creation of new
objects. In this respect, then, we can say that objects become different in psychoanalysis via interpretation – where the analyst
detoxifies the analysand's projections and creates a more digest-
ible introject – and via evocation, in which self and object representations (as images, ideas, or affects) emerge where they have
not existed before.

TRANSFERENCE POSITIONS:
THE USES OF THE OBJECT

I am sure that I am not alone in believing that we can no longer
talk of the transference, unless by that we mean to designate a
genre of diverse but related functions. Some of the theoretical dif-
ferences we seem to enjoy these days occur, in my view, because
different groups are addressing themselves to different transference positions and because our perception of a transference position will imply a countertransference state or disposition, which
in turn has implications for technique.

To define any transference position, the analyst need only inquire into what particular use the analysand is making of the analyst and the analytic process at any one moment. In the past, a
more traditional understanding of transference has been to refer
to that development in an analysis when the analysand begins to
experience the analyst as the father or the mother. It is possible,
then, to speak of oedipal transferences. If the transference relation was characterized by a representation of the father as particularly phallic, or the mother as an anal expulsive figure, it was
possible to discuss pre-genital transference, with the analyst
bearing the projection of earlier infantile parts of the self. Then,
of course, there was the transference of defence when we focused

on the way in which a patient allocated to the analyst a particular defensive function or when he represented a function of the patient's mind, such as the superego.

Such discriminations of the transference (based on what seemed to be passed over to the analyst) were on the right track, I believe. But I should like to talk in more general terms of very different positions taken by the analysand in terms of the use of the analytic object. By object, I mean the total analytic situation, which of course involves the person and sensibility of the analyst, but also includes the analytic setting, the temporal aspects of a session, and the analytic procedure. I also wish to affirm that, although some particularly disturbed analysands may tend to live from within only one transference position, most analysands live through all of the transference dispositions. Indeed in any one session, different types of transference states will be present, some overlapping and contradicting one another. To make this clear, I will now turn to a sketchy description of these different transference states.

TRANSFER TO THE ANALYST'S
DISCRETE IDIOM

All psychoanalysts are different. We have a particular way of setting up our analytic consulting rooms. We differ in the clothes we wear, in our scents, in our way of introducing ourselves to a patient, in the way we walk about our room or end a session, and in the way we speak.

From the moment an analysand enters our space, we influence him. Our presence is an action, and the patient responds. In subtle ways he will inform us of his immediate experience of our precise existence and our idiom. As Langs (1977) and Casement (1985) have emphasized, patients will be affected by our interpretations and attempt to work with us, often, as Searles (1956) stressed, trying to cure us of our error. I believe this is based upon the analysand's 'correct' perception of us and his effort to adapt to the analytic object, situation and process.

TRANSFER TO THE
NARRATIVE OBJECT

243

SELF ANALYSIS
AND
THE COUNTER-
TRANSFERENCE

TRANSFER TO THE NARRATIVE OBJECT

Most patients will talk about events in their lives. They will tell us about wives, husbands, friends and local shopkeepers – in short, the 'stuff' of life. But such narrative objects can also bear the patient's projection of a part of the self or a part of the analytic object. As Gill (1982) has stressed in his recent work, it is important to understand that the narrative object within this transference position may be a metaphor either for a part of the self or for some part of the analyst. For example, an eighteen-year-old patient finds himself worrying excessively about the well-being of other people while he is appallingly indifferent to his own self abuse. A few months before beginning analysis he experienced a profound psychotic decompensation. It is important for him to discover that his worry over the well-being of another person is his own curious way of mourning and caring for the damaged parts of himself which he otherwise refuses to contact. The understanding of patient narrative as a metaphor for self and object declarations is an important part of our work in the transference these days.

TRANSFER OF PARTS OF THE SELF INTO THE ANALYST

This position is characterized by the function of projective identification, a concept that has been developed by the Klein group in London. Ogden has provided the most succinct definition of the term:

> Projective identification is a concept that addresses the way in which feeling states corresponding to the unconscious fantasies of one person (the projector) are engendered in and processed by another person (the recipient), that is, the way in which one person makes use of another person to experience and contain an aspect of himself. (1982, p. 1)

This transference refers to the patient's placement of parts of the self into the analyst. These may be unwanted elements because they are experienced as intrinsically dangerous (such as oral cannibalistic impulses). The schizoid act of splitting off this portion of the self and keeping it inside the other will, of course, bias the subject to a paranoid disposition, as he will fear the recipient object's oral revenge. This transference position is characterized fundamentally by the evacuation of an element of the self into the object by virtue of intense anxieties.

On the other hand, the projected elements may be valued parts of the self placed in the recipient for safe keeping, a splitting of the ego that allows the good parts of the self to survive the bad parts of the self.

TRANSFER OF LIFE HISTORY
VIA THE ANALYTIC PROCESS

Although this transference position may share with the above the function of projective identification, the aim is not to evacuate part of the self to be contained in the other in order to regulate primitive anxieties of a paranoid-schizoid type. This transference state refers to the analysand's unwavering and time-consuming **unconscious effort to reconstruct the life lived within the family of origin** by enacting different roles in the transference (Sandler, 1976). In this endeavour, he invites the analyst to experience himself in roles unfamiliar to him, such as the patient's mother (or a part of the mother), or father, or a part of the child self. This transference is a form of externalization (Giovacchini, 1979), in which the patient creates an environment (see above, chapter 12) in which patient and analyst are meant to pursue a life together.

TRANSFER OF TRUE SELF
VIA OBJECT RELATING

This is perhaps the most difficult transference position to describe because evidence for it is not available in patient narrative, and it requires a countertransference capacity in the analyst for its existence and understanding. Indeed all the above transference positions may occur while yet another transference is developing; namely, the patient is coming into his own being by experiencing himself through his use of the analyst as an object. While we may be interpreting another transference position (for example, the analysand's projection of a part of himself into the analyst or his response to our idiom), the patient gradually and decisively begins to enjoy the aggression of arriving in himself or tries out self states within sessions simply to

experience them and to find what feels right and accurate as an expression of his own personal inner reality and in relation to the real object. This development may take place in complete tranquillity or amidst the hubbub of intense projective and introjective madness. It was this use of the analyst and the process that Winnicott and Khan understood so well. To meet this transference idiom from the countertransference depends on the analyst's ability to take pleasure in its presence and celebrate its development.

TRANSFER OF THE SELF-ANALYTIC ELEMENT

This transference position differs from all of the above in one fundamental respect. The patient is not acting on or using the analyst as a real object in any fundamental manner. If the analyst does feel acted on or used, such use does not imply an intent on the patient's part: it is simply an outcome of the effect of being with the analysand during this experience. The transfer of the self-analytic element amounts to the unconscious **inclusion** of the analyst in the patient's intrapsychic life, in which the analyst may fulfil important and varying psychic functions.

We could say that the patient is not talking to the analyst about the self, but is talking to the self about the self, and utilizing the analyst as part of the mind. The analyst is employed as a mental process, not to contain an evacuated part of the person's psyche, but to hold a function or be an auxiliary (Heimann, 1960) in order to assist the patient in the evocation of new inner experiences and to facilitate the process of new object formation. Such a transference position may follow a period of intense interpretive work by the analyst which will devolve into a self-analytic transference when it can be said that the patient is 'digesting' the interpretation and is now using the analyst as part of the mind in the evocation of new thoughts and feelings.

TRANSFER OF THE
UNTHOUGHT KNOWN

The final transference position I shall take up is the analysand's transfer of what I term the unthought known. This is a form of knowledge that has not yet been dreamed or imagined because it is not yet mentally realized. In part, it corresponds to the primary repressed unconscious, particularly when we take into account that the unconscious ego is itself a memory of ontogenesis. This would be the experience of the inherited disposition (ego idiom at the beginning of life) meeting up with the maternal process through which ego dispositions, feelings and ultimately structure are mutually negotiated between mother and child. A form of knowledge that has not yet been mentally realized, it has not become known via dreams or phantasy, and yet it may permeate a person's being, and is articulated through assumptions about the nature of being and relating.

I also include in the concept of the unthought known those experiences in a child's life that were simply beyond comprehension. As I have explored in chapter 6, I think that all children store the quality of an experience that is beyond comprehension, and hold on to it in the form of the self-in-relation-to-object state, because events beyond comprehension are disturbing and yet seem life defining. I have described this process as the conservative process, and I have defined the event as an internal object: a conservative object because the child's, and then the adult's, aim is to preserve the experience unchanged. There is a wish that some day that which is beyond knowing will eventually be known and then available for forgetting or psychic redistribution (from mood, say, to memory). The transfer of this element may be registered through a particular kind of deep silence on the patient's part or through a struggle within the patient to push forward an internal experience so that it can be thought. The analyst will know it from the countertransference in terms of his own sense that the patient is verging on the introduction of something fundamental and new to the knowing of the person. The analyst, too, will be engaged in an intense effort to facilitate this unthought known into the light of the analytic hour, and it will be important for the analysand's transfer of this element to be witness to the analyst's struggle to think the unthought.

SELF ANALYSIS
AND
THE COUNTER-
TRANSFERENCE

TRANSFER OF THE SELF AND
TRANSFER OF THE SELF AND ITS OBJECTS

We can more or less distinguish between two classes of transference: those which involve the analysand and analyst in the patient's evolved projective and introjective activities lived out in the analytic relationship; and those which make use of the analyst but involve the patient in somewhat private, often unknowable, self experiences within the analysis. It is my view that the first class of transference positions is directed towards the analyst as object, either as an internal object or as an external other. These transferences to the analyst as object are inevitably part of an unconscious phantasy and have an organization to them, even if psychotic processes are involved.

The second class of transference position is characterized by the use of the analytic setting and process. Of course, the analyst is a crucial element in the total picture, but his existence is needed insofar as he is a transformational object, since he **processes** (Winnicott – facilitates; Bion – contains) the patient's thoughts, moods and communications.

As the self-analytic element emerges in transference, we find that the analysand is less inclined towards engaging the analyst as the screen for projections or taking him in for the virtue of introjective qualities, but instead quietly assumes the presence of the analyst as an auxiliary to the process of knowing the self, and therefore as an element not strictly defined as either inside or outside his mind. On the other hand, the analyst is clearly outside the patient, but, as both analyst and analysand are inside the analytic setting and process, they are therefore both inside the same container. The analyst is a transformational object – that is to say, is the trace of the mother's and father's facilitative handling of the infant self. The other is known and needed not as an object, but as a process that perceives, facilitates, remembers, anticipates and gratifies the analysand's personal needs.

With the analyst functioning as the transformational object, the analysand is free to devolve ego activity, to become receptive to news from deep within and to utilize the mental function of evocation. It is as if the ego turns a portion of its perceptive ability towards the primary repressed unconscious, and in its own manner engages the primary repressed in a 'calling up'. Such evocation occurs because the ego establishes a mental space for the collection of psychic news. Without this space, no information would arrive in such a way as to be of ultimate use to the individual. Again, the evocative process is contrasted with projection, although when a new object or self state emerges, it may be instantly available for projecting. The mood of the person in such a state of being, however, is rarely disposed towards the projecting of the newly-arrived self or object experience.

In this place, within such a transference, the analyst is inside the patient's internal world, there in the space of the subject's effort to be available for news from the unthought known. To understand this position of transference to the analytic setting and process within the person's self-analytic existence is crucial for the uses of the countertransference and for technique.

THE COUNTERTRANSFERENCE CAPACITY

A countertransference position is a psychological condition determined by our experience as the object of the patient's use within the transference. It was Racker (1957) who implied that countertransference not only amounts to a recognition of the patient's transference, but also facilitates more articulated transference communications. His point lies at the very heart of the matter. If we believe in countertransference as an ordinary and ever-present state of being, then our conviction creates a space for the reception of communications from the patient, since **the patient unconsciously perceives this belief and space**. The patient's recognition of our internal space for the analysis of transference, which speaks via object usage of our self, permits the patient to utilize this form of relating and knowing. At the very least, more non-verbal or 'primitive' states of being and experiencing will therefore find expression.

Of course, we must all know that this is very different from the view that countertransference is an impediment to the ongoing work of a psychoanalysis. When we take this classical view, we work intensively on the countertransference in order to resolve it and return to the evenly hovering attention that

we value. This understanding of countertransference, and the one I offer above, refer to two fundamentally different psychological phenomena. It is not a question of having to choose between the two theories of countertransference, particularly if we understand that they are not inevitably in conflict with one another. For example, those of us who believe that countertransference can be an impediment are correct when recognizing the arrival of personal psychopathology within the clinical situation, an arrival that may not be at all 'in tune' with the patient's transference communications. Some of us may find that we are resisting our patient's maturation – we may not wish them to leave us, since they have become something of a favoured child. In this case we can, I think, refer to a countertransference that needs to be overcome.

Countertransferences of this kind are indeed resistant impediments to the psychoanalytic situation. What concerns me, however, is that some analysts believe that this is the only possible definition of countertransference and would view any countertransference as an impediment, something to be overcome and worked through. Those who take this view may have a resistance to countertransference experiencing. Their ideal of themselves as an analyst is such that they sincerely believe they must maintain an even state of mind when working with a person, and any disturbance of this even attentiveness is to be corrected so that the analyst can return to listening properly to the patient. I submit that this ideal is necessary, and that evenly hovering attention (close to Bion's concept of 'reverie' (1962a)) is an important frame of mind, but it does not preclude the value of another area of our analytic mind becoming distressed or deformed by virtue of the analysand's object usage of us in the transference.

I think the ideal of always trying to maintain neutrality actually amounts to a resistance in the analyst to countertransference experiencing, which as a consequence forecloses the analysand's use of the transference to articulate more completely internal object relations and to recollect earlier states of childhood.

Capacity permits reception. Reception allows transmission.

Those who disagree and state that countertransference is always a detriment to the analytic process eventually prove themselves prophets in terms of their own clinical work. When we work like this, we do not listen to our shifting states of mind, processing our thoughts and phantasies, and so we shove aside the cumulative accretion of psychic material established in the transference. Eventually, however, the analyst is confronted by his own state of being, and usually analysts of this persuasion will focus on their affects: anger, boredom or affection. Although this recognition is of course of some value, the analyst has usually left his understanding of his countertransference too late. He will not have sufficient information to process his mood. Indeed, the very fact that the countertransference is almost always reported in terms of affect distortion suggests that the psychic content behind the feeling has long been denied, split off, and will most likely not be recovered. Analysts who work with countertransference in this manner aim to abreact feelings (internally) in order to be free of a countertransference position. In effect, the analytic potential goes unrealized.

To my mind, the most regrettable result of such a condition is the analyst's unwitting foreclosure of the analysand's use of the transference. Those who see countertransference as an impediment, who aspire to return to even attention in order to be more in touch with the patient or to be more objective may have, ironically enough, achieved almost the opposite.

COUNTERTRANSFERENCE AS EMPATHY

Transference states that make intense use of the analyst in order to compel him to experience variable, yet unconsciously coherent states of being and thought, amount to a form of infant-child speech. The analysand not only talks to the analyst about the self; he also puts the analyst through intense experience, effectively inviting the analyst to know the analysand's self and his objects.

He not only speaks to the object, he compels the
object to speak to itself.

In such moments, when the analyst simply
does not know what is taking place, he has only
his own internal thought processes to rely on as
the material of the subjective. Indeed only by carefully nurturing
and sustaining an internal mental space for the registration of his
thoughts and feelings can such an analyst reliably provide additional clinical space for the analysand's transference usage. A
patient therefore uses the analyst by coercing the analyst's
internal life, much the way an infant or a small child addresses
the parent by evoking internal responses, enabling such a parent,
through empathy, to provide the right parental act.

Self-analytic activity within the analyst's countertransference is empathic when the analyst provides an internal mental
space for the patient's expressions – not verbally representable,
they can only be discovered in the analyst. For example, a person
comes for a clinical interview to begin an analysis claiming that he
feels life is only just worth living, although he has no intention of
committing suicide. He knows through comments from others
that he is rather dreadfully narcissistic and too thoughtless when
it comes to others. In the course of the interview, however, the
analyst does not feel himself the object of narcissistic relating; he
does not feel either that he has to walk on tiptoe around the
patient or that he is encountered by an obtuse and limited psychic
presence that compels him to try to put himself in the patient's
place. The analyst feels that the patient has looked after the analyst quite well: correcting him thoughtfully when he is in error,
appreciating the moments of understanding, and using the analyst in the transference with a certain urgent skill, as if he has at
last found a source of understanding and almost instinctively
knows exactly how to use the analyst. The analyst might have two
countertransference states. On the one hand, the patient has told
him in all sincerity what he believes – that he is selfish, egotistical
and a problem for others – but the transference evidence belies
this, even though the patient has no knowledge of it. The analyst
might wonder about the patient's self observations, 'Who says
this of you?' and feel a growing sense of disagreement with the

view. On the other hand, the analyst might simultaneously feel a deep affection for the patient's helpless and misunderstood self. If the analyst is comfortable allowing himself variable and diverse internal responses to the analysand, he might already have refused the patient's self-critical mode; he might phantasize about rescuing the patient and looking after him; he might have expressed the thought, 'well, I'm very glad to have you as a patient and I feel fortunate to be your analyst'.

Such responses constitute, in my view, the empathic element of the internal space which makes up the contemporary countertransference facilitation. The analyst **lives through** the patient's internal object relations. He takes sides. In the example above, the analyst's strong sense of refusal is a split-off expression of the patient's nascent and appropriate aggression. Perhaps a 'no' spoken to an overtly critical parent. Of course, later in the development of such an analysis, the analysand may, paradoxically enough, feel himself to be misunderstood by the analyst's understanding, and he may gradually and persistently dement the analyst's frame of mind by sabotaging reverie and the analyst's capacity to think about the analysand's musings or presence, thus bringing into **the life** of the external object relation the presence of a critical and abusive part of the parent. The analyst may well find himself harried and furious with the patient, who may require the analyst to show evidence of having lived this experience with him, evidence that could only be convincing to the patient if the analyst resisted abuse. By resisting abuse, I mean the analyst's saying something like 'nonsense' to a patient's 'trashing' of the analyst in a session. This is a form of counteraggression, but not aggression that inspires greater aggression nor aggression that elicits the patient's sense of guilt, but aggression that relieves the patient who, in such a moment, feels a need to be stopped, or to have someone **stand up with feeling** to the pathological element in the session. I have explored this type of interpretation in the previous chapter, and many analysts have written about such interventions.

This form of empathy involves the capacity of the analyst, through the provision of countertransference experiencing, to

provide sufficient internal space for the analysand to live through all the elements of infant
and child object relations. Inevitably, this means
that the analyst will need to become lost in the
patient's world, lost in the sense of not knowing

what his feelings and states of mind are in any one moment, but
also clear that their registration and storage for potential understanding facilitates the patient's transference experiencing. It is
my view that if the patient senses that the analyst is arresting his
own inner thoughts and feelings, whether ostensibly in order to
listen more acutely to exactly what the analysand is saying or in
order to be more wilfully understanding of the patient's narrative, this will truncate the analysand's transference experience
and deprive both analyst and patient of vital information.

An analyst who is, as far as the patient can see and know,
always helpful, kindly and understanding, may seem to that
patient to be a wonderful man, a man he would like to have had as
a father. He may look back on the analysis as the best experience
of his life and use the internal presence of the good analyst to
lasting effect, but it is my view that nonetheless he may not have
the feeling of having been fully known. This analyst will not have
lived through the patient's childhood. This analyst will not feel
the frustrations of the parents or the destructive ability of the
child who is furious with the parent.

Each person who is characterologically disturbed needs to externalize his pathological object relations, to re-create in the
transference the atmosphere that prevailed in his family and, in
some limited and necessary manner, to force the analyst into the
analyst's own private experiencing of the family atmosphere. The
internal object world does not simply reflect external objects,
such as the inner representation of the father reflecting the
nature of the father. Inner objects are also established by instinctual drives, affects and ego mediations. Nonetheless, in the
course of the externalization of the transference the analysand
will re-present the family atmosphere as he experienced it. Since
this is my focus in the present chapter, I only take up objects that
are fundamentally representations of true external others, such
as the mother and father. This means the analyst has to be the

mother's child, the father's child, and the parent to the enraged and destructive child who in fury refuses any parenting, even if it is good. As we know, such a person does have good objects in his life and yet often cannot use them, because to do so might paradoxically mean to be separated from his origins, to be severed from his sense of self inextricably linked up with his history within the family. Only by making a good object (the analyst) go somewhat mad can such a patient believe in his analysis and know that the analyst has been where he has been and has survived and emerged intact with his own sense of self, an evolution in the countertransference that will match the emergence of the analysand within the transference from his family madness. In this sense, the transference-countertransference lifetime is necessarily a going mad together, followed by a mutual curing and a mutual establishment of a core self.

SELF ANALYSIS AND
COUNTERTRANSFERENCE

Countertransference theory allows the contemporary analyst to talk more frankly about what is taking place in his mind during his work, in this way regaining a function largely lost since Freud's account of his self analysis. No longer do analysts believe that such a task can only be pursued in private. The self-analytic element, derived from our ongoing struggle as people whose lives are devoted to understanding the ways of the mind and the nature of the self, can now be publicly represented in our struggles not simply with the patient but with ourselves as well. In this important respect, the development of countertransference theory amounts to an 'act of freedom' (Symington, 1983) not from the transference intensity of the patient, but from an oppressive element within our own history and within the culture and society of psychoanalysis.

The other important respect in which countertransference experiencing inherits and advances the self-analytic element is the analyst's discovery of the necessity to entertain his experiences as the patient's objects, allowing such moods and thoughts to develop, and considering patiently over time, not urgently, the

meaning of his experiencing. This, of course, is
an act of self analysis within the treatment of a
patient. I believe it should be ongoing and continuous, and in some respects it becomes even
more significant when the analyst may for some

time consciously be unaware of particular thoughts or moods determined by the analysand.

When the analysand discovers through experience that his
analyst is receiving the transference via his own inner experiencing, and when he discovers that the analyst is considering his own
inner life, however distressing, in order to understand his
patient's communications more fully, in that moment he realizes
that both he and his analyst share the self-analytic function. Indeed, the analysand will understand this as an act of empathy and
appropriate identification on the analyst's part. After all, we may
be separated by necessary professional tasks but we both share
the self-analytic function: we undergo experiences and contemplate them as subject and object. When the analysand discovers
that some of his own self-analytic efforts parallel our psychic activity, I believe the patient feels most profoundly supported by
us. He knows us then not to be a distant interpretive presence, or
simply a kind and empathic person, but someone who like himself
struggles to know and may often find the struggle painful and un-
pleasant.

Finally, it is my view that our greatest professional virtue as
psychoanalysts is our commitment to our own personal analysis.
As impressive as our theory is, as important as is the supervisory
process, and as necessary as is our research, nothing approximates the integrity of our experience as the patient. It is this
experience, its nature and its ongoing necessity through self
analysis, which must continue to inform our sensibility. If this
element in the history of psychoanalysis has to an extent been set
aside, as I believe it has, the emergence of interest in the countertransference, in which to some limited but meaningful degree we
recognize ourselves as the other patient in the session, at last re-
dresses a lacuna in our sensibility and brings us closer to the
honesty that characterized Sigmund Freud.

14 *Ordinary regression to dependence*

I N the last chapter I concentrated on how the transference disposition of a patient may be one of several types, and I have distinguished between two fundamental genres of transference: the one involving the self and its objects (internal and external), the other a state of being in which the analyst functions as a part of the patient's self analysis. The former transference class involves projecting, introjecting and projective identifying, while the second class derives from a receptive capacity (in both analyst and analysand) and involves a mental process – evocation – which facilitates the creation of new internal objects. The psychoanalyst's countertransference task within a self-analytic transference is to allow himself to be assumed by the patient and not to interpret unless the patient needs it.

I will focus now on one aspect of a clinical psychoanalysis which may only occasionally develop into its full potential, but which is part of almost all persons' analytic experience: regression to dependence. It is to the work of two members of the British Psycho-Analytical Society, Michael Balint (1968) and D.W. Winnicott (1965), that we owe so much for our understanding of regression. It is they who discovered a special need in certain patients to use the analytic setting and process to be unburdened of the false self and collapse into true self. Later, Margaret Little (1981), Marion Milner (1969), Masud Khan (1974), John Klauber (1981), Harold Stewart (1985), and André Green (1986) further developed our understanding of therapeutic regression.

Winnicott knew that the concept of regression to dependence would face dynamic and almost unceasing misunderstanding from his reading public. His paper on the subject in 1954 is cautious and repetitive. He continually stresses that by regression he means the opposite of progression, that is, a withdrawal in the analysand that becomes favourable if the analyst understands and meets it. He means the latter to be conducted via perception, interpretation, and later what he terms 'management'. Above all, he stresses that he does not mean an instinctual regression, nor a psychotic decompensation. He also emphasizes that in order to meet such a regression an analyst must be experienced at managing a patient during such a state and should be prepared to meet the analysand's needs.

It may well be that some of the more characteristic misunderstandings of his concept are engendered by the laudable but perhaps premature (in precisely the sense Winnicott means by inexperience) efforts of those who worked with R.D. Laing and the Philadelphia Association in the 1960s. For there were regressions taking place in that setting, many of which could not be met by therapists, regardless of how gifted they were. Some of the therapists and analysts who worked in those days with Laing agree with this view, and over the last twenty years they have learned a great deal about the handling of the regressed patient. It is unfortunate that their efforts and accomplishments have been almost entirely divorced from the intellectual world of the British Psycho-Analytical Society.

I suppose it is easy to understand how this topic can become such a volatile one. Winnicott, Balint, Khan and others stressed that during regression to dependence 'ordinary' analytic work is suspended. Many critics have focused on this, as if Winnicott's emphasis was on the complete abandonment of analysis and the enactment of this phenomenon for its own sake. I expect this misunderstanding arises for a variety of reasons. Some classical analysts object to the idea of meeting and managing a regression because they sincerely believe such a notion is ill conceived and potentially dangerous. Other analysts protest because they believe this point of view asks something of them which they cannot possibly fulfil. Furthermore, many analysts who have listened to case presentations where there are reported successes in the management of regression to dependence object because it can force the painful recognition that an analysis working in and with an entirely different model of mind and practice can have a successful outcome. The temptation to dismiss a clinician of another theoretical persuasion by that oft-chimed remark 'but it is not real analysis' is frequently hard to resist.

Another reason why this concept has not been understood is that Balint, Winnicott, Khan and others have tended to describe the more dramatic realizations of regression to dependence and have not focused sufficiently on its simpler, more ordinary manifestations. Ordinary regression to dependence is my focus here.

THE CONDITIONS FOR REGRESSIONS

We cannot understand the intrinsically generative elements of regression to dependence **unless** two factors in the analytic setting are acknowledged. In the first place, when a patient begins to regress in this manner, he experiences the analytic setting and process as an **invitation** to regress. Secondly, the analyst must understand this need and be attuned to the elements of the clinical situation which receive the regressive development. Indeed if the analyst does not 'see this' he will foreclose a generative regressive process and possibly induce (at the worst) a psychotic decompensation, or compel the analysand to act out regressive requirements elsewhere, or collude with the patient to shut off the possibility of the generative regressive process.

To understand how the analytic situation invites regression, let us remind ourselves of certain aspects of the analytic experience: lying on the couch, the physical sensations of being held by this physical object; physical proximity to the analyst and his person; the relief and pleasure (even amidst pain) of the analyst's seemingly undivided attentiveness to our self; the wonderfully secure experience provided by the temporal dimensions (fifty **uninterrupted** minutes, five times a week, for as long as is felt necessary!); our 'cot-like' experience of the objects within the analytic space as we gaze now and again at them, those enduringly familiar objects that come from 'his' or 'her' world; the intrinsic permission given to us to lapse into unselfconscious dreamlike states allowing us simply to feel our being, to find its formations in different experiences, and to report our self to the analyst,

having discovered now and then a surprise from
within. Even when the issues are oedipal, it can be like being held by the mother whilst talking to the father about being his child.

The most important condition for the evolution of the regressed patient is, however, the analyst's understanding of this phenomenon in the first place. It amounts to a capability. If the analyst is capable (through training, his own analysis or some other means) of understanding this phenomenon, then he facilitates the analysand's capacity for its generative realization.

One condition for a regression to dependence is, then, the analyst's frame of mind.

COUNTERTRANSFERENCE AS PROVISION: FROM RECEPTION TO EVOCATION

Once the analyst has discovered the infant or child element within the patient, who is in search of a holding environment that will permit the quiet evolution of other elements of the self (Winnicott's true self), then he will shift his frame of mind. Instead of diligently seeking to understand and interpret the discrete meanings of patient narrative, and rather than using dialogue to involve the analysand in analysis of the transference activity (even if this can be found), the analyst will suspend his interpretation of content or transference. Instead he recognizes that he is needed now as part of the patient's inner processing of known, partly known, and unthought known self experiences. There is little he can do via interpretation to know the patient's inner reality, and this is certainly not the time to organize the experience into an interpretation. But he can assist the analysand by helping the patient to dismiss residual guilt (over saying little to the analyst, for example) or by quietening the part of the patient which feels compulsively obliged to organize matters into self-generated interpretations ('perhaps you need to let yourself be without thinking what it amounts to').

The kernel of regression to dependence in psychoanalysis is an ordinary abandonment on the analysand's part of reporting or thinking oneself out; during silence, he experiences something else. In the previous chapter I termed this a receptive capacity within the patient's relation to himself as object, a capacity that utilizes the mental process of evocation, so that news from within the deeper parts of the self begins to emerge. It has been my observation, based on my own direct experience, and based on the reports of patients who have come out of such 'moments' (either a few minutes in a session, or a few sessions) that the following subjective development takes place:

1. After a period of important analytic work, or after pleasure in looking forward to an analytic session, or after a spell of talking the patient becomes unaware of the analyst's presence as an interpreter.

2. The patient is in a kind of 'twilight state' in which he enjoys lying on the couch, listening to the sounds of the analytic world (such as cars passing by, the ticking of a watch or the sound of voices). Pleasure is found in the analyst's presence, and stomach sounds, breathing and so on are felt to be reassuring and containing.

3. After focusing on the **physical sensation** of pleasure in being held by the couch and on the acoustic sensations of hearing the sounds of the world, the patient lapses into a state when thought processes seem benignly blank. Thoughts **arise in response** to sense stimuli, such as sounds, or objects visible in the analytic room. Patients report that they often look at one of the objects in the room, but gaze in an unfocused manner, not with the aim of interpreting the object, but simply losing oneself 'inside' it.

4. There is a subtle **transition** from hearing, seeing, sensing and feeling the properties of the outside world to hearing, seeing, sensing and feeling the inside world. There may be a continuous interplay between the two. Winnicott terms this the intermediate area of experiencing. This transition is not thought about, however, and is fundamentally pleasurable.

5. The patient reports being amidst the discovery of something important and new. I believe this to be a shift from reception to evocation. It is from within this internal state that a dream may suddenly be recalled or a memory may emerge. Even so, the urge in such a state is not to report. The recalled dream or memory is

part of the arrival of a condition of the self that is

being evoked. Very often, the patient will report that during such a state he found himself dwelling on an image, such as a dresser drawer in a playroom, a garden, a picture book, a car. 'Seeing' these objects does not inspire meaning, but it does feel intrinsically pleasurable and significant. There does not seem to be any urgent need to understand this position.

6. This state which may not be reached, since a person may only come to the above stage before emerging from it to report the dream or work on something important with the analyst. However, on occasion, the evocation of images (as contrasted with thoughts, words or abstractions) inspires some deep affective state. The patient may find himself profoundly moved as a result of the imaging. This in itself seems to **further deepen** the ego's capacity for receptive evocation.

7. It is after the stage of imagining and feeling (probably what Masud Khan means by the experiencing of one's being) that a person in regression to dependence may suddenly 'see' what it is all about. I find this exceptionally difficult to describe. I believe that what happens is almost a metonymic act. The image is part of self-object experience and the affect deepens the memory. At such a moment a patient may suddenly **discover** something **about** the mother, the father and himself which he has never thought before but which has been part of the unthought known. Some patients may break down in tears. Others behave as if they have experienced a revelation. It is very important for the analyst to remain silent and to hold the situation and not to act on his curiosity. Throughout much of the process described above, there is a need to experience this discovery in privacy, as a person may feel he must secure his own private inner experiencing before reporting to the analyst. There can be a fear that to speak the discovery will amount to losing it.

8. Finally, there is an intense need **to tell the analyst.** I have never found this to be accompanied by a fear that the analyst will fail to understand the report. It is as if the patient believes (perhaps necessarily) that the analyst has been in on the experience from the beginning and depends on the analyst's ability to provide

for it. There is great joy at the discovery, even amidst intense grief, and the patient may need to talk at length to the analyst.

Needless to say, if at any moment during the course of these stages of development the analyst asks the analysand what is on his mind, the regression will self arrest, and the process will terminate. I think that analysts who practise classically (and here I'm afraid I really am going on speculation) probably allow their patients to reach the fourth stage, where the patient is in an intermediate area of experiencing. Any question or statement – such as 'what's on your mind?' or 'you seem to have lapsed into silence', or 'perhaps there is something you prefer me not to know' – is an intrusion and may result in the analysand's stating in a somewhat embarrassed manner that actually he has only been thinking of an image.

I can recall interrupting a patient during such a stage when she was imagining her play box in her nursery. She had been recalling the toys one by one, and when I broke in on this, she and I worked a bit on understanding why I thought she was 'in' her nursery at that moment in the transference. I do not disparage the knowledge gained at that moment, nor to some extent the accuracy of the transference interpretation. Nonetheless, I do regret the fact that I interrupted the potential completion of her experience, as I am convinced that she was on her way to experiencing an important self state that lay dormant in the image. Winnicott calls this the freezing of a situation, and I have referred to a conservative object. In a sense, the toy box in her room at that time in her life 'held' a self state (and important experiences with the mother) that was not consciously known by the analysand. Fortunately, she got to this point some six months later. I regret that, so far as regression to dependence is concerned, I know precisely those analysands whom I have failed over the last ten years. There are certain patients who unfortunately cannot trust an analyst to allow the emergence of inner experience such as I have described a second time, and they never use the analytic space for regression to dependence again.

To understand regression to dependence, it is important to differentiate between the analysand's
uses of silence. To be sure, some silences are resistances, and it is quite proper for the analyst to
inquire about the patient's reticence to speak. But the silence
which is a necessary condition for regression to dependence is of a
different kind. Silence becomes a medium through which to experience the analytic holding environment. It is something like
the silence of the small child some ten to twenty minutes before
falling asleep. During this very special transition from wakeful
life lived in relation to important objects, to unconsciousness and
the dream, children lie tranquilly in their beds, eyes open, imagining their life. Sometimes it will be a going over of some of the
events of the day, often it may be wishing for some object, and
there is a consistent interplay between gazing at external objects
and contemplating internal objects. A child may look at a toy
rocket on the desk across the room. For a few moments he may
imagine himself as a space pilot and the rocket is now in outer
space (internal object usage), then he may look at the rocket as an
object in its own right and notice that it has a damaged nose (perception of external object), which may lead to a wish to tell the
mother about this (contemplation of conversation with real object), but may inspire an anxiety that he has not been a good
enough boy that day for the mother to want to do something about
this (reflection on the nature of intersubjective life and the interplay between internal and external). He may become sad. He may
think of asking the father to buy him a new rocket, and he may
imagine the father being quite pleased to do so. He may think of
swapping it the next day with a friend at school and at this point
he might imagine another child's toy. All of this may take only a
few seconds and over the course of twenty minutes many such
musings may take place.

In this experience silence is usually a necessary condition for
the 'processing' of internal world and external reality. This valuable time before sleep is a vital experience for children, and lasts
from early infancy at least through adolescence. It is often accompanied by toys, as some children will have a teddy in bed with

them, and to some extent these 'transitional objects' are part of the nature of the 'intermediate area of experience' which to my mind aptly describes this use of silence.

I have come to value this experience as a feature of regression from three sources: entering this frame of mind during my own analysis; observation of my children who I think were 'there' before bedtime; and subsequently, observation of patients in analysis.

I mention these three different situations because I believe it is necessary for us to address the question of just how we can differentiate the uses of silence, in particular between silence as resistance and silence as the medium for intermediate experiencing.

I will take one of my children as an example. Usually after story time he would ask if I would remain in the room with him when he went off to sleep. I agreed and would sit in a nearby chair. I think he was going through a period of some private anxiety and needed me to be around. After a story, he might ask me something about life: 'Why do parents have children?'; 'where was I before I was born?'; 'why do some of the children at school act dreadfully?'; 'why were you cross with me at the dinner table?' or 'I like being a child, why do I have to be a "bigger boy"?' It is difficult to re-create these questions. Sometimes they emerged after story time, but most often in the course of the ten to twenty minutes before sleep.

During his quiet experiencing during silence, I would sit comfortably in my chair and let my mind wander. It was the end of my day. The family had had supper, and it was now about 7:30. I was content and I enjoyed being with my son. Most nights he would say nothing after the story and just lapse into sleep, and that would be it. But on occasion he would ask some quite profound questions, and I would try in as simple a way as possible to reply. He would then go back into drowsiness and off to sleep. It was only in the writing of this chapter, when I have asked myself to find from ordinary life a normal example of regression to dependence, that I have thought about my child's use of me during this period of his life.

How do I believe I know when one of my patients is in such a

state, and why do I believe it is important not to
intrude on the person's inner experiencing and
inner processing of existence? One patient,
Harold, whom I will discuss shortly, relaxed his
body musculature when on the couch in such a

way as to be floppy. Motionlessly floppy, if that's possible. The
tension of object relating (inevitable with him when he was aware
of me as an object to be related to) would 'go out of his body', and
he would be in a different body mood. This was also true of my
son who would simply relax in his body. It was also the case with
me during a period of regression to dependence in my own analysis.

It is my view that when in the course of a psychoanalysis a
regression to dependence does occur, and when its full transference emergence is not accompanied by psychotic anxieties, it does
so because during the months, possibly years, leading up to such
a transference state, the patient has experienced silences that allow for regressive experiences, when the egos of analyst and
analysand are not at work, but are in a more receptive state: the
analyst in allowing for and upholding the analysand's need for
silence and the analysand by discovering inner experiences
through his silence.

THE ORDINARY COURSE OF A REGRESSION
TO DEPENDENCE

There is no drama to the development in Harold of the full regression to dependence. When he came for analysis, he did so on
the recommendation of his wife who felt he needed something. It
was typical of him in those days that he would act on the desire or
request of another person rather than seriously consider what he
wanted to do. Indeed almost all of his choices in life seemed to
derive from another person's wish.

By no means was this man seriously ill. He suffered an excess
of false self, that is true, and his emotional experiences within
relationships were less than gratifying and somewhat shallow, but
he read a lot, enjoyed concerts, the theatre and galleries, and was
enriched by these experiences. He had hoped to be a creative person and regretted that he was not, but his work was worthwhile

and he was good at what he did, which was selling insurance.

At no time in the course of his analysis did I feel him to be an excessive burden. In the transference, particularly during the first months of analysis, he would heartily praise me for an accurate interpretation and suggest that with just a few more such canny comments his analysis would be over. He sincerely believed that it should take no more than six months. When I persisted in saying that beyond his being anxious with me (which he acknowledged) he also wished to praise me so that he could skim over important issues, he found this true of himself and towards the end of the first year of his analysis he became depressed.

His sessional behaviour, however, was almost always the same during the first fifteen months of analysis. No sooner would he be on the couch than off he went chattering to me about many things. Usually he would begin with some kind of pedantic (though thoughtful) review of the previous session. He remembered my interpretations with almost unerring accuracy and would have thought more about what I had said and inevitably would have added to my comments with more of his own. After a while I said that I thought he was taking flight into his mind to fend off feelings – particularly feelings of helplessness, confusion and despair – but in the early period of his analysis he would spend much of his time detailing events at work and his use of the analysis to understand what was taking place.

It was not the case that I could hardly get a word in edgeways, for he did give me time to say what I thought, but the session seemed to race by. I was aware of a mild hypomanic element to him which I often interpreted. In the first year of analysis he found some of the interpretations very useful in modifying his anxiety about being approved and in controlling grandiose actings out in the office. Such enactments were really not job threatening, but they were sufficient to keep other people slightly aloof from him.

By the second year, however, after considerable work on his early family relations (except the father), his father died. In the year after this he never thought of his father, which initially I

thought was due to denial of affect, but eventually I understood it as due to an impoverishment
of inner object representations of the father. It
was not a denial in the present, if we think of a
negation, but it was a denial from a much earlier
period in his life.

However, as he relaxed more with me in the course of his
analysis, his sessions were less urgently reporter-like and intellectual, and he became capable of using silence. Initially, he
thought this was what I wished, and he tried to apply silence in a
false and adaptive manner. It was some time before he could find
his way to reverie in the session. When he did, it was not difficult
to notice such moments. Ordinarily he gesticulated a great deal,
moving his hands about to punctuate the spaces around his body.
During a generative silence, his hands would flop at his sides, or
would be folded over his chest, and he would turn his head to the
side to look out of the window. There he could see a tree and the
patterns in the sky. When he would emerge from such states, he
would often say how nice it was to look out of the window or bring
to my attention a particular sound he had heard. He also commented now and then on objects within my room, telling me which
painting he liked, and he would tell me on which place in the
painting his gaze had fallen. From my countertransference I
'knew' when he was in such a state, and my intent listening to his
narrative content was not necessary, so I would relax, and then in
such moments I would **consider him**. I do not know how else to
describe it, except that I would think of his entire life, of his body
and how he appeared. I enjoyed these moments.

These relaxed silences were usually brief, lasting only a few
minutes, and then he would be off, telling me about the events of
the day or reporting his self analysis. But in the third year of his
analysis, he became less talkative. He was by nature a very active
person, constantly on the go and quite exuberant, and one of the
first features of his decrease in speech was that occasionally he
would have a sleep on the couch. I never asked him about the
sleep as such, but about two minutes before the end of a session I
would wake him and tell him that soon the session would be
coming to an end. At first he was embarrassed and would sit up

rather red faced and apologize. I told him I did not know why he was apologizing, as he was tired and had simply fallen asleep. I specifically did not want to explore the unconscious meanings; I wanted to defend his right to this experience and allow for its continuation. This behaviour was intermittent. Occasionally he would become less talkative, and maybe once a week he would fall asleep.

At one point the quality of his sessions changed. He was clearly musing on something. He made certain sounds that bordered on talking to himself out loud. In the second session he told me that he was recalling his father's sailboat. It was a lovely boat and yet it was something he had not thought about in years, not since he was a small boy. It was clear from this comment and a few others that he was vividly recalling this object and others. The third session had been spent in silence. In the fourth session he said that he had never actually allowed himself to have what he wanted. He asked, 'why don't I just **do** what I want to?'. There was a weekend break, and on Monday he was ebullient, and told me that he had gone to the shipping yard and ordered himself almost exactly the same sailboat that his father had owned. He was absolutely thrilled and full of himself and over the next months every so often I would hear about the boat and then about his expeditions in it.

It was clear to me that the possession of the boat and its actual use was important to him in terms of his private inner development. I did not interpret the unconscious meaning I thought lay in the buying of the boat, but I did store inside me the belief that he was rediscovering his father through this object.

Approximately a year later, after a spell of useful interpretive activity, he became vulnerable and somewhat helpless. He asked me about my vacations and any breaks from the analysis, questions he had been incapable of putting in the years before. Over the course of two sessions once again he mused on his sailboat. This time, however, he reflected on recent private experiences he had had while in the boat by himself. When he was at the helm and piloting the boat, he suddenly felt an unusual outpouring of affection for his father. He realized that what he was doing his father had done. He wondered why his father had given up on sailing. He marvelled now, as he looked at his and his father's boat, at his father's good taste! His father could not have been the bland character he had always assumed him to be.

It is important to our clinical understanding of a patient in such a frame of mind to know that during such musings on his sailboat and during the sessions, the patient was 'living with' his father. He was of course at times speaking to me, but only in order to move along his own private inner and developing discoveries. At no point did I feel he was requesting an analytical understanding of his experience.

Harold emerged from this regressive use of me in the analytic space having developed an inner relation to his father which ultimately became available for our mutual discussion, as did later the analysis of his intense and bitter destruction within himself of his father and the male elements.

WHERE IS THE REGRESSION AND IN WHAT WAYS IS THIS A FORM OF DEPENDENCE?

I have intentionally selected a clinical example that lacks the dramatic quality of some other reported regressions to dependence in which the analyst actually managed the patient through a period of intense dependence on them. I have done so because I wish to examine ordinary and simple examples of regression to dependence, not just the deep regressions and profound dependence on the analyst which Winnicott, Little and Khan presented.

In keeping with Balint's valuable distinction between a benign and a malignant regression (1968), I believe that a generative regression to dependence is characterized by the analysand's giving over to the analyst certain important mental functions and managerial duties in order to bring the personality back to its childhood moments of origin and experience. This may take the form of the analysand needing the analyst to manage many of his life details (such as travel to sessions, some home affairs and the like) but my emphasis here is on how it involves more frequently the analysand's trust in the analyst's capacity to keep the room, the space, the time and the process going so as to give up certain ego

functions (such as integrative thinking, abstract-
ing, self observing, reporting, remembering details, attending to the analyst's frame of mind
and interpretations, and so on) in order to fall
into a state of intense inner self preoccupation.
The regressive side of the experience is characterized by the giving up of higher ego functions, and the childlike aspect of it is
characterized by a relation to the analyst which mirrors a child's
'good-enough' dependence on the mother who looks after (supple-
ments) the child's ego. This giving up of aspects of the ego to the
analyst induces in the analysand earlier memories and experiences. The dependence on the analyst should be obvious, but
I prefer, in understanding ordinary regression to dependence, to
keep in mind that such examples do not involve the analyst in
actual management of the person, but in holding the analytic process and not intruding with analytic interpretations.

THE PATIENT'S NEED TO MUSE

I come now to a discussion of some of the mental processes involved during regression to dependence. If the psychoanalyst has
the capacity to receive transference states through a form of holding via the countertransference, and if the analysand can yield to
the analyst some of the functions of the ego, then the analysand is
in a position to evoke certain memories, prior self states and new
objects.

In trying to describe the analysand's mental state while silent,
I find it most accurate to say that he is **musing**. The Latin root is
musa, the French **muser**, which *The Oxford English Dictionary*
defines as 'to loiter, to muse, reflect, to rut', a combination of
meanings that suitably describes the patient during regression to
dependence. In a certain sense the patient is loitering, or as Khan
has said is 'lying fallow'. Winnicott speaks of a 'formless state'
(1954), and I believe this describes the moment before and between more active states of mind, which occur when musing
proper takes place. To muse, then, is 'to think closely', 'to study
in silence', 'to meditate' (all *O.E.D.*), or to be 'meditative' or
'thoughtfully silent' (Webster).

If we refer back to the stages of regression to dependence, we

find ourselves identifying important self states
that have less to do with abstract thinking, analysing and the like, and more to do with the poetic
and the sensory. Some of the states of mind during regression to dependence seem to have to do

with the physical properties of objects (including the self) and
with the concreteness of the world. A patient may simply enjoy
the feel of the couch or become aware of the weight of folded
hands on his stomach. His body weight held by the couch may be
an object of attention. He may move from this tactile perception
to a more visual mode of being, and gaze at objects within his
field. A person may move to a more auditory state of mind, listening to the sounds of the room. There are also olfactory sensations
and perceptions. These fundamental modes of perception seem to
be a part of the progress of regression to dependence. It is as if the
patient needs to cohere basic sense perceptions in order to move
inward.

A patient may change from feeling the couch to sensing the
internal states of his body. He may move from listening to the
sounds of the room to hearing a musical strain pass through his
mind, or he may recall the sound of someone's voice. Most typically, however, the analysand reports having almost 'seen something'. This is, of course, very difficult to describe. But I am not
talking of hallucination. It is rather like an eidetic experience,
accompanied by intense feeling and a sense of wonder or discovery. It may not be clear to the person what he has discovered
but the picturing inside the mind of some person or event has the
integrity of memory rather than the fracture of hallucination.

It is important, of course, to be aware that the nature of the
experience at this point constitutes a memory. Like the aesthetic
moment, it is a memory of the state of being a child in the mother's
care. When the patient is musing, with the analyst holding the
space, the time and the process, I believe the adult is 'inside' his
childhood. Therefore, it is more likely that early experiences will
be recalled during such states of regression, although later experiences that constitute part of the 'unthought known' are also
available for evocation, because the state of mind achieved in
regression to dependence may repair a previously damaged

capacity to receive news of the self in this manner. That is to say, the analysand's capacity for musing may have been damaged during the course of childhood and therefore material from the primary repressed unconscious, or even secondary repressed unconscious, will no longer be available. An oedipal catastrophe, for example, can result in a child's taking flight from the mind into mental and physical activity, as with Harold. His discovery during regression to dependence was the nature of his father's personality and his properties as an individual. The patient had known this at one time and had 'lost' it.

This memory of the transformational object can only be recalled if **both** patient **and** analyst are living it through together. We may speak of a progression occurring between analyst and analysand which facilitates those states of self and mental processes that characterize a regression to dependence:

1. The analyst **understands** that silence is not always a resistance, and gradually establishes an ability to perceive when his patient is musing.

2. The analyst's understanding of the patient's use of silence to muse creates the patient's capacity to use this ability within clinical psychoanalysis.

3. Once this is understood by the analysand, the course of regression to dependence is permitted and evolves.

4. Musing is part of the receptive ability, established as a valued part of the analysis by the analyst's capacity to receive the analysand during silent states. The capacity to receive, which enables the mental function of musing, may facilitate another mental process: evocation. Musing is formless, an aimless lingering amidst perceptual capacities, such as imagining, seeing, hearing, touching and remembering. Evocation describes the passive state in which the more active elements from the unthought known arrive. It may have something to do with the return of the repressed. A colleague describes the difference between musing and evoking thus:

In musing, the 'I' actively moves. In evoking, the 'I' receives.

Musing is a state in which I experience myself as active, engaged in movement. In evocation, something emerges into view. I don't feel the force behind the arrival, though I know I have created the state necessary for its emergence. (Laurie Ryavec, Ph.D., 1986, personal communication)

5. The intersubjective process which facilitates this kind of regression depends upon the analyst's function as a transformational object, experienced by the patient in ways similar to the infant's experience of the mother: as an object associated with a process that does not distinguish between internal and external perceptions.

6. The analyst's capacity to become part of this intersubjective process as a transformational object rather than as a separate object amounts to an act of 'provision' within the countertransference; it enables the analysand to deconstruct ego functions in the interest of early states of self.

7. Recovery from regression emerges naturally as a result of the analysand's discovery of something pleasurable or inspiring, even if anxiety provoking, which he wishes to tell the analyst. There is then a need for the analyst's analytic function and a need for the analyst to engage in a discussion with the patient.

CONCLUSION

Analysts from within the British School have rightly emphasized that one of their curative functions is to receive a patient's communication (such as a persecutory introject of the analyst) and to detoxify the introject through interpretations, so that the patient reinternalizes the modified introject and is in possession of a less disturbing internal object. This process is repeated over and over again, so the patient internalizes not only the reformed internal objects, but also the analyst's container function, that is, he takes over the capacity to detoxify bad internal objects.

I believe that it is also important that the analyst should internalize aspects of the patient's self-analytic activity, namely those 'insights' into the self that derive from the regression to dependence and the mental processes of reception, musing and evocation. When such a process occurs and when the patient emerges with the resultant new internal objects, it is important for the analyst to recognize the validity of this discovery and not aim to transform it into his own language or into any psychoanalytical terms, unless the patient needs this.

Regression to dependence allows a person to gain important insights from within the self via fundamentally intrasubjective means. The processes of reception, musing and evoking are crucial elements in the construction of the self-analytic capability and in the thinking of the unthought known. If the analyst understands the patient's need to experience these processes, and if he can use the patient's self analysis as a part of that which is both known and valued (as a continuing source of knowledge), then a psychoanalysis will have sustained and cultivated the analysand's ongoing self analysis.

IV   Epilogue

15   *The unthought known: early considerations*

I T will be months after greeting a new patient before I have some 'sense' of the person's private and unconscious use of me as an object within the field of transference. During the early weeks of an analysis, both the analysand and I are usually taken up with the patient's narrative of his reasons for having sought help, and he 'presents' his life history. This presentation of one's life to the other is a quite special event for the analysand, and its character is as much marked by its eventual dissolution as it is by its early pertinence. For after a while the patient finds he has nothing more to say.

To some extent, this is when free association, or its negation – lack of association – begins. It is also during this period of transition from reporting one's life to discovering life within the analytic space and process that the analysand establishes the nature of transferential object use. Each analysand uses me in a different way. Some patients may elicit my differentiated critical capacity since they seem transferentially confused, while others may not use this capacity much at all. Some analysands create 'points' of empathic identification, enabling the analyst to settle into them for a period of time, while other patients sustain a rigorous affective distance that impoverishes the analyst's emotional life.

As I work to understand what I am in the transference, defined by the function elicited by the analysand, it may be possible in time to discover who I am, even if this 'who' is a composite of the patient's mother, father and former child self.

Our psychoanalytic understanding of the transference has always been that this psychological phenomenon is a re-living in the analytic process of earlier states of being and experiencing. But I wonder now if this is strictly true. Can we say that what is occurring in the analysis has in its entirety **ever been lived** before? I think that in his discovery of psychoanalysis Freud created a situation, now with the person's adult mental faculties present and functioning, in which the individual could live through for the first time elements of psychic life that have not been previously thought.

Such a view of the transference holds that this is not merely a reliving of a relation to the mother or father, or a re-presentation of the child self, but a **fundamentally new experience**, in that 'something' is given a certain dosage of time, space and attentiveness in which to emerge.

I turn quite naturally to Winnicott's concept of the true self to indicate what I believe this previously unlived something is. However, I quarrel with him slightly, in that I do not think this true self should be identified as the id and differentiated from the ego. I think Winnicott was much closer to the truth when he stated that by true self he meant the inherited disposition, and as the id is the psychical presence of the bodily instincts, then all id representations involve ego organization.

Furthermore, if we place greater emphasis on the individual character of the infant, on that organization of the person that is genetically given, and if we understand this core of the person to be the essence of the true self, then it is possible to link up the idea of the ego with the true self and to see how the ego is **in part** the organizational manifestation of the true self.

We can now further link the concept of true self and the ego to the notion of primary repression. The primary repressed must be that inherited disposition that constitutes the core of personality, which has been genetically transmitted, and exists as a potential in psychic space. How this true self will be realized involves consideration of the mother's and father's facilitative logic in their function as the transformational object.

At the very core of the concept of the unthought known, therefore, is Winnicott's theory of the true self and Freud's idea of the primary repressed unconscious. Indeed, I think that Melanie Klein's assertion that infants vary in their fundamental representation of the life and death instincts is determined by the intrinsic

nature of this true self. Phantasy, however, does
not constitute the true self: it represents it. In
this respect, my view differs from the Kleinian
position that early phantasy structures the ego.
Phantasy is the first representative of the un-
thought known in mental life. It is a way of thinking that which is
there. In other terms, it is an expression of the idiom of the infant's being and is the first mental act in the gradual and complex
development of an 'internal' world.

That internal world will process other aspects of human life
through phantasy. Along with the representation of the true self
will be the mental representation of the mother's logic of intersubjectivity. As I have held in the previous chapters, in the early
months and years of a person's life the mother 'instructs' the infant in the logic of being and relating. She does this through
countless intersubjective exchanges in her function as the transformational object. And each exchange is a logical paradigm. It
supports the mother's theory of being and relating, and will in
varying degrees facilitate or forestall the infant's true self, the
unfolding of the person's intrinsic character through object
relations.

Alongside the true self as the core of the unthought known,
one can add the countless rules for being and relating that have
been operationally determined. The mother teaches the infant
her logic, which is partly included in the infant's logic of being
and relating. The infant will alter this logic, or form compromises
between the logic of his being and object need which is fundamentally determined by his inherited disposition, and the logic of the
mother's care. But this continually developed field of knowledge
is not thought. Or to be precise, it is not mentally represented,
even though of course phantasy continues to represent some
aspects of the infant's mental experience of this complex negotiation with the mother. However rich a one-year-old's conscious
or dynamically unconscious fantasy life may be, it is not the con-
stituting factor in the development of the unthought known.

If we combine what we might think of as inherited or intrinsic
logic with intersubjective logic, so that we link a logic that stems
from the given – from the core of being itself – with the logic of the

other, both of which are revealed through operational processes and not via mental representations, then before the small child is capable of topographically significant mental representations (involving secondary repression and preconscious processes) the child already 'knows' the basic essentials of human life, in particular, of his human life. And what is known has not been established via discrete mental representations, in which the human subject forms mental objects in his mind, and abstracts from them theories about existence: that does occur, but much later. Indeed, the oedipus complex engages the subject in the formation of mental representations that do involve unconscious thought as the originating factor, and in this respect the psychic activity in the oedipal phase differs fundamentally from psychic life of the 'preoedipal' phase.

The concept of primary repression does not address early intersubjective contributions to the infant's knowledge of being and relating. It is because we must give room to the infant's internalization of the parent's paradigmatic operational logic that I think a new term, such as the unthought known, is called for. We need a term to stand for that which is known but has not yet been thought, if by thought it is understood that we mean that which has been mentally processed accurately. **Phantasy does give some mental representation to the unthought known, but it is insufficient to process the unthought known, and its liability at times expresses its limitation.**

In what ordinary way, then, does the unthought known become thought? In some respects in the same manner that it partly developed: establishment through object relations. It is only through the subject's use and experience of the other that mental representations of that experience can carry and therefore represent the idiom of a person's unthought known: which, of course, brings us to the transference and the countertransference. I know something about the analysand before I have thought what I know. Through the patient's idiomatic uses of me (both as his internal object and as the other to whom he speaks and from whom he expects), I am instructed in the logic of his intersubjectivity, and gradually I have a sense of the nature of

this person's being. Becoming the cumulative recipient, for example, of the analysand's varied
projective identifications means that I know
something 'about' the patient without it having
yet been sufficiently mentally processed through
my own internal cognitions, reflections and eventual interpretations. Thus a psychoanalysis constitutes a time-consuming
effort, as both the analyst and analysand need to begin to think
the unthought known. Much of my work in the countertransference will be a struggle to put into imagery and language the experience of being the analysand's object.

So an analysis partly recapitulates ontogenesis. In the beginning there may be the word, but there is also the wordless. The
infant–mother dialogue is more an operational and less a representational form of knowledge. And the analyst, like the infant
becoming a child, will struggle **to move** the unthought known into
the thought known.

The role of projective identification in this procedure cannot
be underestimated, particularly if we bear in mind that infants
and children contain unwanted or treasured parts of the parents.
How does an infant or a child think about this? If the mother or
father projectively identifies the element of grief into the child by
isolating any sign of sadness as a major psychic occasion, biasing
the child to be the family bearer of loss, how will the child know
this? Will he know it analytically? Of course not. Will he know it
through the mediative and fecund potential of fantasy? Try as he
might this will not process the content of the known. Then how
will he know what he knows? He knows because he bears a projective identification that will seem to him to be part of the nature of
his being or of life itself. Containing the other's projective identification seems life defining; grief, in this last example, feels like
the essence of his person; it is not to be thought – it cannot be: it is
lived.

Alongside that which is known via the recipient's containment
of projective identification, we must add the child's knowledge of
extractive introjection. The nature of this knowing will not be
identical in both situations: the child who contains split-off fragments of the mother's or father's personality will be under some

kind of pressure to sustain some element of personality in the theatre of family relations, while the child whose psyche has been denuded by a parent's theft of parts of his mind will know this only through a mood based on a primal loss and a sense of a prevailing harm having been committed. Precisely because the nature of extractive introjection occurs in a wordlessly violent manner – so that even adult victims can have a very difficult time identifying the cause of their distress – a small child will be unable to bring this psychic act into thought and speech.

Another element in the unthought known is somatic knowledge. In our work with analysands we experience the patient in our soma. In the most obvious sense, some analysands enable us to feel somatically rested and receptive, while others precipitate complex body tensions within us which we endure but to which we may give very little attention. This is not a peculiarity of psychoanalysis, as in all of our relations with people, we somatically register our sense of a person; we 'carry' their effect on our psyche-soma, and this constitutes a form of somatic knowledge, which again is not thought. I am sure that psychoanalysts could learn a great deal about this form of knowing from modern dance where the dancer expresses the unthought known through body knowledge. And it may well be that musical representation is somewhere between the unthought known and thought proper.

There is in each of us a fundamental split between what we think we know and what we know but may never be able to think. In the course of the transference and countertransference the psychoanalyst may be able to facilitate the transfer of the unthought known into thought, and the patient will come to put into thought something about his being which he has not been able to think up until then. But all analysts will at times fail to transfer the unthought known into thought, and it is important to form a relation to the rather mysterious unavailability of much of our knowledge.

A generative respect towards every representation in thought of the origins of the true self, and of the countless speeches mother and infant make through their curious dialect, enables us to face that knowledge we possess but cannot think. Is it not possible that by eventually developing a limited relation to the

unthought known in ourselves, we can then address the mysteries of our existence, such as the
curious fact of existence itself, particularly the
legacy of our ancestors carried as it is through
the generations via the idiom of the inherited disposition? In
thinking the unthought known we ponder not simply the kernel of
our true self, but elements of our forebears.

1. As I maintained in the introduction, I think by self we mean a set of intrasubjective relations that recur in a person's life and provide him with a sense of presence over time. The phrase 'self as object relation' is therefore apt in its ambiguity, since it may refer either to the specific relation to the self as an object or to the self as an object relation, or inevitably to both ideas.

2. My use of the concept subject is not in the same sense as Lacan's. By subject I mean the arrival of self-reflective consciousness, a process that has many antecedents but that formally begins when the child uses the first person pronoun. This concept of the subject is in some respects similar to Lacan's theory of the ego.

3. By ego I mean the unconscious organizing processes determined by a mental structure that evolves from the inherited disposition of the infant and the dialectic between this intrinsic character of the child and the logic of the parental care system. The ego long precedes the arrival of the subject.

4. If I understand Lacan correctly, the Other is the discourse of the unconscious, the dynamic unconscious of the topographical system. I think we may also argue that another feature of this Other is the primary repressed unconscious which I believe is part of the logic of the ego. Henceforth, I shall give the word an initial capital when employing it in this sense.

5. Bion's theory of mental functioning is complex and challenging. Those unfamiliar with his work may wish to read *Second Thoughts* and *The Seven Servants*. They may also wish to consult *Introduction to the Work of Bion*, edited by Leon Grinberg, *et al*.

    In a psychoanalysis the analyst will note many kinds of verbal and non-verbal communication between the patient and himself. There are many factors involved and, in Bion's theory, factors are elements of functions.

Each person has sense impressions and emotional experiences. There is a specific function of the personality which transforms sense impressions and emotional realities into psychic elements which are then available for mental work, such as thinking, dreaming, imagining, remembering. This element of transformation Bion arbitrarily terms the alpha element.

Beta elements are untransformed sense impressions and emotional experiences which are experienced as things-in-themselves, and which are operated on by projective identification.

6. I have used this term – transformational object – to define the infant's experience of the first object. By this I mean that the infant experiences the mother as a process of alteration. She attends to him in a way that changes his external and inner worlds. Infants do not internalize the mother as a person or imago. They do internalize the maternal **process** which is laden with logical paradigms that contribute to the laws of the child's character. As mother and child are engaged in countless transactions, these become facts of life that contribute to the logic of each person's existence.

7. It may be surprising that I have not mentioned the father, particularly as the father plays a crucial role in the life of the hysteric's desire and in the balance of her identifications. But it is my concern at this moment to concentrate only on the hysteric's sensational grip on the object and on her devolution of personality into eventual theatric. This externalization of self, in my view, expresses the specific nature of the hysteric's relation to the mother.

8. Although I think Freud's metaphor is somewhat unfortunate because a mirror has no feelings with which to register the emotional intent of an act committed in front of it, the analyst is able to facilitate the patient's transference intent the more because he is alive, not inanimate, and it is his aliveness that registers the patient's transference communication.

9. For example, in his letters, the dream book, the joke book, the book on the psychopathology of everyday life, etc.

BIBLIOGRAPHY

Balint, M. (1951) 'On love and hate', in *Primary Love and Psychoanalytic Technique*. London:Tavistock, pp. 121–35.

—(1968) *The Basic Fault*. London:Tavistock.

Bion, W.R. (1958) 'On hallucination', in Bion (1967), pp. 65–85.

—(1961) *Transformations*. London:Heinemann.

—(1962) 'Learning from experience', in *The Seven Servants*. New York:Aronson, pp. 1–111.

—(1962a) 'A theory of thinking', in Bion (1967), pp. 110–19.

—(1967) *Second Thoughts*. New York:Aronson.

—(1977) *The Seven Servants*. New York:Aronson.

Bollas, C. (1974) 'Character: the language of self', *Int. J. Psychoanal. Psychother*. 3:397–418.

—(1978) 'The aesthetic moment and the search for transformation', *The Annual of Psychoanal*. 6.

—(1979) 'The transformational object', *Int. J. Psycho-Anal*. 60:97–107.

—(1982) 'On the relation to the self as an object', *Int. J. Psycho-Anal*. 63:347–59.

—(1983) 'Expressive uses of the countertransference', *Contemp. Psychoanal*. 19:1–34.

Casement, P. (1985) *On Learning from the Patient*. London:Tavistock.

Coltart, N. (1983) ' "Slouching towards Bethlehem" . . . or thinking the unthinkable in psychoanalysis', in Kohon (1986), pp. 185–99.

Donnet, J-L. and Green, A. (1973) *L'Enfant DE CA'*. Paris:Les Editions de Minuit.

Ehrenberg, D.B. 'Psychoanalytic engagement, II', *Contemp. Psychoanal*. 20:560–83.

Erikson, E.H. (1968) *Identity*. London:Faber & Faber.

Fairbairn, W.R.D. (1940) 'Schizoid factors in the personality', in *Psychoanalytic Studies of the Personality*. London: Routledge & Kegan Paul, 1952, pp. 3–27.

Feiner, A.H. (1979) 'Countertransference and the anxiety of influence', in L. Epstein and A.H. Feiner, eds *Countertransference*. New York:Aronson, pp. 105–28.

Fletcher, A. (1964) *Allegory*. Ithaca:Cornell University.

Freud, S. (1900) 'The interpretation of dreams', in James Strachey, ed. *The Standard Edition of the Complete Psychological Works of Sigmund Freud*, 24 vols. Hogarth, 1953–73., vol. 5.

—(1905) 'Three essays on the theory of sexuality'. *S.E.* 7:125–243.

—(1908) 'Hysterical phantasies and their relation to bisexuality'. *S.E.* 9:157–66.

—(1912) 'Recommendations to physicians practising psycho-analysis'. *S.E.* 12:111–20.

—(1915) 'Instincts and their vicissitudes'. *S.E.* 14, pp. 111–40.

—(1915) 'The introductory lectures on psycho-analysis'. *S.E.* vol. 15.

—(1920) 'Beyond the pleasure principle'. *S.E.* 18, pp. 3–64.

—(1933) 'New introductory lectures on psycho-analysis'. *S.E.* vol. 22.

Gear, M., Hill, M. and Liendo, E. (1981) *Working through Narcissism*. New York:Jason Aronson.

Gill, M. (1982) *Analysis of Transference*, vol. 1, New York:International Universities Press, Inc.

Giovacchini, P.L. ed. (1972) 'The blank self', in *Tactics and Techniques in Psychoanalytic Therapy*. London:Hogarth.

—(1979) 'Countertransference with primitive mental states', in L. Epstein and A.H. Feiner, eds *Countertransference*. New York:Aronson.

Green, A. (1981) 'Projection', in Green (1986), pp. 84–103.

—(1986) *On Private Madness*. London:Hogarth.

Greenson, R. (1954) 'On moods and introjects', in *Explorations in Psychoanalysis*. New York:International Universities Press, 1978, pp. 61–74.

Grinberg, L. *et al.* (1975) *Introduction to the Work of Bion.* London:Maresfield Library.

Hedges, L. (1983) *Listening Perspectives in Psychotherapy.* New York:Aronson.

Heimann, P. (1956) 'Dynamics of transference interpretations', *Int. J. Psycho-Anal.* 37:303–10.

—(1960) 'Countertransference', *Br. J. Med. Psychol.* 33:9–15.

Jacobson, E. (1965) *The Self and the Object World.* London:Hogarth.

James, M. (1960) 'Premature ego development', *Int. J. Psycho-Anal.* 41:288–94.

Khan, M.M.R. (1964) 'Intimacy, complicity and mutuality in perversions', in *Alienation in Perversions.* London: Hogarth, 1979, pp. 18–30.

—(1966) 'The role of phobic and counterphobic mechanisms and separation anxiety in schizoid character formation', in Khan (1974), pp. 69–81.

—(1969) 'Vicissitudes of being, knowing and experiencing in the therapeutic situation', in Khan (1974), pp. 203–18.

—(1974) *The Privacy of the Self.* London:Hogarth.

—(1975) 'Grudge and the hysteric', in Khan (1983), pp. 51–8.

—(1976) 'From dreaming experience to psychic reality', *Nouvelle Revue de Psychan.* 12.

—(1976a) 'Beyond the dreaming experience', in Khan (1983), pp. 42–50.

—(1977) 'On lying fallow', in Khan (1983).

—(1979) *Alienation in Perversions.* London:Hogarth.

—(1983) *Hidden Selves between Theory and Practice in Psychoanalysis.* London:Hogarth.

Klauber, J. (1981) *Difficulties in the Analytic Encounter.* New York:Aronson.

Kohon, G. (1986) *The British School of Psychoanalysis: The Independent Tradition.* London:Free Association Books.

Kohut, H. (1971) *The Analysis of the Self.* New York:International Universities Press.

—(1977) *The Restoration of the Self.* New York:International Universities Press.

Krieger, M. (1976) *Theory of Criticism*. Baltimore:Johns Hopkins University Press.

Langs, R. (1977) *The Therapeutic Interaction: A Synthesis*. New York:Aronson.

—(1979) 'The interactional dimension of countertransference', in L. Epstein and A.H. Feiner, eds *Countertransference*. New York:Aronson.

Lewin, B. (1946) 'Sleep, the mouth, and the dream screen', *Psychoanal. Q.* 15:419–34.

Lichtenstein, H. (1961) 'Identity and sexuality: a study of their interrelationship in man', *J. Amer. Psychoanal. Assn.* 9:179–260.

Little, M. (1981) *Transference Neurosis and Transference Psychosis*. New York:Aronson.

McDougall, J. (1980) *Plea for a Measure of Abnormality*. New York:International Universities Press.

Melville, H. (1951) *Moby Dick*. New York:Norton, 1967.

Milner, M. (1952) 'The role of illusion in symbol formation', in M. Klein, P. Heimann and R. Money-Kyrle, eds (1977) *New Directions in Psychoanalysis*. London:Maresfield Reprints.

—(1969) *The Hands of the Living God*. London:Hogarth.

Modell, A. (1969) *Object Love and Reality*. London:Hogarth.

Ogden, T. (1982) *Projective Identification and Psychotherapeutic Technique*. New York:Aronson.

Pao, P.N. (1965) 'The role of hatred in the ego', *Psychoanal. Q.* 34:257–64.

Piaget, J. (1951) *Play, Dreams, and Imitation in Childhood*. New York:Norton.

Pontalis, J-B. (1974) 'Dream as object', *Int. Rev. Psycho-Anal.* 1:125–33.

—(1981) *Frontiers in Psychoanalysis*. New York:International Universities Press.

Racker, H. (1957) 'The meanings and uses of countertransference', in *Transference and Countertransference*. (1968), London:Hogarth, pp. 127–73.

Ricoeur, P. (1970) *Freud and Philosophy*. New Haven:Yale Universities Press.

Sandler, J. (1976) 'Countertransference and role responsiveness', *Int. J. Psycho-Anal.* 3:43–7.

Schafer, R. (1968) *Aspects of Internalization.* New York: International Universities Press.

Searles, H. (1956) 'The psychodynamics of vengefulness', in *Collected Papers on Schizophrenia and Related Subjects.* New York:International Universities Press, pp. 177–91.

Smith, S. (1977) 'The golden fantasy: a regressive reaction to separation anxiety', *Int. J. Psycho-Anal.* 58:311–24.

Sontag, S. (1966) 'The aesthetics of silence', in *Styles of Radical Will.* New York:Dell Publishing.

Stewart, H. (1985) 'Changes of inner space', *Int. J. Psycho-Anal.* 68:255–64.

Stoller, R.J. (1973) *Splitting.* New York:International Universities Press.

—(1976) *Perversion.* London:Harvester.

Stolorow, R.D. (1972) 'On the phenomenology of anger and hate', *Am. J. Psychoanal.* 32:218–20.

Symington, N. (1983) 'The analyst's act of freedom as agent of therapeutic change', *Int. Rev. Psycho-Anal.* 10:283–91.

Tauber, E. (1954) 'Exploring the therapeutic use of countertransference data', *Psychiatry* 17:331–36.

Winnicott, D.W. (1936) 'Appetite and emotional disorder', in *Through Paediatrics to Psychoanalysis.* London:Hogarth, 1975, pp. 33–51.

—(1952) 'Anxiety associated with insecurity', in *Through Paediatrics to Psychoanalysis.* London:Hogarth, 1975, pp. 97–100.

—(1954) 'Metapsychological and clinical aspects of regression within the psycho-analytical set-up', in Winnicott (1975), pp. 278–94.

—(1956) 'The antisocial tendency', in *Collected Papers.* London:Hogarth, 1958.

—(1960) 'The theory of the parent-infant relationship', in Winnicott (1965).

—(1960a) 'Ego distortion in terms of true and false self', in Winnicott (1965), pp. 140–52.

—(1963) 'Psychiatric disorder in terms of infantile maturational processes', in Winnicott (1965), pp. 230–41.

—(1963a) 'The capacity for concern', in Winnicott (1965).

—(1963b) 'Communicating and not communicating leading to a study of certain opposites', in Winnicott (1965), pp. 179–92.

—(1965) *The Maturational Processes and the Facilitating Environment*. London:Hogarth.

—(1968) 'The use of an object', in *Playing and Reality*. London:Tavistock, 1971.

—(1971) 'Playing: A theoretical statement', in *Playing and Reality*. London:Tavistock, 1971.

—(1974) *Playing and Reality*. London:Pelican.

—(1975) *Through Paediatrics to Psychoanalysis*. London: Hogarth.

INDEX

This first edition of
THE SHADOW OF THE OBJECT
was finished in May 1987.

It was phototypeset in 10½/14pt Bodoni
by a CRTronic 300 and printed by a
Harris cold-set web offset press
on 80g/m², vol. 17.5 Chantry Book Wove.

The book was copy-edited by Sara Beardsworth,
designed by Carlos Sapochnik and produced
by David Williams at Free Association Books.